. . . [were] . . . desirable or necessary to secure the constitutional principles of the sovereignty of Parliament and the
supremacy of the law." [9] The response was that the " 'best
exposition of the modern doctrine . . . is that contained in
Dicey's *Law of the Constitution.'* " In treating the same area in
1957, the Committee on Administrative Tribunals and En-
quiries noted that " 'the rule of law stands for the view that
decisions should be made by the application of known principles or laws . . . on the other hand there is what is arbitrary.' " [10] This more modern view of the rule of law as
principled decision-making had two main attractions. It
"legalized" an increasingly important body of rules and institutions that had grown up in the United Kingdom and
the United States since the 1930s. And, perhaps of greater
importance, it liberated the concept of the rule of law from
the particular political culture of late-19th-century England
and brought the common law view of the rule of law into
accord with Continental thinking. This can probably best be
illustrated by comparing the view of the rule of law contained in the 1957 report quoted above with the definition
offered by a leading French scholar: "no act of legal consequence can be done validly unless it does not conflict with
the rules laid down by an authority superior to the author
of the act." [11]

Implicit in the proposition of the rule of law as principled
decision-making are two corollary propositions. The first is
that there must be rules.[12] An ordinance that provides that
"The importation into the Gold Coast of any article is
hereby prohibited except under license granted by the Con-

---

[9] Quoted in Sharwood, *The Rule of Law,* J. GOULD AND W. KOLB, A DICTIONARY
OF THE SOCIAL SCIENCES 611 (1964).

[10] *Ibid.*

[11] WALINE, TRAITE ELEMENTAIRE DE DROIT ADMINISTRATIF 103 (6th ed., 1952).

[12] L. FULLER, THE MORALITY OF LAW 46 (1969) ("The requirement of general-
ity.").

troller of Imports and Exports and subject to such terms and conditions as may be contained therein" [13] is incompatible on its face with the rule of law since it contains no rule that the Controller is to apply in deciding when to issue a license. The ordinance can be read to confer upon the Controller absolute discretion to issue a license whenever and to whomever he chooses upon any conditions, no matter how arbitrary.

The second corollary to the view of the rule of law as principled decision-making is that the rules must be publicized.[14] In the case of the Gold Coast ordinance, for example, it is likely that the volume of import applications will exceed those that the Controller can personally consider. In order to delegate authority to his subordinates, so that they are able to process some of the workload, the Controller would, in the usual course, issue guidelines for decision-making. Thus the more usual case is not that there are no rules, but that the rules are not publicized outside the administration. Now it could be argued that the publication requirement does not necessarily follow from the rule of law as principled decision-making. That is to say, so long as the administration follows rules in making decisions, even if those rules are known only to the administration, the rule of law is satisfied. Experience, however, teaches otherwise. Studies of bureaucracy have now established that exclusive knowledge of rules provides the administrator with an opportunity to apply the rule in some cases and not in others. And the administrator will avail himself of the opportunity presented since this uneven application of the rules is the means by which the bureaucrat enhances his power.[15] This natural tendency toward the expansion of bureaucratic power beyond the scope of the rules can only be guarded against by making the rules known beyond the limits of the

---

[13] Order No. 113 of 1948, LAWS OF THE GOLD COAST.
[14] FULLER, *supra* note 12 at 49.   [15] *Id.* at 233.

bureaucracy.[16] This empirically based conclusion is confirmed by the study team appointed by the Government of India to look into the operations of the Import and Export Trade Control Organization. In order to prevent the abuse of administrative authority, the team concluded that "the conduct of Government business in licensing should be as far as possible open to the public . . . [and] that, as a guiding principle, nothing of interest or relevance to the trade should be kept from publication . . ." [17]

It is in this requirement of publication of rules that one finds the largest gap between the rule of law and the exchange distribution systems utilized in developing countries. For the publication requirement is alleged to conflict with the requirement of flexibility necessary to implement an effective system of exchange distribution. The administrator of such a system has noted that "the degree of control that it is necessary to exercise, and the nature of that control, may vary almost from day to day in the light of such factors as the level and trend of the exchange reserves, the incentives there may be for persons to evade or circumvent the control, actions taken by other countries in the exchange field and changing trends in international dealings." [18] This necessity for expeditious action and reaction is often coupled with the need to discourage speculation to lead to the conclusion that changes in the system must be made "without prior publicity." [19] In the ensuing chapters of this study we shall be concerned with the tension between the requirements of the rule of law and the need for administrative

[16] *Id.* at 51.

[17] Directorate of Commercial Publicity, Ministry of Commerce, Government of India, *Report of the Study Team on Import and Export Control Organization* 6, 11 (1965).

[18] Tarr, *The Administration of Foreign Exchange Control in Canada,* XXVII CAN. BAR REV. 625, 633 (1949). The author was the Secretary of the Foreign Exchange Control Board. See also Viner, *Trade Relations between Free-Market and Controlled Economies,* II LEAGUE OF NATIONS, ECO. AND FIN. A. 4, 14 (1943) (". . . [E]xchange control must by its very nature be administered under discretionary authority.").

[19] Tarr, *supra* note 18 at 633.

flexibility. In particular we shall seek to refine the areas of potential conflict to see whether the two are in fact irreconcilable under various systems of exchange distribution presently in use.

To this point we have relied upon American, English, and French legal philosophers to give content to the concept of the rule of law. But if we are to test the administrations in developing countries against a rule of law standard, an effort must be made to establish that they too subscribe to the concept of the rule as law as a constitutional principle. Given the number and diversity of the developing countries it would be impossible to examine the constitutional practice of each. The best that can be done is to offer such proofs as are available in the belief that a reasonable observer could conclude that the concept of the rule of law as defined is a prevailing norm in the developing world.

To begin one might look to the various "International Congress of Jurists" periodically sponsored by the International Commission of Jurists. Beginning at its Athens Conference in 1955, the ICJ has taken upon itself the task of securing "universal acceptance of these principles [Rule of Law] and . . . [exposing and denouncing] all violations of the Rule of Law." [20] Since that time the ICJ has sponsored Congresses in New Delhi (1959), Lagos (1961), Rio de Janeiro (1962), Bangkok (1965), Dakar (1967), which have reaffirmed and expanded the commitment of the respective participants to the principles of the Act of Athens. Each of these conferences has been attended by prominent lawyers, judges, and government officials from the developing world. In each case, however, attendance has been in an individual capacity rather than as a representative of his government. The most that can be concluded from these conferences, therefore, is that there are in many developing

[20] Act of Athens, June 18, 1955.

countries some prominent individuals who have dedicated themselves to work for the strengthening of the rule of law in their respective countries.

A more fruitful avenue for establishing the existence of a commitment to the rule of law in the developing world begins with a reference to the Universal Declaration of Human Rights. In the preamble to the Declaration, there is the finding that it is essential, "if man is not to have recourse as a last resort, to rebellion against tyranny and oppression, that human rights be protected by the rule of law . . ." A fair reading of this statement would seem to be that no substantive human rights can exist unless there is first accepted the constitutional principle of the rule of law. In fact, the very purpose of the Declaration is the articulation and publication of the principles which are to govern the relations between individuals and their governments. Without the acceptance of the rule of law as a basic premise, there would have been no point to making the Declaration. This is not to say that in adopting the Declaration the parties thought they were making law. For on the face of it the Declaration noted it was to be a "common standard of achievement." In fact, the United Nations effort in human rights was directed first toward the Declaration that was to be, and has been, followed by the drafting of Covenants incorporating in binding form the substantive rights outlined in the Declaration. What the Declaration does represent, for present purposes, is the belief that if certain rights are to be established, that this can only be done by adherence to the rule of law requirements of articulation and publication. The Declaration was adopted in the UN General Assembly on December 10, 1948 by a vote of 48 for and none against. There were eight abstentions, mainly from the Soviet Union and its political allies. In their case, however, as well as in the case of Saudi Arabia and the Union of South Africa, the abstentions were based on objections to one or more of the

substantive rights incorporated in the Declaration. The Soviet Union had in fact participated in the drafting of the
Declaration and there is no evidence that the Soviet representatives objected to the incorporation of the rule of law
principle in the preamble. Indeed even Stalin made clear, in
proposing the 1937 Soviet Constitution, that there was no
incompatibility between a Socialist State and the rule of law
and that in fact the rule of law was a prerequisite for the
building of socialism.[21]

Even in the case that the Declaration has, in fact, recognized the rule of law as a prerequisite to the existence of a
legal right, still one may ask for some evidence indicating
that the rule of law concept has been accepted by the developing countries. After all, the rule of law concept seems to
have been the product of European and American historical experience. Moreover, many of the countries which are
today categorized as developing were not members of the
United Nations when the Declaration was adopted in 1948.
Two sets of response are offered—particular and general.
In particular one might look to specific acts on the part of
individual developing countries which evidence acceptance
of the Declaration. For example, the Declaration appears to
have been treated as binding law in the Supreme Court of
the Philippines in the case of *Chinskoff* v. *Commissioner*.[22] A
commitment to the Declaration is explicit in the constitutions
of Algeria, Burundi, Cameroon, Chad, Congo (Brazzaville),
Dahomey, Gabon, Ivory Coast, Malagasy, Mali, Maurita-
nia, Niger, Rwanda, Senegal, Somalia, Togo, and Upper
Volta. Adherence to the principles enunciated in the Declaration is manifested in the American Convention on Human
Rights, signed on November 22, 1969 by Chile, Colombia,
Costa Rica, El Salvador, Ecuador, Guatemala, Honduras,

---

[21] Hessen, *The Rights of Man in Liberalism, Socialism and Communism* in
UNESCO, HUMAN RIGHTS 108, 138 (1949).
[22] UNITED NATIONS YEARBOOK ON HUMAN RIGHTS 288–289 (1951).

Nicaragua, Panama, Paraguay, Uruguay, and Venezuela.[23]

Considered more generally, there are many legal scholars who consider that the Declaration has become so widely accepted that it has become part of customary international law. This view is shared by such widely diverse authorities as Sir Humphrey Waldock,[24] Professor G. I. Tunkin,[25] and Professor Milan Marković of the University of Belgrade.[26] Their arguments basically follow the same line of reasoning. The Declaration had been adopted without opposition and the effect of the abstentions had been ameliorated by the unanimous adoption of subsequent United Nations' resolutions that were premised on the vitality of the Declaration. Moreover, the Declaration is generally a restatement of existing national law.[27] Finally, the Declaration was specifically incorporated in many international conventions, state constitutions, and judicial decisions throughout the world.[28]

In addition to those developing countries which have pledged adherence to the Declaration in their constitutions, many others have indicated their acceptance of the "rule of law" principle in other ways. The constitutions of Barbados, Guyana, and Trinidad and Tobago incorporate the phrase "rule of law" in their preambles. The constitutions of Kenya, Malawi, Sierra Leone, Tanzania, Turkey, Uganda, and Zambia all refer to the "protection of the law" as one of

[23] Reprinted in A. DELL RUSSO, INTERNATIONAL PROTECTION OF HUMAN RIGHTS 329 (1971).

[24] Quoted in Humphrey, *The UN Charter and the Universal Declaration of Human Rights,* in E. LUARD (ed.) THE INTERNATIONAL PROTECTION OF HUMAN RIGHTS 39, 53 (1967).

[25] *Ibid.*

[26] Marković, *Implementation of human rights and the domestic jurisdiction of states,* in A. EIDE and A. SCHOU (eds.), INTERNATIONAL PROTECTION OF HUMAN RIGHTS 47, 57 (1968).

[27] Statement of Sean MacBride, *id.* at 277.

[28] See statement of Charles Malik of Lebanon, one of the principal draftsmen of the Declaration, UN General Assembly, Official Records, 3rd Sess., 1st Part, Plenary Meetings at 858 (1948) (Declaration based on proposals of member states "but also of the laws and legal findings of member states" of the United Nations).

their guiding principles. Others, like the Afghan Constitution, indicate that "liberty is without limit except . . . as defined by law." Similar general expressions of the supremacy of law are found in the constitutions of Chile, Costa Rica, Ecuador, Guatemala, Honduras, Morocco, Peru, and Tunisia.

Even if there were no Universal Declaration of Human Rights, the global acceptance of the constitutional principle of the rule of law can be established by the existence of government itself. Governments vary in their aims but universally depend on a legal order in the sense of "a system of public rules" for achieving those aims.[29] This is not to say, of course, that every government adheres to the rule of law standard with regard to its every action. In fact, quite the opposite is the case. It would appear rather doubtful that a government has ever existed which did not on occasion depart from previously announced public rules. The point therefore is not whether there are occasional, or even substantial, departures from the rule of law standard but whether those departures are the norm or the aberration. If these departures constituted the norm the result would be not government but anarchy. To the extent therefore that government exists and anarchy does not, the rule of law concept as heretofore defined can be said to be a constitutional precept of a particular state. It is because the concept of the rule of law can be defined so broadly that so distinguished a humanitarian as Professor Wolfgang Friedmann could say that "all modern societies live under the rule of law, fascist as well as socialist and liberal states." [30] It is for precisely the same reason that Stalin could proclaim, with justification, his adherence to the supremacy of law in his introductory speech on the Soviet constitution. To those

[29] J. RAWLS, A THEORY OF JUSTICE 236 (1971).
[30] W. FRIEDMANN, LAW AND SOCIAL CHANGE 281 (1951), quoted in FULLER, *supra* note 14 at 107.

who may find this somewhat disconcerting, it is important to note that the conception of the rule of law adopted here— that is, the articulation and publication of rules—is in no way incompatible with injustice.[31] Whether the rules are just or not is beyond the scope of this study. What will concern us as we look at systems of exchange distribution is whether those systems are compatible with the minimum concept of the rule of law heretofore discussed.

To the extent that systems of exchange distribution depart from the rule of law standard, they present dangers to peaceful political development. A "disregard of the principles of legality may inflict damage on the institution of law itself." [32] This observation has special relevance to exchange distribution since the system affects large numbers of people—particularly the economically powerful business community. It is thus not difficult to conceive of the situation where one's impressions of the legal system and the government are substantially formed for large numbers of persons through the process of exchange distribution. If that area of government activity is "lawless," is there reason to expect that other areas with which one is not in such intimate contact are any more "lawful"? This situation must be viewed against the background of general social instability existing in the developing countries, which is the product of the modernizing process. Now it could be argued that the absence of law and the social instability are, in fact, intimately related and that the absence of law in the exchange distribution area is just one indicator of that general instability. That is to say, if the government were capable of making law it would do so, but the social conflict resulting from modernization prevents it from doing so. The argument is not without persuasive force, particularly in the light of recent work in the political theory of development

[31] RAWLS, *supra* note 29 at 236.   [32] FULLER, *supra* note 12 at 221.

highlighting the fact that it is the *degree* of government, not the *kind* of government, which distinguishes the developing from the developed world.[33] What are nominally called governments in many developing countries lack the power to govern. They will gain that power through a process of institutionalization which will be reflected in a legal system recognized as legitimate. The point to note is that the lack of rules governing exchange distribution may reflect the more general phenomenon of lack of institutionalision in many areas of developing-country life resulting from the process of development itself. Were this the case, however, one would expect to find some correlation between proximity to the rule of law standard and the stage of development of a particular country, assuming, of course, that one could identify an acceptable standard for "stage of development." But by any conceivable "stage of development," the research in the present study shows no such correlation. Instead one finds that a country like India, with a well-developed political system, a long tradition of an elite civil service, and a vital legal system, employed in some areas a system of exchange distribution as far from the rule of law standard as one might go before reaching total anarchy.

The explanation for this phenomenon in India is largely historical, the inheritance of a system designed for England 40 years ago. The more typical case however is an adoption of a system under the influence of forces outside the society. Because exchange distribution affects *international* payments, nations other than the one employing the system are vitally interested in it. As we shall see in chapter 3 this interest has been manifested in bilateral treaties and, of much greater importance, the Articles of Agreement of the International Monetary Fund. These international rules substan-

[33] See generally, S. HUNTINGTON, POLITICAL ORDER IN CHANGING SOCIETIES (1968).

tially affect decisions concerning the necessity for and nature of a system of exchange distribution. Their existence suggests that the rule of law problem is not solely a reflection of the degree of a particular country's development. More important, they raise the possibility that a country's exchange distribution system may be brought closer to the rule of law standard than might be the case without such international interest. They may even suggest that there is a duty on the part of the international community to assist developing countries in bringing their exchange distribution systems within the ambit of the rule of law.

Without such a movement toward the rule of law standard in general the alternative for maintaining public order may be "lawless terror." [34] For the third possibility, anarchy, cannot be tolerated for too long a period. While the possibility of a lack of rules in the exchange distribution area could lead to authoritarian government may seem a bit far-fetched, there is some evidence that this was precisely the case in the Germany of the 1930s.

The New Plan introduced by the Nazi regime in September 1934 had as its objective the reduction of imports of nonessential goods and the restoration of a favorable balance of trade—and thereby to increase employment in Germany. To achieve the desired control over the import mix, 25 "Control Boards" (*Überwachungsstellen*) were established whose function it was to approve or disapprove all imports. The decisions of the Boards were made in accordance with directives issued by the Ministry of Finance. While a good many of these directives were published, others, termed "general confidential orders," were considered "not appropriate for publication." [35] The decisions of the Boards were

[34] FULLER, *supra* note 12 at 107.

[35] Rashba, *Foreign Exchange Restrictions and Public Policy in the Conflict of Laws*, 41 MICH. L. REV., 777, 803, 810 (1943).

final and were not appealable. We do not unfortunately have data on the day to day administration of the system. Professor Howard Ellis, author of the classic study on the economics of the system, concluded however that administrative exchange distribution "was an instrument *par excellence* of political power . . . [which the] National Socialist State developed . . . to one of its most formidable weapons." [36] Further, it was "a device by which a dictatorship achieves and continues to exercise control over the economic and political destinies of the populace."

No one, and certainly not the present writer, has yet asserted that the system of exchange distribution has been used as a weapon of political oppression in the developing world. So the New Plan era in Germany may seem remote from the area of our present interest.[37] But what we consider here are possibilities. The system has in the past been used to build a totalitarian state. Could it not be so used again if it should fall into the hands of a present or future combination of Schacht and Hitler? Perhaps even more chilling is the final sentence in Dr. Ellis' study of German exchange control. "Unfortunately it must also be recorded that, in creating an authority against the decisions of which the law afforded no redress, the political predecessors of Hitler nurtured an institution which paved the way for totalitarianism." [38]

According to Dr. Ellis the venality of a Hitler was not a necessary prerequisite for an exchange distribution system incompatible with the rule of law. For he notes that his study of the Austrian exchange control system in force in 1932—whereby exchange was allocated among competing applicants by "preliminary examination boards" (*Vorpru-*

---

[36] ELLIS, *supra* note 2 at 289.

[37] For the view that certain forms of African nationalism exhibit many characteristics of "the Third Reich," see Seton-Watson, quoted in A. AFRIFA, THE GHANA COUP 15–16 (1967).

[38] ELLIS, *supra* note 2 at 289.

füngstellen)—revealed that decisions were made "by high-handed and arbitrary methods." [39]

CORRUPTION

To this point our treatment of the rule of law has emphasized the two requirements of existence of rules and publication of those rules. From these two propositions flows a third—that the administration apply those rules in dealing with the subject matter concerned. The underlying rationale for this conclusion is a reciprocal relationship between the individual and the administration, whereby the individual has a duty to obey the articulated rules in exchange for a similar commitment on the part of the administration.[40] Without such an understanding, the rule of law requirement of articulated norms would amount to no more than a hollow exercise. The failure to apply articulated norms can be viewed as deviating from the rule of law concept in either of two ways. Either it can be said that the norms upon which decisions are based have not been articulated, i.e., the real criteria for decision are not those incorporated in the statute or regulation, and thus there has been a violation of the first principle of the rule of law. Or it can be said that the deviation represents a violation of the third principle— the implicit social contract that articulated norms will be applied.

Where the deviation from the rule of law standard is motivated by "a desire for personal material gain" it is generally treated in social science literature as a violation of the third principle—the failure to apply articulated norms— and is generally labeled "corruption." [41] The corruption

---

[39] *Id.* n. 1 at 39.   [40] FULLER, *supra* note 12 at 39–40.
[41] A. ROGOW and H. LASSWELL, CORRUPTION AND RECTITUDE 2 (1963). "A *corrupt act* violates responsibility toward at least one system of public or civic

that we deal with here, therefore, is a subspecies of the rule
of law problem. It is the type of corruption that is universally condemned in the world's legal systems. Section 429 of
the Ghana Criminal Code is a typical formulation. That section provides:

A public officer . . . is guilty of corruption in respect of the
duties of his office . . . if he directly or indirectly agrees to permit
his conduct as such officer . . . to be influenced by the gift, promise, or prospect of any valuable consideration to be received by
him, or by any other person, from any person whomsoever.

It is the type of corruption dealt with in this and similar
statutes that is the subject of our case study from Ghana.

Ghana was the first of Britain's colonial territories in
Africa to gain independence. The choice was not accidental.
At the time of independence Ghana had a large body of
well-trained indigenous civil servants and a substantial African middle class. Moreover, although highly dependent on
cocoa exports, profits from those exports in the postwar era
had been substantial so that by 1957 Ghana's monetary reserves were nearly $600 million. The sad shattering of the
hopes of the Ghanaian people is a story that has been told
elsewhere. For the present purposes, the relevant fact in
that story is the overthrow of the Government of Kwame
Nkrumah by a combination of military and police forces in
1966. Subsequent to that event, the National Liberation
Council, as the junta styled itself, began a series of investiga-
tions into allegations of corruption during the Nkrumah
era.

By Executive Instrument No. 93 of March 5, 1966 the
National Liberation Council established a Commission of
Enquiry into Alleged Irregularities and Malpractices in

---

order and is in fact incompatible with (destructive of) any such system. A system of
public or civic order exalts common interest over special interest; violations of the
common interest for special advantage are corrupt." *Id.* at 132.

Connection with the Grant of Import Licences, with Justice
N. A. Ollennu as the sole commissioner. Justice Ollennu
was charged with looking into "alleged irregularities and
malpractices in connection with the grant of Import Licenses during the relevant period perpetrated by persons
paid out of public funds in the performance of their official
duties."

During the period reviewed by the Ollennu Commission,
it was the responsibility of the Ministry of Trade to prepare
an import and export plan at the beginning of each budget
year. This plan was reconciled with the foreign exchange
budget prepared by the Foreign Exchange Committee.
Once the totals for the import side were established, they
were apportioned between commercial and industrial use.
Categories of imports were then broken down "according to
priorities and essential needs of the country." The import
and export plan was sent to the Cabinet for approval. After
approval, the Ministry of Trade was charged with implementation of the plan. The initial step with regard to imports was the publication of a "notice to importers" in the
Ghana Commercial and Industrial Bulletin. Issue No. 46 of the
Bulletin, October 27, 1965 contained a typical "notice to importers" outlining "Import Licensing Procedures for the
Calendar Year 1966." The notice indicated that by statute
"the power to grant licenses and to create exemptions is
vested in the Minister of Trade." Regulations are administered in behalf of the Minister by the Controller of Imports
and Exports, the senior civil servant in the Ministry. Ghana
maintained a two-license system. A limited category of
goods could be imported under Open General License,
which means, in effect, freely imported "without further
written authority." The categories of goods permitted to
enter Ghana under open general license were mainly trade
samples, personal and household effects of visitors and im-
migrants, unsolicited gifts for personal use of value not ex-

ceeding £60 and a weight not exceeding 22 pounds gross, single copies of books and periodicals, pets, certain livestock from neighboring African countries, fish caught by Ghanaian-owned boats, and "headloads" of food stuffs for personal use. All other goods could be imported only under a specific license.

In order to apply for a specific license, an importer had to be registered with the Ministry of Trade.[42] If he were registered, he could apply to import a product for which the Controller had announced in the *Bulletin* that applications were being received. The application would be mailed to the Controller.[43] An applicant could request an interview to discuss his application for a license. In such a case, his request was to be sent to the Chief Commercial Officer, Ministry of Trade.[44] Licenses were distributed based "on the amount of foreign exchange available for each class of commodity." [45] Applicants were notified of the decisions on their applications by "printed standard letters." Apparently, however, the procedures outlined in the statute and notice presented only the formal structure. For it was evident from the testimony taken by the Ollennu Commission that some import licenses were issued according to a different procedure.

J. K. Khubchamdani, managing director of the Glamour

[42] Importers (Regulation and Imposition of Fees) Act, 1963, No. 318 of 1963.

[43] See ¶ 13, Notice to Importers, GHANA COMMERCIAL AND INDUSTRIAL BULLETIN, Oct. 27, 1965 at 762. But see WHITE PAPER 4/67, REPUBLIC OF GHANA, SUMMARY OF THE REPORT OF THE COMMISSION OF ENQUIRY INTO IRREGULARITIES AND MALPRACTICES IN THE GRANT OF IMPORT LICENCES 4 (1967) (". . . Kwesi Armah . . . introduced the system whereby all applications for import license had to be addressed to him personally under registered cover . . .").

[44] See ¶ 29, Notice to Importers, GHANA COMMERCIAL AND INDUSTRIAL BULLETIN, Oct. 27, 1965 at 764.

[45] See *id.* at 760, ¶ 7. "Sometimes when Kwesi Armah came to the office in the mornings . . . he would call upon him [the controller] to produce to him all the applications of a particular importer or importers . . . [U]pon the applications being produced, Kwesi Armah . . . graded the applicant and then minuted on the application the value of license [sic] to be issued; and this had to be carried out." See REPUBLIC OF GHANA, *supra* note 43 at 4.

Garment Factory in Accra, filed an application for import licenses of a value of £1 million for 1965 pursuant to the regulations. Two months went by without Khubchamdani hearing from the Ministry. Finally he received a telephone call in January 1966 from a Mr. Inkumsah, Deputy Speaker of the National Assembly, asking him to stop by the latter's office. At the meeting, Inkumsah indicated that he knew about Khubchamdani's application for an import license and that he (Inkumsah) would "help." Khubchamdani testified, somewhat disingenuously, that "I did not understand how a Deputy Speaker of the National Assembly could help me to get import licenses." That Inkumsah's help would be invaluable became clear at their next meeting when he told Khubchamdani that he had spoken with the Minister of Trade and the Minister had indicated that if Khubchamdani were prepared to pay 10 percent of the value of the licenses needed, they would be issued to him. Khubchamdani's initial reaction was that he could not afford to pay 10 percent. Inkumsah replied to the effect that "no 10 percent, no license." Since the amount of money involved was large, Khubchamdani made one last try to get the price lowered by going directly to the Minister. He was unsuccessful in several attempts to see the Minister at his office. Finally, he met the Minister at a cocktail party and indicated to him that he would like to see him at the office. The Minister responded that it would be very difficult. Khubchamdani then said "I know Inkumsah well." To this the Minister replied, "If you know Inkumsah, then it is not necessary for you to see me." Shortly thereafter, Inkumsah again telephoned Khubchamdani to inform him that, in view of the size of the transaction, the Minister had decided to reduce the "commission" below 10 percent. There ensued further negotiation with Khubchamdani indicating that instead of a license for £1 million he would like a license for £100,000. Inkumsah responded that this was "too small" and that the minimum license "he could get" was £250,000. Further bargaining revealed that the commission would have to be paid in advance "because many people to whom he [the Minister] had given import licenses had failed to pay the commission." Khubchamdani and Inkumsah finally agreed on £250,000 worth of licenses for a commission of £17,000. On February 22 or 24, Khubchamdani received two separate licenses permitting him to import goods to a total value of £300,000. The extra £50,000 was apparently a bonus for Khubchamdani's willingness to make payment in advance. Why had Khubchamdani done it? He related that in 1964 his company received licenses worth £48,000 and in 1965 worth £50,000. These were extremely low in terms of the needs of his business and he was "compelled to close down branches." By 1966 he had apparently learned his lesson.

The Ollennu Commission heard a similar story from Wassif Saldalah Dakmak. Dakmak applied for £210,000 worth of import licenses for the year 1966. While awaiting a response to his applications, Dakmak was visited by Emmanuel Maxwell Omusu Korantang (described in the testimony as "an unemployed") who indicated that the Minister of Trade was a friend of his and that he would see the Minister in an effort to obtain the licenses for Dakmak. About a week later Korantang appeared at Dakmak's house with the licenses, but also with a demand for a commission. According to Dakmak he refused to pay the commission and Korantang took the licenses away. Korantang returned two days later to indicate that if Dakmak did not agree to pay the commission, his companies would be "blacklisted." Korantang returned the following day and indicated that for a fee of £5,000 he would "see the Minister on the matter." Dakmak, fearing for his business, gave Korantang what cash he had available, about £3,333. That same evening Korantang returned with the licenses and Dakmak paid him £15,000 commission.

A similar tale was told by A. Rahman Accad, managing director of Auto Parts Limited of Accra. On behalf of his company Accad applied for import licenses valued at £1 million on October 9, 1965. He heard nothing about his license until the third week in January 1966 when Mrs. Victoria Adubea Akainyah, wife of Justice A. A. Akainyah of the Supreme Court of Ghana, telephoned and invited him to pay a call on her. At her house, Mrs. Akainyah told Accad that the spare parts import allocations were nearly finished and that he had better "hurry up." Mrs. Akainyah indicated that she could obtain the licenses for a fee of 10 percent. Accad responded by offering 5 percent and lowering his requirements to £200,000 worth of licenses. There the discussion ended. A few days later Accad received another invitation to call on Mrs. Akainyah. When he arrived, she told him that the terms for the licenses would be 5 percent when delivered and a further 5 percent after he had received his letter of credit. Shortly thereafter, Accad received in the mail import licenses of a value of £300,000. He then called on Mrs. Akainyah with £10,000 (5 percent of £200,000). The next morning however he received another call from Mrs. Akainyah, who said that she had had a visit from the Minister the previous evening and was told that Accad had been issued £300,000 worth of licenses. He therefore owed her an additional £5,000. This he dutifully paid.

These transactions, as well as others detailed in the Report of the Ollennu Commission, were carried out during the regime of Kwesi Armah as Minister of Trade, which lasted from July 1, 1965 until the time of the coup. In the practice of personally "approving" all import licenses, however, Kwesi Armah was no great innovator. The Ollennu Commission found, for example, that A. Y. K. Djin, a previous Minister of Trade, had a similar practice. In fact, there was testimony indicating that Djin's regime could be characterized as much more imaginative than Kwesi Armah's. Djin, for example, was the proprietor of the Ghana Trading Enterprise, a small trading firm. In 1963, the firm received import licenses with a total value of £35,000. Following Djin's assumption of office in October 1963, it enjoyed great prosperity. In 1964 the firm received licenses worth £90,000 and in 1965 worth £722,226!

In considering the background that gave rise to this sort of corruption, Justice Ollennu found that it was directly attributable to the shortage of foreign exchange which made it essential to limit imports to necessities—"import licenses ought not to be given for the importation of canned potatoes and artificial jewelry when the more pressing needs are for rice, sugar, milk, and medicine to maintain a healthy working population." To implement such a policy, "the concept of *specific licenses* becomes apparent and meaningful." Yet "the inauguration of a system of specific licenses, however necessary, can, in the hands of incompetent enthusiasts, bedeviled by an overwhelming desire to maintain arid formalities in the processing and issuing of licenses, or heartless individuals preoccupied with fraudulently enriching themselves or promoting their own personal aggrandisement through patronage, be so maneuvered as to lead to complete economic chaos and bankruptcy. This in fact is what took place during the period under review."

One can readily agree with Justice Ollennu that no system is workable in the hands of "incompetent enthusiasts" or of "heartless individuals." Yet to attribute the cause of such flagrant corruption to "heartless individuals" seems too simple a diagnosis.[46] It is to say that a Kwesi Armah or a Djin would be corrupt in any circumstances and that if we can only develop a system for identifying such "bad men" early

---

[46] See also W. CROCKER, ON GOVERNING COLONIES 22 (1947) ("Experience in all colonies to date is that once you entrust an African with authority that is not his traditionally . . . he will in the majority of cases abuse it for his own interest.").

enough, Ghana and developing countries generally will be well on the road to eliminating the corruption that has plagued many of them since independance. Surely there is more to it than that. For an intelligent response to the "corruption problem" it is necessary to probe more deeply into the circumstances in which the corruption took place.

The conventional wisdom is that corruption is an undesirable phenomenon.[47] One would think that there could be little quarrel with this seemingly commonplace idea. Yet there could be some legitimate questioning of it. As one writer has noted, in "a very real sense corruption, as beauty, is in the eyes of the beholder." [48] To illustrate the meaning of this somewhat cryptic phrase take the case of money or other valuable consideration paid to a bureaucrat to do what he is supposed to do in any case. Under most laws, this would constitute the offense of bribery and be a corrupt practice. The student of political behavior may be a bit more tolerant. If, for example, one applies for a driver's license the normal waiting period may be five weeks. Although essentially a simple transaction, the volume of requests for driver's licenses may be so great that the staff is inadequate to handle the requests in a more expeditious manner. If one is impatient and does not wish to wait the normal five weeks, one may offer the clerk who accepts the

[47] Early in his administration President Nkrumah was himself a vigorous opponent of corruption. See *Ghana Today*, June 22, 1960 and *Sunday Times*, April 19, 1961 (London), cited in McMullan, *A Theory of Corruption*, 9 (N.S.) SOCIOLOGICAL REVIEW 181, 201 n.s. 2 and 10 (1961). President Nkrumah was ostensibly so zealous in his effort to root corruption out of his government that he caused to be enacted the Corrupt Practices (Prevention) Act, 1964, No. 230 of 1964. That Act provides that upon receipt of an allegation of corruption on the part of a public official, the President "may . . . appoint a Commission . . . to enquire into the truth of the allegation." Section 1. Section 5 of the Act does away with the usual presumption of innocence in criminal cases by providing that "the findings of the Commission shall be *prima facie* evidence of the facts found, and the accused shall be called upon to show cause why he should not be sentenced according to law for the commission of the offence charged."

[48] Tilman, *Emergence of Black-Market Bureaucracy: Administration, Development and Corruption in New States*, PUB. AD. REV. 437 (1968 Sept./Oct.).

application 5 shillings or 5 rupees in exchange for which he will place the application on top of the pile instead of at the bottom. This type of payment, called "dash" in West Africa, "tea money" in Asia, and most appropriately, "speed money" in India, is almost universal in those areas. The widespread nature of the practice is itself strong evidence that it is not considered "corrupt" in the society in which it operates. In Nigeria, for example, "dash" is apparently considered a part of the normal compensation for a job, much the same as the use of a company car. Examples of the "dash" in Nigeria in 1952 were found "in hospitals where the nurses require a fee from every in-patient before the prescribed medicine is given, and even the ward servants must have their 'dash' before bringing the bed-pan; it is known to be rife in the Police Motor Traffic Unit, which has unrivalled opportunities on account of the common practice of overloading vehicles; pay clerks make a deduction from the wages of daily paid staff; produce examiners exact a fee from the produce buyer for every bag that is graded and sealed; domestic servants pay a proportion of their wages to the senior of them, besides often having paid a lump sum to buy the job." [49] Some Western scholars have looked on the "dash" or "speed money" system as a means "of building rewards into the administrative structure in the absence of any other appropriate incentive system." [50] Others, however, have found that the term "speed money" is an ironic misnomer. The Santhanam Committee in India found that speed money "has become one of the serious causes of delay and inefficiency" in government for the obvious reason that deliberate delay gives rise to the claim for it.[51]

An analysis of the elements of speed money or dash gives

[49] Commission of Inquiry into the Administration of the Lagos Town Council (Lagos 1954), quoted in Leys, *What Is the Problem About Corruption*, 3 JR. MOD. AF. STUDIES 215, 218 (1965).

[50] Prof. Myron Weiner, quoted in G. MYRDAL, ASIAN DRAMA 953 n. 3 (1968).

[51] Quoted in *id.* at 953.

some indication of why it may not be considered a corrupt practice. The critical factor is that the benefit is conferred to accelerate the performance of an act which it is the duty of the actor to perform in any event. That is to say, the act is *ministerial*. Upon receipt of a properly completed application, the clerk is obligated to issue the driving license. No discretion is involved on his part. His function is very much that of a mechanical device, with the dash serving to lubricate the mechanism. The second observation is that the payment of the dash is normally to a civil servant at the lowest level. This follows from the fact that his function is ministerial, since the usual organization of a civil-service hierarchy reflects a general widening of the area of discretion as one moves toward the peak. Finally, the value of speed money or dash in a single transaction tends to be rather small. In part this is a reflection of the low value placed upon the service that the recipient is called upon to perform. More probably, however, it is due to the low salary scale of the recipient so that a small payment on the part of an applicant may loom much larger as a given percentage of the recipient's total income. Because the incomes of the recipients are low and the amounts involved in individual transactions rather small in the eyes of the more prosperous elite groups, dash or speed money tends to be shrugged off more as a nuisance than as a subject of vital concern.

The type of corruption that generally disturbs involves larger sums of money and higher-level civil servants who possess a wide latitude of discretionary authority. Larger sums are involved in the first instance because they must be made attractive to parties whose incomes are more substantial. More important in this instance, however, would seem to be the fact that the value of the benefits capable of being conferred by the higher civil servant may be substantially greater than the civil servant lower down on the scale. Thus at the initial rungs of the civil service ladder one could find

that the higher of two civil servants has an income from
50–100 percent greater than his subordinate, but his authority to issue import licenses, for example, may be 1000
percent higher in terms of the amounts involved. Moreover,
at this level one is dealing with civil servants whose authority is more discretionary than ministerial and the benefit
conferred by the civil servant is normally not to do what he
was obligated to do anyway, but rather to *deviate* from the
pattern he would have followed absent the bribe. This is the
situation that seems to be more offensive to societies generally, although whether this is because of the absolute
amounts of money involved, or because the pattern of behavior is in conflict with the scope of his authority, is difficult to establish.

In his landmark study of political development and political decay, Samuel Huntington suggests why there may be
more general concern about corruption at this high level
than at the lower echelons of the bureaucracy. Corruption
at low levels and relative freedom from corruption at
higher administrative levels are characteristic of societies
with well-developed national political institutions. In such
societies "rising political leaders [are socialized] into a code
of values stressing the public responsibilities of the political
leadership." [52] In societies where corruption infects the
highest levels, as in Ghana, the level of political institutionalization tends to be very low. The correlation is not
meant to separate the two phenomena into cause and effect.
For it seems clear that the relationship is symbiotic. That is,
a low level of political institutionalization makes it more
likely that the leadership will succumb to corruption. And
corruption will undermine the process of political institutionalization.

Huntington goes on to indicate that a pattern of high

[52] HUNTINGTON, *supra* note 33 at 68.

level corruption "is not necessarily incompatible with political stability." While one could cite several examples in support of that proposition, Ghana is, of course, not one of them. For corruption was clearly one of the reasons for the overthrow of the Nkrumah regime.

Ironically enough, President Nkrumah himself supplied the reasons for the coup, which occurred 24 days after he had made the following analysis:

[The root cause of military coups] can be found not in the life and tradition of the African people, but in the maneuvers of neocolonialism. . . . Corruption, bribery, nepotism, shameless and riotous and ostentatious living become rife among the leaders of [a neocolonialist] regime. This brings untold suffering on the workers and people as a whole . . .

The masses have then nowhere to turn for redress. They therefore have no choice but to organize to isolate the army from the corrupt regime, if the army itself is free from the taint of corruption.[53]

In the light of the reasons given for their action by the leaders of the coup, Nkrumah seems to have correctly identified the conditions that would give rise to a coup, although he seems to have erred in attributing those conditions to the machinations of the neocolonialists. The coup leaders pinpointed the issuance of import licenses as an area where they believed corruption was rampant. In his first major radio address following the overthrow of the Nkrumah regime, the Chairman of the National Liberation Council, Lt. Gen. J.A. Ankrah, noted on March 2, 1966: "Import controls would be maintained, but it would be the policy of the NLC to eliminate as soon as possible the shortages that have been occurring in certain essential commodities. Many

[53] Parliamentary Debates, official record, Feb. 1, 1966, cols. 2 and 3, quoted in E. LEFEVER, SPEAR AND SCEPTER 58 (1970).

irregularities had been noticed in the issue of import licenses for 1966, and it had, therefore, been decided that all licenses issued after January 4, 1966 . . . should be returned immediately to the Ministry of Trade."

A thorough review would be carried out without delay and the necessary adjustments made to enable orders to be placed by importers. The NLC had decided that in the future every license the value of which exceeded 5,000 cedis should be published in the *Commercial Bulletin* for everybody to see.

Referring to the "chaotic foreign exchanges position," General Ankrah said this made it impossible for the NLC to remove exchange controls at present. However, "the Council was aware of the hardships that those controls are causing and are determined to introduce measures which will ultimately lead to their abolition."

Political scientists have warned of accepting "postcoup rationalizations" for the causes which led to a coup.[54] Some argue that it is not so much corruption as a "total distaste for the messiness of politics—whether honest or not—and a tendency to blame civilian politicians for failures to meet overly optimistic popular aspirations which would be impossible of fulfillment even by a government of angels."[55] Clearly there were reasons in addition to corruption in the issuance of import licenses that prompted the Ghana military and police officials to act. Economic conditions in Ghana were bad as a result of a decline in the price of cocoa, the principal foreign exchange earner. Moreover the elite was disgusted by extravagances such as the expenditure of almost $20 million in the construction of a Palace of African Unity as a suitable place to hold a one-week conference. And the elite was increasingly uneasy about the grow-

[54] Nye, *Corruption and Political Development: A Cost-Benefit Analysis*, 61 AMER. POL. SCI. REV. 417 (1967).
[55] *Id.* at 422 (footnote omitted).

ing ties between Ghana and the Soviet Union and in particular the growing influence of the latter in the Ghana
security services.[56] Nonetheless the attention paid to the
subject of import licenses in the first major address by the
coup leaders seven days after the coup took place is some
evidence that it was a subject much on their minds. The
subsequent appointment of the Ollennu Commission also
provides some justification for concluding that corruption
in this area was one of the motivations for the coup.[57]

The ill-will generated by open corruption has proved rich
soil for nourishing discontent in other areas. With a focus
such discontent can turn into a powerful weapon against
the government. Sir Robert Thompson has pointed out that
corruption "was an important factor in the downfall of Nationalist China." [58] Widespread corruption in Burma and
Pakistan were principal causes in the overthrow of their civilian governments.[59] The same thing appears to have been
true in Sierra Leone. Following the coup which overthrew
the government in March 1967, Lt. Col. Juxon-Smith announced that his purpose was "to eradicate bribery, corruption and neopotism 'which have besmirched the name of
Sierra Leone and most of Black Africa.' " [60] Even if one accepts the proposition that these are "postcoup rationalizations," the prospects for the military takeover enjoying a
substantial measure of public support are undoubtedly
greater if the view that the fallen government was corrupt is
widely accepted among the populace. History is replete with
instances of authoritarian regimes whose initial acceptance is

[56] These causes and others are given in E. LEFEVER, supra note 53 at 43–57. See
also A. AFRIFA, supra note 37 at 13 ("The Rhodesian crisis of late 1965, and
Nkrumah's wild plans for military intervention, led directly to the overthrow of
the Ghanaian dictator."). On the reasons given for the 1972 coup, see p. 31 supra.

[57] See also P. BARKER, OPERATION COLD CHOP 21, 58 (Accra 1969). For a theory
indicating why corruption may lead to violence see A. ROGOW AND H. LASSWELL,
supra note 41 at 73.

[58] R. THOMPSON, DEFEATING COMMUNIST INSURGENCY 51 (1966).

[59] MYRDAL, supra note 50 at 937.   [60] 4 AFR. RES. BULL. 739 (1967).

based on disclosures of corruption and punitive action against those responsible.[61]

Even if corruption leads to military coups, one must consider whether all coups are inherently undesirable. It is possible, for example, that a coup will result in the creation of viable political institutions which will result in the country's being better able to cope with the stresses resulting from the effort to modernize. This would be particularly true if the junta in power devoted itself to its own dissolution in favor of a more representative system of government. The cases are few, however, and the more likely result of a coup is the whetting of the appetite for political power on the part of the military. The history of the developing world seems to evidence the validity of the argument that military coups do not generally result in political modernization.

Against the risk of the violent overthrow of the government or the replacement of a civilian by a military regime, we must consider the possible "benefits" of corruption. Some argue, for example, that experience shows that the planners are not very good at their jobs and the corruption actually facilitates a more rational allocation of goods in the society. Not only more rational, but more developmental. To cite a case, it has been argued that the "honesty and efficiency" of the French civil service did a great deal to discourage "economic innovation and progress during the 18th century." [62] The first argument here goes that the man who offers a bribe for an import license has calculated the potential profit he can make from the scarce import, that a man who thinks about profitability is really thinking about the efficient allocation of resources, and that the efficient allocation of resources is the way in which economies grow. This argument is especially persuasive with regard to locali-

[61] MYRDAL, *supra* note 50 at 938.

[62] Leff, *Economic Development Through Bureaucratic Corruption,* 8 AM. BEHAV. SCI. 8, 12 (1964).

ties in which the entrepreneurial group is closely identified
with a racial or religious minority. Corruption of officials
charged with implementing policy that discriminates against
those groups may result in a more economic allocation of
resources.[63] Secondly, the bribe for an import license is said
to reflect the market value of the benefits conferred by the
license. The more efficient entrepreneur is thus able to give
the larger bribe. In effect, then, the corruption associated
with the distribution of import licenses functions very much
like an extralegal auction with the license being distributed
by market demand.[64] This argument assumes, however,
that the market for licenses is a free one with each entrepreneur having equal access to the decision-maker, each having
the same degree of insensitivity to the moral aspects of the
practice, and each having the same willingness to take the
risks of the imposition of legal sanctions. A related argument is that a government may "overregulate" an economy
in the interest of detailed planning and that such over-
regulation hampers economic development. "Corruption in
government may be an efficient compromise between the
desire of public opinion and legislators to regulate economic activity and the needs of business to avoid punctilious
compliance with each and every regulation in the interest of
efficiency." [65] This argument has been made with particular
force with regard to developing countries whose economic
development strategy is ideologically determined and
thereby produces an inefficient allocation of resources in
market terms.[66]

The fruits of corruption may also be looked upon as a tax

[63] Bayley, *The Effects of Corruption in a Developing Nation,* 19 WESTERN POL. QUART.
719, 728 (1966). See Nye, *supra* note 54 at 420 (Nye cites the survival of the Asian
minority entrepreneur in East Africa via corruption of local officials as possible evidence here).

[64] Leff, *supra* note 62 at 8.

[65] H. JOHNSON, ECONOMIC POLICIES TOWARD LESS-DEVELOPED COUNTRIES 44 n.
1 (1967).

[66] Nye, *supra* note 54 at 420; Bayley, *supra* note 63 at 729.

on economic activity.[67] It has also been suggested that bribery is a means of facilitating entry into a field of economic activity, thus functioning as an antimonopoly device.[68] Moreover, corruption in the form of bribery is a resource allocation device in another way. It transfers goods from the briber to the bribed official. Some have argued that if the bribed officials are more "development minded" than the bribers, it may well be that bribes will lead to more economic growth in the society. "The key elements in this determination are the marginal propensities of the corrupted and the corruptor to consume and invest." One reason for the possibility that officials are more "development minded" is the likelihood that government servants represent "an educated elite with unique access to information about prospects for economic development." [69] There is some evidence that corruption has resulted in concentrations of capital in the hands of the recipients of bribes. In Indonesia, three ex-ministers of the Sukarno government managed to accumulate about $100 million out of commissions paid on import licenses. The difficulty is that this money was not invested in Indonesia, but rather in accounts in Swiss, German, and Hong Kong banks. Presumably the funds were invested by the banks, but the growth they financed most likely occurred in Hong Kong, Western Europe, or the U.S. This transfer of the proceeds of corrupt activity out of the country seems to be the rule rather than the exception. It has been estimated, for example, that Peron, Perez Jiménez, and Batista transferred out of Argentine, Venezuela, and Cuba respectively a total of $1.15 billion during the period 1954–59.[70]

Corruption also leads to economic waste in another way.

---

[67] Leff, *supra* note 62 at 8.   [68] *Id.* at 10.

[69] Bayley, *supra* note 63 at 728.

[70] E. Lieuwen, Arms and Politics in Latin America 149 (1960), cited in Nye, *supra* note 54 at 421 n. 22.

The scarce resource of administrative talent is utilized by the corrupt to arrange for their self-enrichment instead of helping to solve the country's problems. And the administrative skills of others must be utilized to seek out corruption instead of being similarly devoted to more pressing government tasks.[71] A counter argument here is that corruption may actually increase the quality of civil service. Civil servants are generally poorly paid. Their economic problems are compounded by the fact that they are probably the one group from which the government can be certain of collecting an income tax. In an environment of large and rapid inflation associated with development civil servants find themselves gradually being reduced to the lower economic echelons of society. Economically at any rate, they are a group very susceptible to being corrupted. But if bribery is substantial it transforms posts in the civil service from low-paying ones to quite lucrative ones. To the extent that financial emolluments are an element that affects the quality of the civil service, the service is upgraded by means of corrupt practices.[72]

Aside from its economic effect, however, one must consider the potential political benefits of widespread corruption. It has been argued that corruption enables the new political elite to "bridge the gap" between themselves and the older elite whose status derived from private wealth. There is some evidence in Central America, for example, that the corruption of the leaders of military juntas has been a means of integrating them into the existing upper class.[73]

It has also been argued that corruption may provide the finance for political organization so necessary to the development of political institutions in developing countries. The argument here is that once the nationalist party has brought

---

[71] Nye, *supra* note 54 at 422.
[72] Bayley, *supra* 63 at 728.   [73] Nye, *supra* note 54 at 420.

the country to independence and itself to power, its sup-
porters are less willing to finance it, usually in the belief that
a party in power has no need of private contributions.[74] Evidence exists that the proceeds of corrupt practices have
served the cause of political development in this manner in
East Africa [75] and Mexico.[76] On the other hand, it was certainly not the case in Nigeria where the Action Group di-
verted nearly $12 million from the Western Region Market-
ing Board into the party treasury.[77]

Then again it has been argued that corruption enables
groups to participate in the government decision-making
process "to a greater extent than would otherwise be the
case." [78] This is true almost by definition. Such participation
will presumably further the interests of the participants.
And if the private interests of the participants should coin-
cide with the "true" public interest—as opposed to the public interest as expressed in the policies being deviated
from—the corruption may be a good thing. And even if it is
not, it has been argued that eliminating corruption should
not be a high-priority item for the governments of developing countries. The argument is that the interplay of colonialism, independence, and the drive for modernization inevitably result in government corruption.[79] In part this is a
definitional argument. The political system of a state is defined as underdeveloped when there is a wide gulf between
bureaucratic norms and societal norms. In an underdeveloped society, the bureaucratic norms of equity and ra-
tionality are in basic conflict with the societal norms which
place great value on family and communal loyalty. "Corrup-

[74] *Id.* at 421.
[75] Greenstone, *Corruption and Self-Interest in Kampala and Nairobi,* 7 COMP. STUD.
IN SOC. AND HIST. 199–210 (1966), cited in Nye, *supra* note 54 at 421 n. 19.
[76] Needler, *The Political Development of Mexico,* 55 AM. POL. SCI. REV. 310–311
(1961), cited in Nye, *supra* note 54 at 421 n. 18.
[77] See Sklar, *Contradictions in the Nigerian Political System,* 3 JR. MOD. AF. STUDIES
206 (1965), cited in Nye, *supra* note 54 at 421.
[78] Leff, *supra* note 62 at 8.   [79] McMullan, *supra* note 47 at 200.

tion thrives in such conflict of values simply because there is no agreement as to what corruption is." [80] To fully appreciate the other elements in this argument for the inevitability of corruption, it is necessary to look in particular at the interplay between the colonial experience and the drive toward independence.

A favorite explanation for widespread corruption in newly independent countries is grounded in their colonial history. During the colonial period, the laws were made by aliens presumably interested only in the confirmation of their rule over the subjugated inhabitants of the country. The resentment that the colonial system engendered led the local inhabitants to attempt to evade the colonialist rules in every possible way. More colorfully, "cheating of 'foreign devils in government' became admired as a patriotic virtue." [81] This attitude carried over to the new government which in many cases was equally alien. Much of the corruption in the Philippines, for example, is attributed to the lingering on of the wartime patriotic duty to disobey the rules laid down by the Japanese occupiers. Others have attributed it to the corruption endemic in the prewar American colonial regime.[82]

A second thesis based on colonialism has to do with the attitude of the colonial leaders toward political activity on the part of the "natives." It is a sweeping but essentially valid generalization that such activity was discouraged. To the extent local inhabitants of the colonial territory were educated, they were co-opted into the colonial administration. Those, on the other hand, who chose political agitation as a profession were generally persecuted. To treat preindependence politics as criminal had two effects. It discouraged from political activity those who could become civil

---

[80] Braibanti, *Reflections on Bureaucratic Corruption*, PUB. AD. 357, 360, 366 (1962).
[81] *Id.* at 359–360.
[82] Nye, *supra* note 54 at 423, citing HIGGINS, ECONOMIC DEVELOPMENT 62 (1959).

servants and it, therefore, left the field of politics to those who had little or nothing to lose. When the latter came to power with independence, they naturally sought some compensation for their years in the wilderness. In addition, they strongly distrusted the senior civil servants whom they regarded as black, brown, or yellow "Englishmen" or "Frenchmen."

A similar argument has been made with regard to the civil servants. In India, for example, it was observed that after independence new groups came to occupy posts in the civil service, groups different from the traditional sources, i.e., families of "wealth, learning, landholding, or hereditary tribal leadership." The civil servants of the old school were secure in their posts because of their social status and "the public naturally accorded such officers esteem and obedience." The new recruits, however, being far less secure, were "easily flattered by postures of obeisance" and presumably were easily corrupted as well.[83]

One cannot, however, make too much of the colonial argument. Thanks to the researches of Professor N.G. Smith, we have a fair amount of knowledge concerning corrupt practices in Nigeria that existed long before the British arrived on the scene.[84] In his study of Hausa political organization Smith indicates that by 1800 the practice of *gaisuwa* (literally, greetings) or bribery was so widespread that it was condemned by the Shehu Othman dar Fodio, who was to lead a war against the Habe Government in 1804 and by 1808 had conquered an empire 1,100 miles east to west and 400 miles north to south. During Othman's rule he concerned himself with developing an effective administration. But when he died, the succession of his brother Abdullahi to the Sultancy was contested by Abdullahi's son,

[83] Braibanti, *supra* note 80 at 368.
[84] Smith, *Historical and Cultural Conditions of Political Corruption Among the Hausa*, 6 COMP. STUD. IN SOC. AND HIST. 180 (1964).

Mohammed Bello. In the ensuing period of strife many of the ruling Fulani leaders sought to reintroduce traditional Habe "forms" so as to rally the subject Habe people to their side in the dispute. By 1827 the bribery and the making of gifts was again current in northern Nigeria. Thus by the time Lugard arrived in Nigeria in 1900, he would observe that "it was the custom for all men visiting their superiors to bring a *gaisuwa* or present." [85] If the British are to be condemned with regard to widespread corruption in Nigeria, it can only be on the ground that they were not vigorous enough in attacking the evil. And it is not surprising to find that they have been attacked on just these grounds. With regard to India, for example, the colonial administration has been accused of racism for failing to be more vigorous in condemning bribery and corruption among the "natives" while condemning these practices among themselves.[86] In failing to do so, the argument goes, they allowed the corruption to be "institutionalized" and "carried over even after independence." [87]

Another historical argument goes back to the precolonial days. In Burma before the British came, officials were compensated on the basis of a percentage of revenues collected, fees paid by the parties to a case, or local tolls on the transport or sale of goods. In each case, the charges were established by the officials themselves. This customary system of officials paying fees for services developed into a tradition which survived the colonial era.[88]

Given this context, can one rationally argue that the blame for corruption in exchange distribution systems is anything more than simply another manifestation of corruption endemic in the development process? It is the thesis

[85] *Id.* at 185, quoting M. PERHAM, NATIVE ADMINISTRATION IN NIGERIA 51 (1937).

[86] Dwivedi, *Bureaucratic Corruption in Developing Countries,* VII ASIAN SURVEY 245, 246 (1967).

[87] *Id.* at 247.   [88] MYRDAL *supra* note 50 at 949.

of this study that one can and that, in fact, the incidence of corruption in such systems is a result of two inputs—the context and the process of exchange distribution itself. An obvious reason is that the rewards are easily valued. The bribe given in exchange for the issuance of a driver's license will provide the recipient of the license with a benefit difficult to value in monetary terms. The proper "price," therefore, will reflect a subjective determination on the part of the briber as to the value of the license. The value of an exchange distribution for financing imports, on the other hand, has a readily calculable value to the importer. Thus he would be more willing to pay $100 for an import license entitling him to import goods on which his profit potential is $1,000 then he would be to pay $100 for a driver's license. The facility with which one can weigh the results of corruption is therefore one reason why one finds corruption associated with exchange distributions.

Perhaps more important is the magnitude of both bribe and reward. The amounts involved in exchange distributions are generally large and the potential profits enormous. For government exchange distribution is really an effort to distribute a limited supply of *goods* in the face of a large demand for those *goods*. The value of the distribution will reflect both these supply and demand factors. Some degree of the gap is indicated by the finding of an investigation into corruption in the issuance of import licenses undertaken by an Indian Government committee which indicates that import licenses were commonly resold for anywhere from 100 to 500 percent of face value.[89]

A third reason that one finds corruption associated with exchange distribution is that the typical system reserves a substantial degree of discretion to the distributing authorities. This is particularly true with regard to decisions con-

[89] J. Monteiro, Corruption 44 (Bombay, 1966).

cerning which applicant is to receive exchange, as opposed to higher level decisions such as the total supply of exchange to be set aside for government imports or private sector imports and decisions with regard to the supply of exchange to be allocated to particular commodities. A further reason is that decisions with regard to individual recipients are usually not subject to public scrutiny and/or review by an agency independent of the deciding authority. Finally, "(m)any persons otherwise law-abiding feel no moral compunction about breaking or evading currency laws or cooperating with others who do so." [90]

These factors would seem to explain the close association between exchange distribution and corruption in the developing world. A substantial amount of the commentary on this phenomenon is conclusary. In numerous interviews conducted by the author in India in 1966, the point was repeatedly made that it was "common knowledge in the business community that bribery was needed to obtain an import license." [91] There are, however, well-documented episodes in addition to that of Ghana. In Pakistan, for ex-

[90] That the problem is not endemic to developing countries is well illustrated in W. RUNDELL, JR., BLACK MARKET MONEY: THE COLLAPSE OF U.S. MILITARY CURRENCY CONTROL IN WORLD WAR II (1964).

[91] See also Marshall, *Exchange Controls and Economic Development*, in ELLIS, ECONOMIC DEVELOPMENT FOR LATIN AMERICA 430, 436 (1966) ("[I]nherent temptation to corruption . . . among the worst features of quantitative exchange controls."); Schott, *The Evolution of Latin American Exchange Rate Policies Since World War II* 10 (Princeton Studies in International Economics, No. 32, 1959) (Large windfall profits "provide the leverage for extensive illegal connivance between importers and the administrators of exchange-control machinery."); ELLIS *supra* note 2 at 192 ("Costs of exchange control . . . [include] fees and bribes"); Felix, *An Alternate View of the "Monetarist"-"Structuralist" Controversy*, in A. HIRSCHMAN, LATIN AMERICAN ISSUES 81, 90 (1961) (". . . [E]xchange controls had become . . . a prime source of corruption by the 1950's. . . ."); Banez, *Exchange Control and the Social Interest: A Reconciliation*, 32 PHIL. L.J. 621, 627 (1957) ("Exchange control . . . lends itself to corruption . . ."); MYRDAL, AN INTERNATIONAL ECONOMY 283 (1956) ("The system tends easily to create cancerous tumors of partiality and corruption in the very center of the administration, where the sickness is continuously nurtured by the favors distributed and the grafts realized and from which it tends to spread out to every limb of society.").

ample, of the 1,134 persons prosecuted under the Foreign Exchange Regulations Act and the Hoarding and Black Marketing Act, 735 were civil servants of whom 136 were senior officers.[92] And following the 1958 military coup, 75 senior government officials involved in exchange and trade matters were dismissed.

Exchange distribution systems and developing countries are a volatile combination. This study is aimed at identifying the blend least likely to undermine the rule of law and give rise to corruption and its negative consequences. What we shall be searching for is a middle ground between the views of developing country economists who argue that "control on foreign exchange is an integral part of policy as long as development is consciously pursued" [93] and "exchange control becomes an indispensible tool in the planner's kit bag" [94] and those who warn that "foreign exchange control must be limited as otherwise it will lead to a totalitarian control which could infringe upon the individual liberty of the citizen." [95] In particular we should bear in mind Robert Triffin's admonition that "the statesmen who introduced exchange control in so many countries were not at all blackguards or fools. Their motives should be understood. . ." [96] Chapter 2 provides a brief introduction to those motives.

[92] G. PAPANEK, PAKISTAN'S DEVELOPMENT, SOCIAL GOALS AND PRIVATE INCENTIVES, 126 (1967). See also S. YANG, A MULTIPLE EXCHANGE RATE SYSTEM 35 (1957) (Post-war attempt to control foreign exchange distribution in Thailand ineffective due to corruption).

[93] Djojhadikusumo, *Fiscal Policy, Foreign Exchange Control and Economic Development*, VII EKONOMI DAN KEVANGAN INDONESIA 211, 216 (1954).

[94] Nair, *Exchange Control and Economic Planning in Underdeveloped Countries*, 40 IND. JR. OF ECON. 153, 154 (1959).

[95] FINANJE (Yugoslavia) (Sept.–Oct. 1952).

[96] Triffin, *National Central Banking and the International Economy*, in INTERNATIONAL MONETARY POLICIES, POSTWAR ECONOMIC STUDIES No. 7, 66 (1947), reprinted in R. TRIFFIN, THE WORLD MONEY MAZE 142, 163 (1966).

Chapter 2

Why Developing Countries Ration Foreign Exchange

THE BALANCE OF PAYMENTS CRISIS

Foreign exchange is a medium of payment not issued by the debtor country which is accepted internationally in satisfaction of claims on the government and nationals of a debtor country. International acceptability depends upon a number of factors including history, custom, psychology, and the economic strength of the issuing country. Since Bretton Woods international acceptability has also been related to adherence to certain standards prescribed in the Articles of Agreement of the International Monetary Fund (IMF). At any given point in time a country's available supply of foreign exchange is indicated by the level of its reserves. Increments to the reserves and depletion of the reserves are closely related to the balance of payments.

Although widely used, balance of payments is not a term of art. It may represent one of three different concepts. Most commonly, the term is used to refer to the *accounting* balance of payments. As so used it is "a systematic record of all economic transactions between the residents of a country and foreign residents." [1] Its principal components are transactions on current account (primarily imports and exports of goods and services), unilateral transfers (e.g., private gifts, government grants), and a capital account recording overseas investment by local firms and individuals and local investment by foreign firms and individuals. By definition the accounting balance of payments always balances. That is to say, balances on goods and services, capital accounts, and net unilateral transfers will be offset by changes in official reserve assets and in a line for "net errors and omissions," which is generally believed to be a rough approximation of unrecorded private short-term capital transfers. Since it is the case that the accounting balance of payments will always be in balance, a payments deficit or surplus referred to in the accounting balance of payments is directed not at the totals but at the relationship between certain kinds of transactions. The effort is to segregate out the significant transactions. These are the so-called autonomous transactions that in the "basic" balance of payments are the current account transactions and long-term capital movements.[2] The remaining lines on the overall balance—errors and omissions, official reserve transactions, and short-term capital flows—are generally considered accommodating, i.e., they respond passively to the autonomous transactions or to changes in monetary and fiscal policy. Although a useful concept, the basic or accounting balance suffers from the fact that this division between autonomous and accommodating transactions is tenuous at best. For it has been established that some long-term capital transfers, particularly portfolio investment, do respond to monetary policy measures and some types of short-term capital flow do not. A refinement of the accounting balance of payments system is

---

[1] B. COHEN, BALANCE OF PAYMENTS POLICY 1 (1969).   [2] *Id.* at 42.

the official-settlements balance, which focuses not so much on transac*tions* as on transac*tors*.[3] The refinement is to consider only official reserve transactions as accommodating. The reason for this view is that "these are the transactions of the only transactors whose *function* it is to be accommodating under the present international financial system." [4] While the system is also subject to the criticism that other types of transactions may be accommodating, and certain official transactions are not, it appears to be the most accurate reflection of the balance of a country's international transactions. In general discussions it is the accounting balance proper or the official settlements balance variation that is meant by the term balance of payments.

From the planners' point of view, however, the accounting balance suffers from the fact that it describes past events while their principal preoccupation is with the present and future. The accounting balance may be likened to the income statement or balance sheet of a private economic unit. The analogous summation of present and future resources is the budget. The statement which serves as a budget in foreign exchange planning is the program balance of payments. As we shall see, it is the formulation of the balance of payments most widely used in the developing countries for planning purposes since it is "based upon a calculation of domestic consumption and investment requirements." [5] In particular it is useful in projecting the amount of foreign financial assistance which will be necessary to sustain a given level of economic growth. Since, however, the supply of such foreign assistance is highly dependant on political factors, it does not provide a reliable basis on which to construct a balance of payments policy, as opposed to, say, a foreign policy.

The better measure of present and future activity in

[3] *Id.* at 43.   [4] *Id.* at 44.   [5] *Id.* at 52.

foreign exchange is the *market* balance of payments. The
market balance is a model incorporating the effective demand for and supply of foreign exchange at the current
rate (and at various hypothetical alternative rates). While
not as all encompassing as the accounting balance of payments, the market balance has the virtue of focusing on a
country's autonomous intended transactions which are the
critical element for policy-making. For it is the relationship
of these transactions that will indicate whether there is pressure on the existing rate of exchange.

Our interest in these differing concepts of the balance of
payments is their relationship to exchange distribution.
That relationship is direct and immediate. For it is the perception of the balance of payments as "negative" that normally leads to the implementation of an exchange distribution system. As is evident from the various conceptions of
the balance of payments, the same set of economic circumstances may indicate that the balance of payments is negative
or positive. And even if one conception were adopted as
reflecting the "true" balance of payments, definitional pecu-
liarities may give rise to anomalous situations. For example,
in the accounting balance of payments if a deficit in the
trading account is offset by borrowing from private sources,
the borrowing is treated as a capital inflow, so that the deficit in the current account is offset by a surplus in the capital
account and the country is not in balance of payments deficit. "On the other hand, when a trading country draws
down its reserves or secures reserve credit [borrowing from
the IMF or other central banks] its overall balance of payments is in deficit." [6] This matter will not be further pursued as our central concern is with the cure rather than the
disease. At this point we may conclude only that there is a

[6] Bernstein, *Does the United States Have a Payments Deficit?* in L. OFFICER AND
T. WILLETT (eds.), THE INTERNATIONAL MONETARY SYSTEM 54 (1969).

need to be aware of the assumptions which are implicit in the identification of an economic situation as manifesting a balance of payments deficit.[7]

Assuming that one can identify a payments deficit, the next question is what is to be done about it? A response will depend on whether the deficit is considered undesirable. The conventional wisdom indicates that it is undesirable because a deficit enables a country to "live beyond its means," and suggests certain courses of action to be explored in this chapter. But note should be taken of the fact that the conventional wisdom has been challenged. Tibor Scitovsky, for example, has noted that the issue is not so much one of economics as of ethics. "Not only is it perfectly good economics occasionally to get something for nothing; it is or should be one of the economist's main preoccupations." [8] It is, indeed, the subject matter of welfare economics. It is further argued by some that the United States' payments deficits in the 1950s provided the liquidity in the international monetary system needed to foster the expansion of the West European and Japanese economies.[9] And it could be maintained that persistent payments deficits enable developing countries to grow at a faster rate than would pursuit of equilibruim exchange policies. Nonetheless, the conventional wisdom about the undesirable nature of payments deficits is the prevailing view. When a country runs a deficit, it more often than not recognizes this as a situation requiring remedial action.

Corrective action usually comes about when an existing or projected deficit reaches "crisis" proportions. Here again we find a subjective term conditioning economic and political

[7] For the view that "most" developing countries suffer from "persistent" payments deficits, see, e.g., Wadhva, *Regional Payments Arrangements, An Application to Asia and the Far East,* 10 YALE ECO. ESSAYS 149, 150 (1970).

[8] Quoted in COHEN, *supra* note 1 at 126.

[9] See, e.g., COHEN, *supra* note 1 at 127.

activity. For a crisis is more a state of mind than an objective fact.[10] The conditions adding up to crisis in the mind of one observer may be shrugged off with equanimity by another. This simple observation explains a good bit of the controversy which, as we shall see, surrounds the concept of exchange distribution. For there is substantial agreement that a balance of payments crisis will justify strong measures, but far less agreement on what factors add up to a crisis. In modern times the widespread use of exchange distribution is associated in the developed world with the First and Second World Wars and the intervening depression. While distribution of foreign exchange has been criticized, to say the least, with regard to the latter set of events, its use in wartime is tacitly, if not explicitly, accepted as legitimate. But war in the sense of open conflict is such a cataclysmic event that if it were accepted as the degree of crisis necessary to justify the introduction of an exchange distribution system, such systems would be rare indeed. But they are not. Empirically, one thus finds that there is a degree of crisis somewhat less than war that has triggered the utilization of exchange distribution. The nature of that kind of crisis and its underlying causes are the matters we shall now briefly take up.

The initial thrust of most development efforts is an increased investment in social overhead capital. Substantial expenditures are planned to increase the number of roads,

---

[10] Cooper, *Contingency Planning in International Finance,* in CONTINGENCY PLAN-NING FOR UNITED STATES INTERNATIONAL MONETARY POLICY, Statements by Private Economists Submitted to Subcommittee on International Exchange and Payments of the Joint Economic Committee, 89th Cong., 2d Sess., p. 18 (1966) ("At the outset, it is worth recalling that a 'crisis' is defined by the dictionary as a 'crucial time' and a 'turning point.' Any social or economic crisis involves a violent disturbance to the mental frame of reference and the conventions of behavior of the people involved in it. As such, crises are uncomfortable. But they are not things always to be avoided at absolutely any cost. The turning point can be in a desirable direction as well as an undesirable one; and the shakeup to the conventional wisdom and modes of behavior may have some value.").

power stations and educational facilities. These expenditures require large amounts of local financial resources to cover their local costs and foreign exchange to cover the cost of imported machinery and equipment. Putting aside for the moment foreign exchange needs, the government is faced with the task of generating the local funds. Normally governments raise revenues by imposing taxes. But one of the characteristics of developing countries is that their tax administrations are not terribly efficient. Thus while the typical developed country raises in taxes an amount equal to 25 percent of its Gross National Product (GNP), the average for the developing countries is less than 15 percent of GNP. Moreover, while developed countries' *direct* tax portion of their total tax proceeds averages about 50 percent, the equivalent figure for developing countries is about 30 percent.[11] A variety of explanations have been offered for this poor tax performance. Some are technical and relate to the inability of administrators to effectively tax barter transactions or the value of home-produced and consumed commodities. Others relate to "social codes of behavior" and the unwillingness of governments to make "a determined effort to improve collections." [12] In Gunnar Myrdal's phrase, they are "soft states."

As an alternative the government could borrow the money. Borrowing on the local market would be a more palatable technique than taxation but in developing countries may come down to the same thing. The credit of newly independent states is not terribly good almost by definition. Thus some deficit-finance techniques open to the developed countries are not generally available in the developing

[11] See, e.g., Chelliah, *Trends in Taxation in Developing Countries*, XVIII STAFF PAPERS 254, 269–271, 277 (1971). More recent figures give the developed country tax ratio at 26.2 percent and the ldc ratio at 15.1 percent. See III IMF SURVEY 162 (1974).

[12] Wai, *Taxation Problems and Policies of Underdeveloped Countries*, IX STAFF PAPERS 428, 430, 445 (1962).

world. Although a good deal of government "borrowing" goes on in developing countries, much of it is really a sort of round-about taxation. Moreover, to borrow money the government must pay interest. There is a cheaper and more politically palatable way to raise money. Since the government has control over its money supply, the path of least resistance is to expand bank credit, i.e., print money.[13] This new money is then utilized to finance development. To the extent that the country's supply of resources remains the same, the general price level will rise unless voluntary saving takes place in the society to offset the increased government expenditures. Given the high propensity to consume of most of a developing country's population, this is unlikely.[14] The great problem of the developing countries is just this problem of *undersaving*. And even were it the case that much of the increased government expenditure were directed toward that small strata of a developing society which has a higher propensity to save, their savings are more often than not turned into unproductive investments in precious metals and real estate. Thus the government utilizes inflation as a means of forced savings which are invested in development projects.[15]

Our interest is not, however, in the causes of inflation in developing countries but rather in the impact of inflation on their foreign exchange position. Higher money incomes from inflation and a fixed exchange rate result in an in-

[13] Bernstein and Patel, *Inflation in Relation to Economic Development*, II STAFF PAPERS 363, 368 (1952).

[14] See, e.g., Marwah, *An Econometric Model of Colombia: A Prototype Devaluation View*, 37 ECONOMETRICA 228, 234–235 (1969). (Per capita marginal propensity to consume in Colombia is .747; for seventeen Latin American countries .769.)

[15] See, e.g., INTERNATIONAL MONETARY FUND, SEVENTEENTH ANNUAL REPORT ON EXCHANGE RESTRICTIONS 22 (1966); Bernstein and Patel, *supra* note 13 at 367; R. MIKESELL, FOREIGN EXCHANGE IN THE POSTWAR WORLD 445 (1954); E. SOHMEN, FLEXIBLE EXCHANGE RATES 132 (1961); R. HARROD AND D. HAGUE (eds.). INTERNATIONAL TRADE TRADE THEORY IN A DEVELOPING WORLD 189 (1966). For an extensive discussion of inflation and development, see A. HIRSCHMAN, LATIN AMERICAN ISSUES (1961).

crease in imports as foreign goods become cheaper relative to domestically produced goods. Exports, on the other hand, fall as their price to foreign buyers increases. In addition, capital flight accelerates as those with savings rush to put their funds into a more stable form. Shortly the government is faced with a deficit in its international payments.

REINFORCEMENT AND RESISTANCE

As indicated *supra*, whether the situation is considered a "crisis" is a subjective determination. Given a fixed exchange rate, the government could, if it chose, ignore the payments imbalance since it should eventually correct itself. The rush to exchange local currency for foreign should lead to a decrease in the domestic money supply. With the decline in purchasing power prices and incomes should drop, imports appear less attractive, and the balance of payments should eventually reestablish itself at a new equilibrium level.[16] The word "should" is used advisedly to emphasize the manifest disparity between textbook models and the real world. Most governments will not stand by while the model plays itself out but will instead act in the face of a payments imbalance. They do so primarily because their international reserves may be such a small proportion of the domestic money supply that the reserves would disappear "well before the running down of money balances had any significant corrective effect." [17] In choosing to act, governments have a choice of two basic strategies—either to

[16] The converse is also true with regard to payments surpluses. While there is no external pressure to force a currency revaluation, a country running a persistant payments surplus finds that the surplus generates increased purchasing power. If this tendency toward inflation is not checked by monetary and fiscal policies, the result will eventually be the same as that described above.

[17] Johnson, *Towards a General Theory of the Balance of Payments*, in R. COOPER (ed.) INTERNATIONAL FINANCE 237, 241 (1969).

reinforce the self-correcting market action or to *resist* it.[18] *Reinforcement* is effected either by adoption of deflationary monetary and fiscal policies—the conventional wisdom [19]— or by altering the exchange rate, i.e., devaluation. *Resistance* involves altering the market distribution of foreign exchange. Resistance strategies are employed because the government wishes to avoid, for reasons that we shall now explore, reinforcement policies.

DEFLATION

Asking the government of a developing country to employ deflationary policies is almost disingenuous. For the government more often than not has consciously embarked on a policy of forced savings through inflation precisely because of the ineffectiveness of its monetary and fiscal apparatus. Moreover "since only a fraction of the country's total income is spent abroad," restrictions to control inflation must contract the national income by an amount several times the size of the payments deficit in order to have the desired effect.[20] For example, if 5 percent of a nation's income is spent on imports (more correctly, if the *marginal* propensity to import is .05), national income would have to decline 20 times the proposed decrease in imports.

Such a deflation could be politically devastating as it would result in substantial unemployment. This comes about because wages are not as downwardly flexible as assumed in illustrative models. Thus, while a deflationary policy should result in lower wages, it rarely does so. This was

[18] COHEN, *supra* note 1, at 90.

[19] See, e.g., Host-Madsen, *Balance of Payments Problems of Developing Countries*, Part II, IV FIN. AND DEV. 304, 307 (1967) ("Deficits that have arisen as a result of excessive credit creation by the domestic monetary system can be corrected, if the stability of the exchange rate is to be preserved, *only* through measures to reestablish monetary equilibrium.") (emphasis added).

[20] R. TRIFFIN, THE WORLD MONEY MAZE 165 (1966). See also *The Application of Multiple Exchange Rates in Selected Asian Countries*, ECAFE BULL. 19, 21. (Reluctance to deflate since marginal propensity to import "around 0.20 to 0.25.")

the experience in the nineteenth century and it is just as true today.[21] Instead, because of rigidities built into the system, deflation results in widespread unemployment. The cost of unemployment can be calculated in terms of man-hours lost. What is not subject to calculation is the "welfare losses in the form of frustration and loss of dignity experienced by those willing but unable to work." [22] While these latter losses were tolerated during the 19th and early 20th century, the traumatic effect of the Depression was such that full employment has become a principal goal of governments since the Second World War—a goal more often than not accorded priority over goals of monetary stability or external equilibrium.[23]

DEPRECIATION

The postwar prescription for a long-term balance of payments deficit caused by inflation is a combination of deflation and exchange depreciation.[24] The reason for the combination is readily apparent. Although deflationary fiscal and monetary measures could, if given sufficient bite, right the balance of payments, their general application would be a classic case of "overkill." A more precise strategy, which immediately and directly affects the payments situation, is exchange depreciation. But a depreciation cannot in and of itself remedy a payments deficit caused by inflation. If the

---

[21] Triffin, *Myth and Realities of the So-Called Gold Standard*, in COOPER, *supra* note 17 at 38, 41.

[22] J. GRUBEL, THE INTERNATIONAL MONETARY SYSTEM 49 (1969).

[23] See, e.g., Haberler, *Quantitative Trade Restrictions*, II LEAGUE OF NATIONS, ECONOMIC AND FINANCIAL 44 (1943); Fleming, *On Making the Best of Balance of Payments Restrictions on Imports*, 61 ECO. JR. 48 (1951) (". . . [T]he principal stabilising devise of the old system—variation in employment, production and incomes—is now generally regarded with disfavour. . .").

[24] See, e.g., Hemming and Corden, *Import Restriction as an Instrument of Balance of Payments Policy*, 68 ECO. JR. 483, 495 (1958).

A downward alteration in the exchange rate is a depreciation. When the alteration is also reflected in an alteration in the par value of the currency the term devaluation is used. See I IMF SURVEY 32 (1972).

inflationary pressures continue to exist, it will be a short time until the payments accounts are again out of balance and depreciation is again called for. This phenomenon reached the point in many countries in Latin America where any exchange depreciation was rendered "almost immediately ineffective." [25] The depreciation must, therefore, be combined with deflationary measures. The advantage of the combination is that the deflationary measures need not be so severe as would be the case were they relied on as the sole remedy for correcting the payments inbalance. The depreciation will restore the payments equilibrium at a new rate, and the role of the deflationary measures will be to contain future inflationary pressures within reasonable limits. The difficulty with this happy combination is that many governments seek to avoid exchange depreciation even more than they shun the deflation strategy.

The reasons for the view that exchange depreciation is a course to be avoided are manifold and mostly economic. But the principal one is psychological. Nations do not like to depreciate their currency.[26] It smacks of economic failure.[27] There is a widespread notion that "there . . . [is] something fundamentally wrong and wicked in changing the value of your currency." [28] This aversion to depreciation has been

[25] Power, *Import Substitution as an Industrialization Strategy,* Papers of Society For International Development 28 (1966).

[26] See, e.g., Katz, *Devaluation—Bias and the Bretton Woods System,* BANCA NAZIONALE DE LAVORO 178, 180 (1972) ("In practice, the less-developed countries have often been reluctant to devalue their currencies because of the high domestic political costs of such a decision."); J. BHAGWATI, TRADE, TARIFFS AND GROWTH 60–61 (1969); R. GARDNER, STERLING-DOLLAR DIPLOMACY lxx (2d ed.) ("For reasons of prestige, national leaders tend to postpone rate changes . . .").

[27] Woodley, *Some Institutional Aspects of Exchange Markets in the Less-Developed Countries,* in R. ALIBER, THE INTERNATIONAL MARKET FOR FOREIGN EXCHANGE 177, 178 (1969).

[28] Testimony of Assistant Secretary of State Dean Acheson, Hearings before Senate Banking and Currency Committee on the Bretton Woods Agreements, 79th Cong., 1st. Sess., quoted in Metzger, *Exchange Controls in International Law,* in P. PROEHL (ed.) LEGAL PROBLEMS OF INTERNATIONAL TRADE 313 (1959). See also Johnson, *The International Monetary System and the Rule of Law,* XX JR. LAW AND

described as "pathological." [29] Reluctance to depreciate is not, of course, a characteristic solely of developing countries. Great nations have in recent years postponed what seemed an inevitable devaluation for months and even years at great cost to their domestic economy and international markets.[30] They have at times pursued such stringent deflationary policies, resulting in underemployment of manufacturing facilities and unemployment of millions of workers, that they have been driven from office. And even where they have not been, the economic losses caused by underutilization of human and material resources cannot be recovered. All this in the name of protecting the value of the currency.[31]

Even if a government were willing to face the political consequences of depreciating the currency, selecting the new exchange rate is fraught with uncertainty. It is exceedingly difficult to know in advance the degree of depreciation that will bring the balance of payments into equilib-

---

ECON. 277, 288 (1972) (". . . [P]ropensity of governments, Treasuries, and central banks to take the view that devaluation is a confession of sin in policy-formation. . . ."); Harrod, *Imbalance of International Payments,* III STAFF PAPERS 1, 25 (1953) ("In the old days devaluation was regarded as a form of currency debauchery; this was a healthy view of it.").

[29] Viner, *Trade Relations Between Free-Market and Controlled Economies,* II. A. 4. LEAGUE OF NATIONS, ECONOMIC AND FINANCIAL 10 (1943) ("On the continent of Europe in particular there was an almost pathologically extreme determination to maintain, at whatever cost, the official gold values of the national currencies because of the memories of the havoc which had resulted from the extreme inflations following the first World War.") (footnotes omitted). See H. JOHNSON, ECONOMIC POLICIES TOWARD LESS-DEVELOPED COUNTRIES 59 (1967) (". . . [U]niversal fetishism that surrounds exchange rates in the present international monetary system.").

[30] In a reference to the "second half of the 1920s," Pierre-Paul Schweitzer, Managing Director of the IMF, noted that "in many countries it became the primary purpose of monetary policy to defend unrealistic exchange rates through deflation at a high cost to production and employment, that is, to human welfare." Supplement to XXIII I.F.N.S. 377 (1971).

[31] See, e.g., *They were Swamped, Too,* 239 ECONOMIST 74 (1971) (". . . [G]iven the almost religious attitude of the Swiss to their currency . . . made parity changes virtually impossible.").

rium.[32] More often than not, the figure is an "educated guess." A more precise means of selecting the right figure is to let the rate find its own level, i.e., float. While this technique raises some problems with a country's commitments as a member of the IMF,[33] it has been utilized by the United States, the United Kingdom, Canada, the Federal Republic of Germany, and Japan.

A much more difficult question is the timing of a depreciation.[34] The reason is the existence of currency speculators. If currency X is going to be devalued, one converts one's holdings of that currency into dollars or Swiss francs, only to reconvert after the devaluation, gaining a substantial profit in the process. But liquidating one's holdings in currency X may involve selling off profitable investments and one would hesitate to do this prematurely. An alternative would be to borrow large amounts of currency X for conversion and reconversion. In both cases, the objective is to convert out of currency X as close to the time of devaluation as possible. While currency speculation may not be evil per se, its consequences for a developing country can be quite serious. During the period when Brazil suffered from almost permanent inflation, the influx of foreign capital followed a wavelike pattern with large amounts flowing in immediately after a devaluation and diminishing over time. When there was a rumor of an impending devaluation, funds flowed out of the country with increasing momentum. Because this outflow was financed by local borrowings, it had the side effect of severely restricting the amount of credit available to small local firms.[35]

---

[32] For the view that devaluations tend to result in a new par value *lower* than needed to correct existing price disparities, see Katz, *supra* note 26 at 179.

[33] Chapter 3 *infra*.

[34] See, e.g., R. HARROD AND D. HAGUE (eds.). INTERNATIONAL TRADE THEORY IN A DEVELOPING WORLD 556 (1964) ("Most of the legitimate objections to devaluation rested on the necessary unpredictability of its timing and extent.").

[35] 2 BOLSA 629–630 (1968).

Central bankers are of course aware of this speculative activity and, to combat it, the timing of a depreciation must be kept secret until the last possible moment. "In the forlorn hope of avoiding or preventing further embarrassment and injustice, governments refuse even to discuss devaluation proposals and problems except in darkest secrecy, thus reducing the communication, interchange, and cross-fertilization of ideas, information, and interests to a bare minimum. It is small wonder that in selecting a new official rate of exchange, harried officials and their economists, working against deadlines and faced with inadequate information and knowledge, have been known to make the final choice by the flip of a coin." [36]

A graphic illustration of these problems is the British devalution in 1967. With pressure against the pound severe, a cabinet meeting was scheduled on Thursday. On Wednesday evening the BBC relayed a rumor of an international loan to save the pound. The Treasury would neither confirm nor deny the rumor. On Thursday the cabinet decided to depreciate by 14.3 percent. Thursday afternoon, the Chancellor evaded a direct answer to a question about the loan. On Friday approximately £300 million in reserves left the Bank of England. On that same day, a British Minister announced in Paris that "there is no plan to alter the exchange rate." On Saturday evening the devaluation was announced. After the fact, critics and commentators were left to wonder why the depreciation was not announced Thursday evening, saving the Bank of England a substantial portion of its reserves and at least one of the Ministers his credibility.[37]

Despite the harrowing nature of the experience governments do depreciate their currency, once convinced that

---

[36] USAID/ANKARA, INSTITUTIONAL REFORMS FOR THE DEVELOPMENT OF TURKISH EXPORTS 147 (1968). See Wallich, in CONTINGENCY PLANNING, *supra* note 10 at 153.

[37] *Britain: Will the Bungle Work?* ECONOMIST, Nov. 25, 1967, in OFFICER AND WILLETT, *supra* note 6, at 110–111.

depreciation offers a way to ameliorate a crisis situation. The economic aspects of the decision are resolved primarily by an analysis of the effect of the projected depreciation on the balance of trade. For the purpose of a depreciation is to encourage exports by lowering their price and discourage imports by increasing their price. The advantageous consequences of a depreciation on exports depends upon the relative elasticity of demand for those exports. The demand for developing-country primary products is relatively inelastic.[38] Thus, a given rise in price will not result in an equivalent fall in demand so that export proceeds will remain constant. Instead, increases in export prices may lead to only slightly diminished demand thereby raising total export earnings. For purposes of discussing the feasibility of devaluation, however, our concern is with the other side of this equation. Where demand is inelastic, a depreciation that *lowers* the unit price of exports will not necessarily lead to a proportionate increase in demand for those exports. To put it a bit more concretely, the point being made is that the world demand for coffee will be nearly the same at $60 per bag as at $55 per bag. There may be no close substitute for coffee so that the consumer is willing to pay the higher price rather than switch to drinking something else.

[38] See, e.g., G. MYRDAL, ASIAN DRAMA 2080 (1968) ("The relative price inelasticity of the supply of export goods even in the long run constitutes, however, a valid reason why devaluation would not be much of a remedy for a South Asian country's exchange difficulties.").

The impact of elasticities on the effect of a depreciation is expressed in the Marshall–Lerner Condition:

$$\frac{Fi}{Fe} \, ni + ne > 1$$

where Fi is the initial foreign value of imports, Fe the initial foreign value of exports, ni the home country's elasticity of demand for imports and ne the elasticity of demand by the rest of the world for the home country's exports. If the trade were initially balanced $(Fi = Fe)$ depreciation would improve the balance of payments only if the sum of the absolute value of the elasticities was greater than unity. It would have a perverse effect if the sum was less than unity.

It is important to note that the general proposition that primary products have relatively inelastic demand curves has been challenged by some economists. Professor Gottfried Haberler has indicated that "today most economists are convinced that the actual elasticities are in practice always sufficiently large to guarantee stable equilibrium in the balance of payments, except perhaps in the very short order and under very unusual circumstances, which may exist in highly specialized raw material–producing countries during depression periods." [39] He attributes the notion that demand elasticities for developing-country primary products are low to the fact that exchange depreciations in developing countries are not accompanied by deflationary policies, so that the expected favorable effect of the depreciation on exports is short-circuited by immediate cost increases. Thus the "downward shift in an *elastic* demand curve creates the erroneous impression that the curve is *inelastic*." [40] Moreover, even if the demand for a given commodity is inelastic the demand for a particular country's exports of that commodity may not be inelastic. For example, it was suggested above by way of illustration that coffee appears to be a commodity with a relatively inelastic demand. But if Colombia depreciates its peso so that Colombian coffee is cheaper than similar coffee from other sources, the demand for Colombian coffee would probably increase considerably as against similar coffee from other sources. But the devaluation would not benefit Colombia if other coffee producers also devalued, i.e., engaged in a competitive devaluation. Thus in the 1930s most of the major coffee exporters depreciated their currencies in an effort to increase their export sales. What happened instead was a general decline in coffee prices and lower export proceeds for all of the

[39] Haberler, *A Survey of International Trade Theory* 38 (Princeton University, International Finance Section, Special Papers in International Economics, No. 1, 1961).
[40] *Id.* at 39.

depreciating countries.[41] Depreciation will not work to increase exports, therefore, where it is likely to be followed by depreciation on the part of other leading suppliers. Where, on the other hand, the depreciation is the consequence of particular economic conditions affecting only one exporting country, it is less likely to be imitated and most likely to work to increase export proceeds.

The second factor to be considered, in determining the utility of a currency depreciation where a primary product export is involved, is the ability to increase the export volume once the price has been lowered. Where the *supply* is relatively inelastic, a depreciation would not be particularly useful.[42] Again referring to the case of coffee, the current supply of that commodity is determined by planting decisions made six years previously. Coffee trees take that long to mature. An increased demand is unlikely to call forth a greater supply, but only increased plantings that will not mature for another six years. On the other hand, if a country has stockpiled coffee, so that the stockpiles could be liquidated to fill the increased demand, the depreciation may prove beneficial.[43]

From the point of view of a developing country's *manufactured* exports, the effect of a depreciation may be more beneficial. The demand for manufactures, unlike primary products, is generally considered elastic. At the time of the

[41] Triffin, *Exchange Control and Equilibrium,* in S. HARRIS (ed.) FOREIGN ECONOMIC POLICY FOR THE UNITED STATES, 413, 418 (1948).

[42] See, e.g., Sweeney, *The Mexican Balance of Payments,* III STAFF PAPERS 132, 139–140 (1953); Address by Dr. Puey Ungphakorn, Governor, Bank of Thailand, reprinted in XI BANK OF THAILAND MONTHLY BULLETIN 14 (April 1971) (Thailand had payments deficit of $48 million in 1969 and $128 million in 1970, but would not devalue. "On the earning side, all our main commodities, with the exception of rice, are already competitive in price. I am referring to maize, rubber, tin, tapioca products, tobacco, soya beans, timber and minerals. The obstacle in all of these cases lies in the limitation in production and supply. . . . To sell them cheaper would not bring in more dollars; on the contrary, we would in fact lose by devaluation.").

[43] Triffin in S. HARRIS *supra* note 41 at 418.

British devaluation in 1967 it was estimated, for example, that a 1 percent drop in export prices would lead to a 2 percent increase in export volume.[44] For developing countries, however, different considerations may apply. For it may well be that particular manufactured exports face such a wall of protection in their prospective markets that they must be considered to have an inelastic demand curve. There are some indications that this may be true with regard to labor-intensive manufactures, which are the most likely exports in this category for developing countries.

To summarize briefly, the effect of currency depreciation on the balance of payments will depend in large measure on the elasticity of demand for a country's exports and the elasticity of the supply of primary-product exports. Although open to challenge, the prevailing view among planners in developing countries is that primary-product exports are inelastic, both as to demand and supply, and manufactured exports face an elastic demand. Accepting these generalizations it will be seen that the developing country that wishes to lessen its dependence on primary-product exports, and increase its volume of manufactured exports, is thus in a dilemma. For the currency depreciation that is likely to promote manufactured exports is also likely to reduce the proceeds of primary-product exports. But this portrayal of the dilemma is itself an oversimplification.

Many developing-country manufactured and semimanufactured exports utilize foreign raw materials, technology, and capital equipment. The effect of the depreciation is to increase the cost of these imported components. And this increase in the cost of exported products will offset to some extent the price advantage gained by the depreciation. In 1966 some estimates were made of the effect on export prices of a 50 percent devaluation of the Pakistan rupee. If

[44] ECONOMIST, *supra* note 37 at 112.

production costs were constant, a 50 percent devaluation was projected to reduce export prices 33.3 percent. The rise in the cost of imported components, however, would have limited price decreases for plastic products to 25 percent, nonelectrical machinery to 26.5 percent, canned fruits and preserves to 25.5 percent, and wearing apparel to 25 percent.[45]

Costs of production will also increase where a significant proportion of imports consists of foodstuffs. The increase in the price of imported foodstuffs consequent upon depreciation will eventually work through the economy in terms of higher wages and therefore higher costs. But the consequences may have far wider ramifications than on the costs of processed exports. In Sri Lanka, for example, to cut down on foreign exchange expenditures for rice, the government of Prime Minister Senanayake reduced the rice ration from four pounds to two pounds per week. In the May 1970 elections, Senanayake was swept from office and the opposition party of Mrs. Bandaranaike won with the largest parlimentary majority since independence. The "issue believed most responsible for her landslide" was the promise to restore the rice ration to four pounds per week. To fulfill this promise, however, it was necessary to redistribute exchange from the importation of raw materials. This resulted in factory closings and slow downs, aggravating an already grave unemployment problem.[46]

A more recent example can be taken from Ghana. On January 13, 1972 the civilian government was again overthrown by a military coup. One of the first steps taken

[45] Sanders, *The Short-Run Impact of Development* [sic] *on The Cost of Production*, VI PAK. DEV. REV. 580, 582–83 (1966). See Cohen, *Measuring the Short-Run Impact of A Country's Import Restrictions on its Exports*, 80 QUART. JR. ECON. 456, 462 (1966). That a devaluation would raise the price of imported raw materials was one of the German Government's principal arguments against such a move in 1933 and 1935. See ELLIS, EXCHANGE CONTROL IN CENTRAL EUROPE 228 (1941).

[46] Schanberg, *Ceylon's Leftist Government Finds Its Promises Have Added to Economic Problems*, New York Times, Oct. 18, 1970 § 1, p. 14.

by the junta was the revaluation of the cedi, which had been devalued 44 percent by the civilian government. Ghana is heavily dependent on imported foodstuffs and the devaluation had sent food prices soaring. "Everything's coming back down, and people are happy! reported a grocery clerk. . . ." [47] From an economic point of view, what the civilian government had done was correct in the sense that the maintenance of an exchange rate, which overvalued the cedi in terms of other currencies, meant that food imports were being subsidized by the reallocation of resources from other parts of the economy. Nonetheless, in the face of the reaction in Ghana, and similar though more orderly experiences in other countries, it is easy to understand why governments of countries that import substantial quantities of their food supply are reluctant to devalue.

More generally, the effect of a depreciation on imports will be directly related to the elasticity of demand for those imports. If import demand elasticities are low, a depreciation will result in an increased proportion of national income being devoted to foreign as opposed to domestic goods.[48]

Even if we put aside considerations of imported supplies and equipment as well as food imports, a depreciation may result in an increase in the costs of producing manufactured exports in another way. For if we assume that primary-product exports face a relatively inelastic demand, a depreciation will result in increased local currency proceeds

[47] *Ghana in Firm Hands 2 Months After Coup*, New York Times, March 20, 1972, p. 6, cols. 1–4. See also *Bolivian Tension Tied to the Peso*, New York Times, Nov. 26, 1972, p. 30, col. 1.

[48] Shah observes that India's import mix is relatively inelastic because (1) government imports more than 60 percent of total imports and government is expected to purchase "all possible requirements from the domestic market" and (2) private sector imports are only permitted when there are no indigenous substitutes available. See Shah, *Devaluation—The Indian Case*, 18 IND. ECO. JR. 117, 122 (1970). For similar observations, see Blades, *Devaluation and the Direction of Malawi's Import Trade*, 4 E. AF. ECON. REV. 63, 69 (1972).

for those engaged in that sector of the economy. This can have two effects. The increased profitability of primary-product exports may result in switches of land use from food production to cash crops, thus reducing the food supply and thereby increasing its price. In addition, to the extent that the proceeds are passed on in the form of increased wages to employees in the primary product export sector, their high propensity to consume will also result in upward pressure on food prices. Increasingly food prices will soon translate themselves into increased wage demands in all sectors and thus adversely affect the costs of manufactured exports.[49] As an illustration we again refer to the hypothetical calculations done in Pakistan in 1966. It was estimated that a 50 percent devaluation of the rupee would increase the value-added component of export costs by the following percentages: plastic products 14.5 percent, non-electrical machinery 13.0 percent, fruits and preserves 6.5 percent, wearing apparel 7.5 percent, jute textiles 100 percent, cotton textiles 6.5 percent, and woolen textiles 11 percent.[50] The 1966 Indian devaluation of 36.5 percent resulted in an increase in the domestic price of manufactured goods of 15.7 percent by the end of 1967.[51] More generally, estimates for a 1963 devaluation of the Colombian peso by 25 percent indicate that the price level would have increased by 12.82 percent and a 35 percent devaluation would have resulted in a 17.65 percent price-level increase.[52] Thus a

[49] Kaldor, *Dual Exchange Rates and Economic Development,* IX Econ. Bull. for Latin Amer. 215, 218 (1964).

[50] Sanders, *supra* note 45 at 583.

[51] Marwah, *Measurement of Devaluation Impact: Indian Case Study,* 17 Ind. Eco. Jr. 737, 744 (1970).

[52] Marwah, *supra* note 14 at 247. In the first two months following the Indian devaluation in 1966, food prices rose 15 to 30 percent although only a small percentage of food was imported. That portion of the increase attributable to the rise in the price of imported grains was apparently offset by a food subsidy. See Shah, *supra* note 48 at 125 n. 12.

depreciation unaccompanied by some effort to control subsequent price increases may confer little advantage on the export of developing country manufactures. This may explain why a government lacking the power, ability, or will to impose a deflationary domestic policy will avoid depreciating as long as possible.

Although the impact or lack thereof of a currency depreciation on the trade balance is the critical policy determination, other economic factors may also militate against a depreciation. If the aim of the development effort is to increase social overhead capital, the heart of a country's development imports are capital goods imports. A depreciation would increase the cost of these goods in local currency. To keep the costs low, governments may avoid depreciations. In Pakistan's First Five-Year Plan, for example, note was taken of the fact that when sterling was devalued in September 1949, the Pakistan rupee was not. The reason was that "[t]his held down the rupee costs of industrial machinery." [53] This argument is not unique to Pakistan. *The Bulletin of the United Nations Commission for Asia and the Far East* for November 1956 indicates that "a strong argument for the maintenance of an overvalued currency" is "the need to keep the cost of imported development goods low." [54] While valid with regard to the individual firm, this argument is unsound from a national planning standpoint. Just as in the case of cheap food imports, maintaining an overvalued exchange rate means that favored imports are being subsidized by other sectors of the economy. While this may be and often is the true intent of government policy, it is erroneous to believe that this enables a de-

---

[53] National Planning Board, Government of Pakistan, *The First Five Year Plan 1955–60*, p. 179 (1957), quoted in MYRDAL *supra* note 38 at 2079 n. 2.

[54] ECAFE BULL., 57 (Nov. 1956), quoted in MYRDAL, *supra* note 38 at 2079 n. 2.

veloping country to import capital goods at a lower cost to
the economy than would be the case were the exchange rate
set at equilibrium levels.

One other category of imports is of vital concern to the
planner contemplating a depreciation. This import is one of
the so-called "invisibles"—principally debt service payments.
The developing countries have borrowed enormous sums
for the financing of development projects from both public
and private lenders. A depreciation means that repayment
of the principal and interest of these loans becomes more
expensive in local currency terms.[55] Here again the same
fallacy occurs as in the case of food and capital-goods imports. But it is a fallacy widely accepted, or at least, widely
utilized to disguise the true cost of such development
assistance.

Another factor taken into consideration by a developing
country contemplating depreciation is the income redistribution effect of such a course. Currency depreciation redis-
tributes income to exporters and away from importers. This
may or may not be desirable from the government's point
of view. It will be considered useful if the exporters are society's entrepreneurs and the government wishes to put
capital in their hands. But it is not easy to identify entrepreneurs, let alone decide whether importers or exporters contain the preponderance of such individuals. And
in some ex-colonial territories, where both the import and
export sectors of the economy are largely in the hands of
nonindigenous people, the government may favor neither
group. Moreover, because they maintain economic planning
organizations, governments may believe that the real entrepreneurs who will lead development are within the government. Or, for ideological reasons, the government may wish
to reduce the role of private entrepreneurs within the soci-

[55] This was also an argument used in Germany in 1933 and 1935 to oppose
devaluation. See ELLIS *supra* note 45 at 228.

ety. Here again if the income redistributing effects of the depreciation are not those desired by the government, it must accompany depreciation with other policy measures.

The availability of supplementary measures can assist in limiting the undesirable economic consequences of a currency depreciation. The primary supplement is a general deflationary policy. Without effective deflationary action, any benefits gained from a depreciation will be lost in the near future. As we have seen, however, such a policy runs counter to the growth philosophy of most developing country planners. More selective controls may achieve some of the same ends. The most obvious are price and wage controls with which most developed and developing countries are currently experimenting. The verdict is not yet in on their ability to substantially limit inflationary tendencies. For the developing countries, however, there is the added disadvantage of requiring large numbers of administrative personnel—a scarce commodity in most of them.

Selective controls that have worked in developing countries have been directed primarily to siphoning off the increased profits in the primary export sector by the imposition of export taxes or by channeling these products through government marketing boards.[56] Even here however the government need proceed with caution. When Uruguay imposed an export tax on wool, many sheep owners reacted by driving their flocks to Brazil for shearing.[57] More generally, the imposition of export taxes may discourage production of primary products. As the IMF has pointed out "it must not be assumed that the traditional ex-

[56] See generally, Goode, Lent and Ojha, *Role of Export Taxes in Developing Countries*, XIII STAFF PAPERS 453 (1966).

[57] *The Non-Taxpayer, New York Times*, Jan. 28, 1966, p. 49. In the late 1940s Thailand was plagued with "large-scale smuggling of rice out of the country" due to the unattractive price offered by the Thai Government. See *Application of Multiple Rates, supra* note 20 at 30.

port sector will take care of itself and can always stand heavy taxation." [58] The increased cost of essential imports consequent on a depreciation could be offset by a series of import subsidies. As we shall see, many exchange distribution systems function to just this effect. Their distinction from direct subsidies is primarily that the latter are somewhat more difficult to administer and are too visible for the liking of many political leaders. While the open subsidization of food imports may be politically attractive, the same policy applied to imports of raw material and equipment for the private sector may involve negative political repercussions.

The limited ability of developing country governments to fashion viable selective fiscal and monetary programs, combined with the psychological inhibitions against currency depreciation, have militated in favor of most countries adopting *resistance* strategies to balance of payments difficulties. The object of a resistance strategy is to achieve the favorable consequences of currency depreciation without the trauma of a devaluation. Thus a resistance strategy aims at increasing exports and decreasing imports without affecting the value of the currency.

The classic means for reducing imports is raising the tariff. For historical reasons, however, this is difficult for developing countries. Developing countries that were former colonies generally have low tariffs because the customs tariffs were not used as protective devices to encourage the development of local industry. The colonial strategy was quite the opposite. The colony was to be the market for the manufactures of the metropole and thus import duties on manufactures were kept low in the colonies.[59] This presents problems for developing countries which are members of the General Agreement on Tariffs and Trade (GATT). For it

[58] INTERNATIONAL MONETARY FUND, EIGHTEENTH ANNUAL REPORT ON EXCHANGE RESTRICTIONS 44 (1967).
[59] MYRDAL *supra* note 46 at 2083.

is the general purpose of the GATT to reduce the level of tariffs. This is accomplished at periodic negotiating sessions generally known as "rounds," e.g., Dillon Round, Kennedy Round. These negotiations result in agreements binding tariffs not to rise above specified maximum levels. Although there are exceptions in the GATT to deal specifically with developing-country problems, and there is, in addition, a general waiver provision, these require the country to submit to scrutiny by GATT members of its proposed course of action.[60] Although these confrontations have hardly been rigorous and searching, they apparently have discouraged developing countries from attempting to deal with payments problems by increasing tariffs. Through the 1960s only Sri Lanka, Chile, Peru, and Uruguay have sought and received waivers to raise duties above bound rates. And the latter three developing countries have sought such waivers on only one occasion each. This reluctance to increase tariffs can be explained by the basic GATT philosophy of dealing with balance of payments problems by means of quantitative restrictions.[61] The caveat that need be added here is that GATT has increasingly tolerated the imposition of "temporary import surcharges" by, e.g., Canada, the United States, and the United Kingdom, to deal with *temporary* balance of payments problems. These import surcharges are, of course, increases in tariffs which are prohibited by the GATT.[62]

A further drawback in the use of import duties is that their rates are usually incorporated in legislation and are therefore not amenable to frequent change. As Professor Jacob Viner noted in the early 1940s "in countries with democratic procedures there is everywhere a marked jeal-

[60] GATT, Article XVIII. And see K. DAM, THE GATT: LAW AND INTERNATIONAL ECONOMIC ORGANIZATION 91–94 (1970).

[61] K. DAM, *supra* note 60 at 29–33; Triffin in HARRIS, *supra* note 41 at 424.

[62] A GATT Working Party found the 1971 imposition of a "temporary import surcharge" by the U.S. to be a violation of the U.S. obligations under Article II. See XXIII I.F.N.S. 302–303 (1971).

ousy on the part of the elected legislature with respect to
authority over the tariff. . . ." [63] If one is of the view that
most developing countries do not maintain "democratic
procedures" the weight of this argument can be discounted.
It could in fact be argued that the desirability of utilizing
tariff changes for balance of payments adjustments leads to
the conclusion that what the developing countries need is
less democracy rather than more. Needless to say, this argument will not be developed here. A more substantial consideration is the fact that where legislatures have significant
authority, the executive arm of the government is generally
reluctant to raise tariff questions for fear of opening a Pan-
dora's box of regional and parochial interests.

Tariffs suffer from imprecision in that they are sometimes cast in terms of broad categories of goods. This is
largely a function of the fact that they are the product of
the legislative process. Although precise tariff classifications
are conceivable, the process of defining the categories and
nursing them through the legislature is, at best, "labori-
ous." [64] In addition, since they are a cost restriction, the effect of increasing tariffs on imports depends on the elasticity of demand for those imports. In the view of many
planners the data at hand is simply inadequate for them to
predict with a reasonable amount of precision the effect of
a given tariff increase.[65]

Finally, raising import duties to combat balance of payments problems is sometimes no easy task. In 1966 Ecuador

[63] Viner, *supra* note 29 at 14. See also König, *Multiple Exchange Rates Policies in
Latin America,* 10 Jr. of Inter-Amer. Stud. 35, 45 (1968).

[64] Viner, *supra* note 29 at 14. See also V. Salera, Exchange Control And The
Argentine Market 205 n. 11 (1941).

[65] See, e.g., Thomas, *Import Licensing and Import Liberalization in Pakistan,* VI Pak.
Dev. Rev. 500, 523 (1966) ("The removal of licensing requires an alternative form
of rationing to prevent imports from exceeding available foreign exchange resources, and although tariffs and credit controls have been increased, they were
not and they are not adequate to reduce demand to the available supply of foreign exchange."); Fleming, *supra* note 23 at 67.

faced an increasing balance of payments deficit. To close the gap, the ruling military junta ordered an increase in import duties. In response the "powerful import houses in Guayaquil" called a general strike. During the course of the strike two persons were killed at the Central University "during an exchange of shots between soldiers and students . . ." Civil strife resulting from attempts to raise import duties is not new to Ecuador. In 1961 Dr. José Maria Velasco Ibarra was ousted as President of Ecuador over that issue.[66]

A second means of limiting imports, widely used by developing countries, is the advance deposit system. Under this system an importer places on deposit, with the central bank or its agent, local currency equal to a specified percentage of the value of the goods to be imported prior to importation. Once importation is completed the deposit is returned to the importer. In a typical case the deposit might be 200 percent of the value of the import to be deposited 150 days before importation. The added cost, which would deter imports, would be the loss of the income that would have been earned on the deposited sum or the interest paid to finance the deposit. In addition to the immediate import-discouraging effect, advance deposits also tend to freeze a portion of the existing money supply to the extent that they are not financed by the creation of bank credit. Thus they can play a dual role in moving the balance of payments toward equilibrium for they can be both import restricting and deflationary. A final advantage is that advance deposit requirements seem to offend neither GATT nor IMF obligations.[67] On the other hand, unlike tariffs and certain

---

[66] *New York Times,* March 27, 1966, p. 4, col. 1.

[67] Birnbaum and Qureshi, *Advance Deposit Requirements for Imports,* VIII STAFF PAPERS 115, 117 (1960). But see GATT, Article II:1 (bound duties include "charge of any kind imposed on or in connection with importation . . ."). Advance deposits would appear to fit within this category of "charge." Article II of the GATT is, however, subject to Article XV:9(a) which permits the use "of exchange controls

types of exchange distribution systems to be discussed, advance deposit systems do not provide the government with revenues. Moreover, the impact on those in the import trade tends to favor those who are well established and well financed. Perhaps the most serious disadvantage of advance deposits is the corollary of their attraction as a deflationary device. While an advance deposit system will tend to absorb excess liquidity, the liquidity remains as a cloud on future fiscal stability. If, for example, the authorities find the advance deposit system is not biting deeply enough into imports, a decision to increase requirements or impose new import restrictions will lead to a release of advance deposits and thus return to the economy some of the liquidity formerly absorbed. The problem becomes acute when a decision is made to terminate an advance deposit system and the authorities then face the problem of a large injection of liquidity into the economy. This "side effect" of advance deposit systems has led some knowledgeable observers to conclude that their merits are "strictly limited." [68]

A third technique for curbing the flow of imports is through the use of excise taxes. They offer a selective instrument which facilitates import control on an item-by-item basis. Their utility, however, is also limited by the GATT. To the extent that the taxed item is imported and a "like" product is produced domestically, the domestically produced item must also be subject to the tax. Thus the "incidental" effect of protecting local producers that would result from an attempt to curb imports by means of increased tariffs would be absent were internal taxes utilized. Since this "incidental" effect is, in fact, quite important in

---

or exchange restrictions in accordance with the Articles of Agreement of the International Monetary Fund." On the status of advance deposit requirements under the Fund Agreement, see p. 195 *infra*.

[68] Birnbaum and Qureshi, *supra* note 67 at 125.

many developing countries, other means are preferred than a sole reliance on excise taxes. Moreover, experience indicates that short-run elasticities tend to be low for most products, so that "the magnitude of a tax required to provide a given measure of relief may be extremely large." [69] This is particularly true with regard to luxury imports. It has been found that partly because of " 'a conspicuous consumption' psychology" among the upper-income group, as well as the great disparity of wealth in developing countries, the demand curve for luxuries is "rather inelastic at high prices." [70] Finally, excise taxes share with tariffs the dual characteristics of imprecision, due to the fact that they are cost restrictions, and inflexibility, due to the fact that changes in rates are normally the subject of the legislative process.

A resistance strategy to offset the disadvantages suffered by semimanufactured and manufactured exports due to an overvalued exchange rate would be to subsidize those exports. Although export subsidies are in general condemned by Article XVI of the GATT, their use by developing countries is not prohibited unless the developing country in question has explicitly agreed to the prohibition.[71] Subsidies are a double-edged sword from the domestic political point of view, however, in that they bring home in graphic form the cost to the country of its manufacturing sector. Moreover, utilization of subsidies may invite retaliation from two

[69] COHEN, *supra* note 1 at 114 n. 17.

[70] Schlesinger, *Multiple Exchange Rates and Economic Development* 10 (Princeton Studies in International Finance, 1952).

[71] *Declaration Giving Effect to the Provisions of Article XVI:6,* 9s, GATT, BASIC INSTRUMENTS AND SELECTED DOCUMENTS 32 (1961). But see Art. 52, Treaty Establishing a Free-Trade Area and Instituting the Latin American Free Trade Association, *done* in Montevideo, Feb. 18, 1960, reprinted in UNITED NATIONS, MULTILATERAL ECONOMIC COOPERATION IN LATIN AMERICA 57, 63 (1962): "No Contracting Party shall promote its exports by means of subsidies or other measures likely to disrupt normal competitive conditions in the Area."

groups of countries. Countries importing subsidized goods may offset the subsidy by imposing a countervailing duty.[72] And as in the case of competitive devaluations, competing exporting states may also install a subsidy system. As we shall see, certain exchange distribution systems function as export subsidies but somewhat more indirectly. The semi-disguised nature of these subsidies may make them more politically palatable, both domestically and internationally, and thus may account for their relative prevalence as compared to more direct export subsidy techniques in developing countries.

EXCHANGE DISTRIBUTION

Exchange distribution is also a resistance strategy. It is widely utilized because it is thought to offer one or more advantages over other resistance strategies. As compared with tariffs it does not run directly afoul of international legal norms; it is more precise because it is a quantitative rather than a cost restriction; and its design and implementation are a product of the administration rather than the legislature, therefore it is both more flexible and less visible in its impact.[73] Exchange distribution systems purport to be easier to administer than excise taxes, and unlike those taxes can act exclusively on imports. Finally, exchange distribution can be used to the same effect as export and import subsidization, but again with more flexibil-

[72] See GATT, Article VI. See also Section 303 of the United States Tariff Act of 1930, 19 U.S.C. §1303 (1965).

[73] Machlup attributes the administrative preference for what I have termed exchange distribution to the "bureaucratic mind" and its preference for "a more direct approach." Machlup, *Adjustment Problem and Balance of Payments Policy,* in OFFICER and WILLETT *supra* note 6 at 97. For a general summary of the advantages of exchange distribution, see e.g., *Application of Multiple Exchange Rates, supra* note 20 at 37.

ity and less publicity than would attend the employment of direct subsidization techniques.

The utility of exchange distribution goes beyond these factors. And the preference for this resistance strategy can be explained on quite different grounds. For the issues we have been considering deal with the balance of trade components of the balance of payments. While the trade figures are the largest debits and credits in calculating the balance of payments position, the latter includes nontrade payments and capital movements. In particular, neither deflation, devaluation, nor any of the alternative resistance strategies offer a means of controlling capital flight. And capital flight is the situation which has, as a matter of history, led to the introduction of exchange distribution.[74]

CAPITAL FLIGHT

The Great Depression of the 1930s saw the first widespread use of exchange distribution. It is difficult to convey in statistical terms the disastrous effects on the world economy caused by the Depression. There are, of course, many well-known works describing this period most graphically. For present purposes we may note simply that between 1929 and 1932 the world price index fell 47.5 percent, the price index for raw materials and partly manufactured goods fell by 56 percent, the value of manufactured products by 37.5 percent, and the amount of world trade fell by 63 percent. Internally, savers and investors saw their fortunes collapsing around them. In their panic they rushed to withdraw their funds from the banks, the foolish ones to hide their funds under the mattresses, the more clever ones to change their local currency into gold or, if gold was not available, into the hardest currency obtainable. Foreign investors sought to

[74] NURKSE, INTERNATIONAL CURRENCY EXPERIENCE 164 (League of Nations 1944); ELLIS *supra* note 45 at 299.

liquidate investments and repatriate their capital in the hardest form possible. Foreign creditors demanded immediate repayment of loans. The demand for gold and foreign exchange on the major central banks became unbearable. In May 1931, one of the most respected of European central banks—the Austrian Credit Anstalt—collapsed. The introduction of sweeping exchange restrictions can be dated from the collapse of Credit Anstalt.[75] On August 1, 1931, Germany introduced exchange distribution. One week later, on August 8, Hungary did the same. Greece, Yugoslavia, Czechoslovakia, Austria, and Bulgaria introduced exchange distribution by the middle of October. These countries were followed in short order by Denmark, Estonia, Latvia, and Lithuania. In the spring of 1932, Romania introduced distribution. Japan followed in July of that year.[76] In addition to these countries, the years 1931–32 saw the introduction of exchange distribution by Argentina,[77] Bolivia, Brazil, Chile, Colombia, Paraguay, and Uruguay. Italy introduced distribution in 1934 and Poland in 1936.

In virtually every case the introduction of exchange distribution systems was to prevent capital flight. Some detail on the situation in Germany provides a good illustration. The collapse of the Austrian Credit Anstalt found Germany in a severe case of economic depression. German prices for raw materials and finished goods in June of 1931 stood at 61.4 percent of their 1926 values. In February 1931, the number of unemployed stood at 5 million. In the elections of 1930, the National Socialists and Communists increased their seats in the Reichstag from 12 to 107. Following the elections, massive amounts of foreign capital were withdrawn

---

[75] *Exchange Control, Freezing Orders and the Conflict of Laws*, 56 HARV. L. REV. 30 (1942).

[76] Report on Exchange Control, LEAGUE OF NATIONS, II ECO. AND FIN. A. 10 p. 10 (1938).

[77] See, e.g., DIAZ ALEJANDRO, EXCHANGE-RATE DEVALUATION IN A SEMI-INDUSTRIALIZED COUNTRY 57–58 (1968).

from the economy. In the second half of 1930 alone, over a billion and a half marks of foreign capital was exported. Despite efforts by the German Government and some emergency assistance by the central banks of England, France, and the United States, the outflow of capital from Germany continued during the winter and spring of 1931. In the middle of July, a leading German bank—the Darstader-und-Nationalbank—failed. This event seemed to be the last straw for the Reichsbank. It gave up trying to stem the tide of capital withdrawals. The banks and stock exchange were closed. And a series of decrees were introduced culminating in the law of August 1, 1931. That law provided that the Reichsbank be given a monopoly in dealing in foreign exchange. The object was to permit the Reichsbank to repay Germany's foreign creditors in an orderly manner and limit the utilization of exchange for other purposes.

In a very real sense the existence of exchange distribution systems in the developing world is directly related to the events in Europe that began in 1929. As we have seen, several countries in Latin America adopted exchange distribution in response to its adoption in Europe. For the then colonial areas of Asia and Africa the effect was even more direct for the systems of the metropole were automatically extended to the colonies. Thus at the time they became independent the former colonial territories inherited, *inter alia*, an exchange distribution system. And with the approach of independence, the colonies found themselves afflicted with the very illness for which the mechanisms had originally been designed—capital flight.

The colonists, by and large, viewed independence with trepidation. Many thought that the "locals" were not ready for self-rule. Some were certain of it. This view was often shared by the wealthy trading classes. The latter were, in many cases, like the colonists in that they were not indigenous to the country in which they resided and they feared the consequences of rule by the "have-nots." In a period of uncertainty and fear prudence dictates that one transfer one's wealth to a more secure haven, either the metropole or to that classic sanctuary for fleeing capital, the Swiss bank. The determination of which haven to seek was based primarily on the membership of the colony in a currency zone. Thus British overseas territories were members of the sterling bloc and transfers within the bloc, i.e., to the U.K., were virtually unrestricted. A transfer outside the bloc, e.g., to Switzerland, generally faced the same restrictions as those facing a resident of the U.K. Of course, few of the wealthy chose to liquidate their investments in toto. They had been very profitable in the past and there was the chance that they would continue to be so in the future. And panic selling led to extremely depressed prices. A favorite technique for many was to secure loans against locally held assets and transfer the loan proceeds to overseas accounts. The object was to mortgage property to the hilt. This process had the added advantage of ensuring a minimal loss in the event of nationalization or expropriation of one's property. There was little the developing countries could do about stemming this leakage of capital prior to independence. It was, on the other hand, an area where they could and did act soon after independence.

Prompt action against capital flight was facilitated in most newly independent states by the existence of preindependence exchange distribution legislation. Exchange control offices in the former colonies were staffed by ex-colonial administrators familiar with the intricacies of such systems. Also, the local banks were more often than not branches of banks headquartered in London or Paris and were familiar with administering an exchange distribution system. The crackdown on capital flight was, therefore, easy to implement. This is not to say that capital flight ended simply because it was now restricted or prohibited. In fact the restrictions may have accelerated the flight of capital by having exactly the effect those sending their capital abroad were fearful of. Nonetheless capital transfers were now illegal and other more devious routes had to be found to get one's wealth out of the country.[78]

Experience establishes that attempts to control capital flight quickly expand to systems regulating all outflows of foreign exchange. The reason for this development is almost self-evident. When restrictions are placed on outward capital transfers, the almost immediate reaction of those wishing to remove their capital to a safe haven is to evade the controls through the vehicle of unregulated foreign payments.[79] The most important avenue is to utilize payments for imports as a means of "disguised" capital flight.[80] The favorite technique is the overinvoicing of imports, i.e. paying a "premium" for imported goods, with the premium being deposited by a confederate in the overseas bank account of the buyer. To deal with this situation, the authorities need therefore to closely supervise imports and import payments. They will normally require the submission of the documents evidencing the bona fides of the transaction and will themselves obtain independent price information to verify the price being paid for the import. Before importing goods into Brazil, for example, it was at one time necessary for importers to submit to the Brazilian authorities a pro forma invoice, including the price and description of the

[78] Capital flight is not, of course, uniquely the result of decolonization. It is associated with political instability in general.

[79] E. SOHMEN, FLEXIBLE EXCHANGE RATES -120 (1961) ("Administrators of exchange controls have had ample opportunity to learn that enforcement of restrictions on capital movements is ineffectual unless they are accompanied by an equally detailed supervision of commodity trade and invisible items."); see also NURKSE, *supra* note 73 at 165; Machlup, *supra* note 73 at 97.

[80] The term "disguised capital flight" is sometimes used to describe the movement of capital out of the economy as well as out of the country. Thus the practice in India of purchasing smuggled gold as a hedge against inflation is a form of capital flight.

goods, which had been "legalized by the Brazilian Consulate or Chamber of Commerce within the country of origin." [81] The Kenya Government went a step further when it required importers to obtain a clearance certificate verifying price, quality, and quantity from a firm of Swiss cargo superintendents before importers were allocated foreign exchange.[82] Efforts directed at establishing the bona fides of import transactions involve inevitable delays in payments for goods and tend to disrupt the normal commercial life of the country. But the difficulties may go beyond this. In Venezuela, in 1961, the authorities attempting to regulate overinvoicing became concerned about the fact that drug prices quoted by American companies were "substantially higher than prices quoted by suppliers in Czechoslovakia and Italy." [83] The American companies claimed the higher prices reflected a pro rata allocation of research and development costs. The authorities may have suspected an overinvoicing arrangement. But how to prove it without an examination of the financial records of the U.S. drug companies? And the issue may be even more complicated where part or all of the consideration paid for the import is merchandise rather than cash.[84] Similar problems arise with the underinvoicing of exports. Thus Article 35 of the Colombian Exchange Control Law of 1959 provided that exporters must turn in to the authority not merely their export proceeds but "foreign exchange received from exports in a quantity not less than that of the official price list for export product [sic]." [85] In fact all external payments need to be supervised to detect unauthorized capital movements. And efforts to restrict capital flight may go beyond the examination of authorized payments. To reach the resident

[81] 2 Bolsa ii (July 1968).   [82] II IMF Survey, Jan. 3, 1973, p. 15.

[83] Woodley, *Exchange Measures in Venezuela*, XI Staff Papers 337, 342 (1964).

[84] See, e.g., I. Meade, On the Theory of International Economic Policy: The Balance of Payments 266 (1960).

[85] Colombian Law Bulletin, p. 13 (Law No. 1 of 1959) (mimeo).

who acquires foreign currency, or claims to foreign currency, on the local black market and simply mails the exchange to a bank account he secretly maintains abroad, it may be necessary for the authorities to monitor outgoing international mail. This is fraught with difficulties. It would be possible to examine only those letters the senders were foolish enough to address directly to overseas banks or sent in registered form. During the 1930s for example, Austria censored all registered letters addressed to foreign countries.[86] And during World War II, the United Kingdom maintained a system of postal censorship for security purposes which had the added advantage of enabling the Treasury to detect evasions of the exchange regulations. Some governments maintain such systems at present, but in a free society it is not a welcome move. Another obvious possibility for getting exchange out of the country is for a resident to leave with the foreign exchange in his possession. Needless to say, this technique appeals only to the stout of heart or the desperate. Nonetheless declarations are required and physical examinations of baggage and persons are occasionally made at airports in an effort to detect illegal capital flight. In addition to preventive checks, illegal capital outflows are subject, as are all violations of exchange distribution laws, to criminal sanctions.

To the extent that sanctions do not deter, and procedures do not prevent illegal exports of foreign exchange, developing countries try from time to time to "bring home" capital held abroad. One way to do this is to permit importers to freely purchase goods from abroad provided the imports are not financed from official exchange sources. This system provides an inducement to the extent that the goods imported are those normally restricted or prohibited. The importer will be able to market those imports locally at a

[86] ELLIS, *supra* note 45 at 73.

high profit in local currency terms. Many exchange distribution systems contain an escape clause of this nature. It
constitutes a recognition of the fact that no matter how tight
the system and how severe the sanctions, some exchange
will always be in local hands. Once this is accepted the
choice of having those funds invested overseas or being
utilized to supply items not otherwise available in an illegal
way seems less desirable than legalizing the inevitable. In
January 1971, for example, the Syrian Government issued a
decree permitting Syrian nationals to import "primary
products, spare parts, agricultural machinery, and transport
equipment" provided these imports are financed by foreign
exchange held by the importers abroad. (A companion decree suspended all penalties for illegal export of capital
prior to December 31, 1970).[87] Such escape clauses however
are not usually sufficient to repatriate substantial amounts
of capital held abroad. The more usual technique is to declare an amnesty and allow repatriation of foreign balances
without penalty. The Pakistan Martial Law Foreign Exchange (Surrender and Declarations) Regulation, 1958,
permitted surrender of overseas holdings of foreign exchange and promised that "No action of any kind whatsoever shall be taken against a person in respect of the holdings so surrendered or declared, and no tax of any kind
whatsoever shall be levied on or in respect of the amounts
so surrendered or declared." The moratorium was to last
approximately 30 days.[88] Amnesties like this one issued after
Ayub Khan's seizure of power generally follow an abrupt
change of government. In the ensuing period of uncertainty,
the holder of foreign exchange balances is likely to be even
more inclined to maintain them abroad rather than less so.[89]

---

[87] Reported in XXIII I.F.N.S. 27 (1971).

[88] Published in the *Gazette of Pakistan*, Nov. 4, 1958, reprinted in AHMAD, THE
LAW OF FOREIGN EXCHANGE IN PAKISTAN 133 (1963).

[89] The decree apparently resulted in the repatriation of approximately $16 mil-

Thus despite the threat in the amnesty announcement that anyone holding balances abroad who does not repatriate them "shall be punished with rigorous imprisonment which may extend to seven years and with confiscation either of the whole or part of his property in Pakistan," the policy is unlikely to have the effect of bringing back to the country substantial amounts of illegally held foreign balances. Nonetheless governments keep trying. The revolutionary Command Council of Iraq, for example, issued a decree on June 28, 1970 that allowed Iraqis six months to repatriate funds held abroad without incurring the heavy penalties provided for exporting capital or maintaining balances abroad.[90] And Peruvian Decree-Law No. 19266 of January 11, 1972 declared a 90-day amnesty "to enable Peruvian residents to repatriate foreign deposits." [91]

CONVERTIBILITY

Since it is difficult to repatriate capital, most developing countries focus their efforts on limiting capital flight. To do this effectively requires an apparatus for monitoring all external payments. It is not surprising therefore that a country preferring a resistance strategy for dealing with a balance of payments crisis would prefer to utilize its already existing capital control apparatus as the means of implementing that strategy. There is yet a third reason why developing countries utilize exchange distribution. Exchange distribution is a means of coping with a world economic situation in which some of the world's currencies are convertible and some are not.[92] From an economic point of view a currency is convertible when it "can be bought and sold

lion. See G. PAPANEK, PAKISTAN'S DEVELOPMENT, SOCIAL GOALS AND PRIVATE INCENTIVES at 109 (1967).
   [90] XXII I.F.N.S. 259 (1970).
   [91] Reported in BOLSA (April 1972).
   [92] International Monetary Fund, FOURTH ANNUAL REPORT ON EXCHANGE RESTRICTIONS 3 (1953).

freely at the prevailing price, regardless of the residence or purposes of the transactors." [93] Legally, a currency is considered convertible when the country whose currency it is formally accepts the obligations of Article VIII, Section 2, 3, and 4 of the Articles of Agreement of the International Monetary Fund. The test of that provision as well as the central role of the Fund in the exchange distribution picture will be considered in detail in chapter 3. At this point we may accept the following explanation. A currency is *externally* convertible when "all holdings of that currency by nonresidents are freely exchangeable into any foreign (nonresident) currency at exchange rates within the official margins . . . all payments that *residents* of the country are authorized to make to nonresidents may be made in any externally convertible currency that residents can buy in foreign exchange markets. On the other hand, if there are no restrictions on the ability of a country's *residents* to use their holdings of domestic currency to acquire any foreign currency and hold it, or transfer it to any nonresident for any purpose, the country's currency is said to be *internally* convertible. Thus *external* convertibility alone is tantamount to *partial* convertibility whereas *total* convertibility involves both *external* and *internal* convertibility." [94]

Currencies which are not externally convertible, i.e., inconvertible, may be of rather limited value to their holder. An export from a developing country to the U.S.S.R., for example, may be paid for in rubles or a currency of a country which has accepted the obligations of Article VIII. If the latter, the proceeds may be used to purchase goods anywhere. If, however, the proceeds are in rubles, they may only be used to purchase goods of the U.S.S.R.[95] A country

[93] COHEN, *supra* note 1 at 75.

[94] de Vries, *Exchange Restrictions: The Setting*, II IMF HISTORY 1945–1965, 217, 226–227 (1969). On "official margins" see pp. 305–6 *infra*.

[95] On a trend toward "convertibility" in Comecon see, e.g., Wilczynski, *Towards Multilateral Payments in Comecon Trade*, CEDA (1971).

whose exports go to states some of whom enjoy convertible currencies and some of whom maintain inconvertible currencies, thus needs to separate out its transactions with the latter group as the export proceeds there earned are not fungible. Those proceeds can normally be used only to import goods from and/or repay debts from the issuing country. In considering possible import suppliers, therefore, a developing country will have some interest in directing its importers to those countries whose inconvertible currencies are in large supply. This is, of course, a case of trade discrimination which is condemned by traditional trade theory. For it means that goods are not being purchased from the cheapest source. Recent economic writing has, however, reopened the question in view of the continued existence of inconvertible currencies. Some writers would draw a distinction between the sources on the grounds that since a credit balance with a source whose currency is inconvertible can only be used to buy goods from that source it is better to use that balance where one can, holding one's supply of convertible currency in reserve for purchases in other markets.[96] A government could avoid this kind of problem by cutting down on its exports to countries whose currency is not convertible, thereby eliminating credit balances of limited utility. But that policy would be advisable only if there were alternative markets for the goods. Frequently there are not. Also, some international arrangements like the International Coffee Agreement encourage sales to countries with inconvertible currencies by establishing a list of "nonquota" countries whose content is closely correlated with inconvertible currency countries. Where it is profitable on the export side to trade with countries maintaining inconvertible currencies, and the government wishes to encourage imports from those countries to offset its credit balances, it

[96] G. PATTERSON, DISCRIMINATION IN INTERNATIONAL TRADE, THE POLICY ISSUES 1945–1965, 25 (1966).

will utilize its exchange distribution mechanism to limit the availability of convertible exchange where there are alternative suppliers of the same type of goods in inconvertible currency countries.[97]

COLLECTING THE FOREIGN EXCHANGE

In establishing an exchange distribution system the first essential is for the distributing authority to become the depository of all foreign exchange within its jurisdiction. In order

[97] Trading with countries whose currencies are inconvertible is usually carried out by means of clearing accounts. Each trading partner maintains an account in the other so that all trade and other payments between the two countries are handled at the local level. International monetary transfers to balance out these accounts take place once a year or, sometimes, not at all, if the parties decide that the balance is to be eliminated by shipments of goods. This process of settling clearing accounts by transfers of goods has been subject to much abuse, particularly during the interwar period. An analogous situation arises where one or both of the currencies are convertible but one of the parties wishes to limit the use to which its payments for imports will be put. These are the so-called payments agreements which came into wide use during the 1930s between countries in Europe and Latin America. The European countries generally imported more goods from Latin America—mainly foodstuffs and raw materials—than they exported to Latin America. At the same time, the Latin American states introduced exchange restrictions in the 1930s, they limied the amounts of exchange which could be used to pay their European debts. In retaliation, the Europeans brought pressure on the Latin-American states—usually by threatening to reduce purchases of goods from Latin America—to sign payment agreements. Once the agreement was in operation, however, the doubled-edged nature of the threat became apparent. For the payments arrangement only worked so long as the creditor country imported more than it exported to the debtor country. This circumstance gave rise to the saying "to have a good clearing system you must have a bad balance of trade." Moreover, the system adversely affected third countries. In the League of Nations it was noted that "Third parties are adversely affected because a country with a weak currency will tend to buy as much as possible in the country with which it has a clearing agreement. Lacking free exchange, the weak-currency country will buy in the other country even goods which, in the ordinary way, they might have bought in third countries on more favorable terms. This leads to diversion of commercial trends to the detriment of these last-mentioned countries. . . ." (Joint Committee on the Inquiry into Compensation and Clearing Agreements, II LEAGUE OF NATIONS, ENQUIRY INTO CLEARING AGREEMENTS, ECON. & FIN. 1935, B.6., 15). For the case against trading by means of clearing accounts, see VERBIT, TRADE AGREEMENTS FOR DEVELOPING COUNTRIES 100–102 (1969).

to do this, the government will require that all foreign exchange or claims to foreign exchange in the possession or under the control of residents of the country will be declared to the government and *may* require that such exchange be sold to the government or its agent. Thus, the Foreign Exchange Regulation Act of India provides in Section 4(1) that "[e]xcept with the previous general or special permission of the Reserve Bank no person other than an authorized dealer shall in India, and no person resident in India other than an authorized dealer shall outside India buy or borrow from or sell or lend to, or exchange with, any person other than an authorized dealer any foreign exchange." Section 4(3) provides that "Where any foreign exchange is acquired by any person . . . the said person shall without delay sell the foreign exchange to an authorized dealer." While the coverage of the statute is very broad and its language sweeping, it is important to note that for the average person it requires no more than the usual behavior. When an individual obtains foreign exchange, he normally deposits it in his bank or exchanges it there for local currency. The law thus makes mandatory what would otherwise be done, in most cases, voluntarily. The restrictive nature of the legislation is felt when one wishes to use foreign exchange for some purpose.

Note that the law affects different groups of "persons." First it governs the conduct of all persons *within* India without regard to nationality or residence. There is no question that a state can exercise authority over all persons within its jurisdiction. The legislation also covers persons who are residents of India no matter where they are located. Thus the exchange distribution system exercises jurisdiction either with regard to the *situs* of the transaction or the *status* of the transactor. It is the latter category that causes confusion since residence is a question of fact and a very confused one at that. This vexed question is a bit beyond our immediate area of interest and it will suffice to state at this point that the system will reach *residents* of the state regardless of their location.

Similar surrender requirements are typical of most exchange distribution legislation. Article 60 of the Yugoslavian Exchange Control Law provides that a citizen who brings in or receives foreign exchange from abroad must offer it for sale to an authorized dealer or deposit it in a foreign exchange account in "an authorized bank or the National Bank of Yugoslavia." While the citizen may use such balances "in accordance with ordinances adopted by the Federal Executive Council," foreign exchange accounts are "considered deposits of the National Bank of Yugoslavia." And Article 35 of the Colombian Exchange Control Law of 1959 provides that "exporters must sell to the Bank of the Republic, at the rate of exchange periodically set by the Board of Directors . . . the foreign exchange received from exports. . . ." [98]

Despite the fact that the surrender requirements codify what the recipient of foreign exchange would normally do, most governments rely on confirming procedures and criminal sanctions to enforce those requirements. For export proceeds the usual practice is for a government to require that all exporters register their exports, specifying value, destination, means of payment, and so on and agree to turn over their export proceeds to the government or its agent. No goods are permitted to pass through the customs without a registration statement or export license. Thus, if an exporter does not present the foreign exchange proceeds of his exports to the government voluntarily, the government has a ready means of becoming alert to that fact. As a means of encouraging tourists to exchange their foreign currency at authorized dealers, each tourist entering India

[98] See also, e.g., Ecuador Decree No. 5, June 22, 1970, reported in IV BOLSA 458 (1970).

is given a card on which there is to be entered each transaction in which he converts foreign exchange into Indian rupees. When the tourist leaves India, he presents the card to the emigration officials who can readily determine if the tourist has officially exchanged the "usual" amount of exchange for the duration of his stay in India. While prosecutions for converting too little foreign exchange at official exchange agencies are unusual, the existence of the card and the knowledge that it will be checked when the tourist leaves India is sufficient to keep most tourists away from the "black market." A related system used by other developing countries to ensure that tourist expenditures are converted at the official rate is to require that bills at certain hotels frequented by tourists be paid only in foreign currency. When such systems fail, the government must then rely on its criminal sanctions. The *Indian Act* provides that "any person [who] contravenes the provisions . . . shall upon conviction by a Court, be punishable with imprisonment for a term which may extend for two years, or with fine, or both." Persons who retain foreign currency in Peru are subject to up to five years imprisonment, confiscation of the currency, and a fine of ten times the value of the amount involved, according to Decree-Law No. 18275 of May 17, 1970.[99]

Having gathered into its coffers the available supply of foreign exchange the government must then distribute it. In his 1944 study of the prewar international monetary system, Professor Nurkse identified four kinds of decisions involved in the distribution process. The authorities must decide "(1) how much to allot for different *purposes* (com-

---

[99] Reported in 4 BOLSA 345 (1970). In Nazi Germany, a decree issued on December 1, 1936 made "economic sabotage" a capital offense. Among the acts constituting economic sabotage was the transfer of property abroad "consciously, without scruple or conscience, for clearly egoistic purposes, or other base purposes." *New York Times*, December 2, 1936, quoted in ELLIS *supra* note 45 at 68 n.42. Contracts which involve evasions may be void. See, e.g., *Sharif* v. *Azad*, reported in *The Times* (London), Oct. 6, 1966 at p. 6.

modity imports, debt service, tourist traffic, etc.); (2) how
to distribute the exchange available for imports among different *commodities;* (3) how to ration exchange among different *firms;* and (4) how to distribute the total among
different *countries."* [100] The present study will concern itself with the types of decisions Professor Nurkse numbered (1)–(3) and particularly group (3), the rationing
among firms. At the outset we will look at the general political, economic, and legal constraints operating on a developing country in its choice of distribution systems.

[100] See NURKSE, *supra* note 73 at 173.

Chapter 3

The International Legal Framework for Exchange Distribution

Restrictions on the free use of foreign exchange have a long history. Professor Paul Einzig's researches go back to ancient Lydia where coins were made of two different weights, one for use on the eastern caravan routes toward Mesopotamia, which conformed to Babylonian weight standards, and the other for the western route conforming to Æginetan standards.[1] Plato advocated a system of coins with no intrinsic value, with ownership of gold and silver being confined to the state for use in the prosecution of wars and the requirements of foreign embassies. His proposals may have been based on the Spartan practice of issuing iron bars for currency, with a corollary prohibition on holding precious metals. A similar system was employed by the Ptolemies in Egypt.

From time to time controls were attempted on the importation, exportation and circulation of foreign coins and pre-

[1] P. Einzig, The History of Foreign Exchange 50 (2d ed. 1970).

cious metals in Tudor England. During this period all foreign payments and receipts had to pass through the hands of the "Royal Exchanger." [2] And in the Statute of Staple, 1353, King Edward III provided that "merchant strangers" could take out of England only the same amount of money they had brought in.[3] These attempts were mainly short lived because of the protests of the increasingly important class of merchants and bankers. Restrictions in the use of foreign exchange did not become generally significant until World War I.

The modern use of controls can be traced to that war when belligerent states sought to conserve their supplies of foreign exchange for the purchase of military equipment and cargo space. It was, however, the depression of the 1930s that first saw exchange distribution introduced on a wide scale. And the world war that followed which prompted the first effective multilateral action to limit the influence of such systems. The motivation for international action was well summarized by the then U.S. Secretary of the Treasury, Henry Morgenthau. "We saw currency disorders develop and spread from land to land, destroying the basis for international trade and international investment and even international faith. In their wake, we saw unemployment and wretchedness—idle tools, wasted wealth. We saw their victims fall prey, in places, to demagogues and dictators. We saw bewilderment and bitterness become the breeders of fascism and, finally, of war." Secretary Morgenthau may have overdramatized the effect of exchange restrictions in this statement, for currency disorders were not the sole cause of World War II. But they undoubtedly contributed to the general economic instability

---

[2] See *id* at 158.

[3] See Metzger, *Exchange Controls and International Law*, in P. PROEHL (ed.), LEGAL PROBLEMS OF INTERNATIONAL TRADE 310, 312, n.4 (1959) (citing NUSSBAUM, MONEY IN THE LAW 447 [rev. ed. 1950]).

that reduced large numbers of people to such desperate straits that they were willing to turn to radical leadership. And Secretary Morgenthau's views may reflect the fact that the Roosevelt Administration had done much more thinking about economic policies for the postwar world than about its political composition.[4] Nonetheless the belief that economic factors were critical in reconstructing a peaceful world was a very real one. And these views were shared by the representatives of the developing countries who participated in the Bretton Woods Conference. The Hon. Arthur De Souza Costa, head of the Brazilian delegation, noted at the time that "There are still in the memory of all of us the drama of all sorts of international blocked currencies, of economic isolationism, of competition instead of cooperation among central banks, and of general unemployment. The civilized world must not permit a repetition of this tragic situation." Given these views, it is not surprising that statesmen devoted much time and energy to bringing forth new institutions which would prevent a reoccurrence of these conditions. The story of these extraordinary men and the institutions they created has been splendidly told elsewhere.[5] Our immediate concern is with the product of their efforts.

The Articles of Agreement of the IMF incorporate three separate concepts.[6] First, the Articles provide a *code of conduct* in international monetary affairs. The code of conduct aspect of the Agreement is the one with which this study is immediately concerned. The draftsmen of the Articles how-

[4] R. GARDNER, STERLING-DOLLAR DIPLOMACY 8 (2d ed. 1969).

[5] I IMF, HISTORY 1945–1965 (1969); GARDNER, *supra* note 4. See also Fleming, *Developments in the International Payments System*, X STAFF PAPERS 461, 462 (1963) ("The general aim of this system was to adjust payments disequilibria with the least possible impairment of full employment, of freedom of international trade, and, in a sense, of exchange stability. It was designed to avoid the faults alike of the gold standard, of Schactianism, and of the currency chaos of the 1930's.").

[6] Evans, *Current and Capital Transactions: How the Fund Defines Them*, in FIN. AND DEV. 30, 31 (Sept. 1968).

ever were wise enough to see that it was not sufficient to prohibit certain practices. They knew that compliance with the code of conduct would be facilitated if members were provided with access to resources that would tide them over the financial crises which had hitherto been dealt with by the newly prohibited practices. The draftsmen thus provided that the IMF would be a source of short-term support for countries whose *reserves* were falling to a critical level. Finally, the Articles established the Fund Secretariat to administer the code of conduct and the financing operations. Taken together, the package has worked extremely well. The financing operations have given the Fund authorities the leverage needed to encourage compliance with the code of conduct. At the same time, the profits from the Fund's financial operations have provided a means of funding the organization itself and thereby keeping it remarkably free of outside political pressures. The availability of internal funding has also enabled the IMF to recruit a staff unrivaled in quality. And they have, in turn, dynamically interpreted and implemented the provisions of the Articles of Agreement so as to enable the Fund to deal with a different world than the one which existed when the Articles were drafted in 1944.

The code of conduct incorporated in the Articles of Agreement provides the outer limits within which a member may establish or maintain a system of exchange distribution. For present purposes the most significant section is Article VIII, Section 2(a), which provides that "no member shall, without the approval of the Fund, impose restrictions on the making of payments and transfers for current international transactions." Read literally, this looks like an outright prohibition on exchange distribution systems. This was certainly the original aim of the American delegates at Bretton Woods. For in their view, "in the hands of Nazi Germany exchange control and exchange discrimination had become the handmaidens of military aggression." [7] In the original American draft for the Fund, therefore, members were to abandon *all* exchange restrictions.[8] The distinction between "current" transactions and other types of international transactions is one that will be discussed in detail later in this chapter. At this point it is sufficient to note that confining the prohibition against restrictions to current transactions did not seriously compromise the aims of the American draftsmen of the Articles since their ultimate goal was to restore "multilateralism" to world trade.[9] Multilateralism has been defined as a "system . . . in which barriers to trade and payments are reduced to moderate levels and made nondiscriminatory in their application." [10] The object then was not the elimination of all controls, but the more realistic goal of their reduction to a reasonable level.[11]

From the point of view of legal history, the general prohibition in Article VIII, 2(a) is remarkable. For the principal draftsmen of the Articles of Agreement were British and American, whose legal background was in a common law system built largely upon precedent. Yet there was little precedent available to aid in formulating a policy on exchange restrictions.[12] The experience of the 1930s was considered such an aberrational situation that it provided little data for the formulation of a standard that was to operate in more "normal" times.[13] The pre-Depression adherence

---

[7] GARDNER, *supra* note 4 at 76.

[8] The original proposal was for the abandonment of "all exchange restrictions within six months after joining the Fund or after the cessation of hostilities, whichever was later." GARDNER, *supra* note 4 at 89.

[9] Ironically enough, there is language in the Articles of Agreement which goes to strengthen the use of exchange distribution in contrast to the somewhat sweeping prohibitions incorporated in Article VIII, 2(a). The very next paragraph, 2(b), provides that "[e]xchange contracts . . . contrary to the exchange control regulations . . . of [a] member maintained or imposed *consistently* with this Agreement shall be unenforceable in the territories of any member." (Emphasis added.)

[10] GARDNER, *supra* note 4 at 13.

[11] *Ibid.*   [12] Metzger, *supra* note 3 at 313.   [13] *Ibid.*

to the gold standard, and widespread notions about the evils of impairing the values of one's currency, meant that exchange restrictions were not widely used before the 1930s. The straightforward prohibition of Article VIII, 2(a) was thus a statement of general intention whose interstices were meant to be filled in by experience. To understand the meaning of Article VIII, 2(a) it is necessary therefore to examine the jurisprudence that has resulted from its interpretation over the years.

The language of Article VIII, 2(a) has been subject to only one official interpretation in the twenty-nine years since the Articles have come into force. That interpretation, to be discussed below, was nine years in the making. The Committee on Interpretation began looking into the question of the meaning of Article VIII, Section 2(a) in June of 1951. The decision was published on June 1, 1960. As will be seen below the decision is of a very general nature. In effect, the staff has decided to treat the matter of the interpretation of Article VIII, 2(a) on a case by case basis.[14] This approach has had the meritorious effect of allowing both the Fund and the members to respond to new and changing situations in a flexible way. Despite the absence of definitive interpretations however there is a large body of unofficial doctrine consisting of the published work of the Fund staff. Each word in the critical sentence has been subject to at least some exigesis by members of the staff. Although these interpretations are not binding on the Fund, they do provide some insight into the institutional views on the meaning of Article VIII, 2(a).

Recall that the critical language is that "no member, shall, without the approval of the Fund, impose restrictions on the making of payments and transfers for current international transactions." Starting with the first word—"restric-

---

[14] I IMF HISTORY 1945–1965, 311 (1969).

tion"—the General Counsel of the IMF has written that "The word 'restriction' must, however, be distinguished from 'control.' The former means a real interference with payments and transfers for current international transactions, and therefore something more than imposing on parties the nuisance of having to go through some procedure that is not unreasonable as a condition precedent to a payment or transfer." [15] The Agreement does not, therefore, prohibit exchange controls, but only exchange restrictions. Note however that the phrase "controls" is given a very narrow meaning as contrasted with the more usual practice of utilizing "exchange controls" as synonymous with exchange restrictions.

We know further that an unreasonable condition precedent, i.e., a restriction, will "involve suppression (or delay) of the transaction, or limitations as to its volume, direction or terms." [16] What we do not know is the nature of a "reasonable condition precedent" to payment or transfer, i.e., a control. The only clue provided by the General Counsel indicates that one way to test the reasonableness of a condition precedent is to look at the ostensible purpose. A required procedure is not a restriction, for example, if the purpose is the gathering of statistics. There is thus a two-factor test to determine whether a procedure is a "restriction" within the meaning of Article VIII. One first looks at the *purpose* of such a restriction. If the purpose is to interfere with payments, the procedure is a restriction. If, on the other hand, the purpose is a legitimate one, e.g., gathering statistics on the nature and volume of international trade and payments, the procedure will not be a restriction. The second part of the test of a restriction is the *effect* of the procedure. If the effect is to interfere with international

[15] Gold, *The International Monetary Fund and Private Business Transactions: Some Legal Effects of the Articles of Agreement* 8, (IMF Pamphlet No. 3, 1965).
[16] I IMF HISTORY 1945–1965, 311 (1969).

payments, the procedure is a restriction within the meaning of Article VIII. Where this effect is not present, there is no restriction. Thus procedures that at first impression may appear to be restrictions, e.g., prior licensing or prior registration of import or export transactions, will not be "restrictions" if they do not unduly delay or limit the making of payments or transfers. This leaves two other possibilities. First, the case where a requirement is intended to limit payments but does not have that effect. Such a case of ineptitude is likely not to run afoul of the Agreement. Conversely, a requirement that has a legitimate purpose but the prohibited effect is likely to be condemned. For it would appear that the Fund is less interested in the *mens rea* of the offender than in the impact on international payments. If this is the case we might then reconstruct our definition of a "restriction" to mean a procedure which has the prohibited effect of interfering with international payments. And the quantum of effect that will amount to interference will be greater where there is a legitimate purpose for the procedure than would be the case where there was no such purpose. To take a crude illustration, let us assume that a requirement of prior registration of all import payments that delays those payments two days from the time period when they would ordinarily be made would amount to a restriction. If, however, the basis for the requirement was the gathering of statistics, the two-day delay might not be a restriction.[17]

[17] This seems the only rational means of reconciling the General Counsels observation that a "nuisance . . . procedure" will not be a restriction if imposed "to assemble statistics" with the language of Decision No. 144–(52/51) of August 14, 1952 indicating that Article VIII, Sec. 2 (a) "applies to all restrictions . . . irrespective of their motivation and the circumstances in which they are imposed." See V. SALERA, EXCHANGE CONTROL AND THE ARGENTINE MARKET 199 (1941) ("In the preamble to the decree of November 7, 1938, which set up a universal import system, the sole statement that was strictly related to the text of the decree itself declared that 'a general application of the system of exchange permits to all imports would permit the obtaining of complete statistical information regarding the probable future development of our purchases from abroad.' The subterfuge of an undefined statistical hiatus of course deluded none in informed circles in Buenos Aires.").

There is yet a third aspect of "restriction" as used in Article VIII, 2(a). In their only official interpretation of this provision, the Executive Directors have indicated that the prohibited restrictions must be limitations imposed by government action.[18] The impositions may be administrative in form and need not, in fact, be formally promulgated. This interpretation would seem to include within its ambit the so-called voluntary restrictions currently in use in some countries. And government includes independent agencies such as central banks to whom the political authority may have delegated the power to supervise exchange transactions. In sum therefore, a procedure falling within the ambit of Article VIII, 2(a) is one which is imposed by government and which exhibits the prohibited effect.

A restriction prohibited by Article VIII, 2(a) must be on "payments" (or "transfers.") The Fund lawyers considered three possible interpretations of the phrase "restriction . . . on payments." [19] The first possibility was a broad interpretation that would have condemned all restrictions—direct or indirect—on the making of payments. An indirect restriction would, for example, be a regulation prohibiting the importation of shoes. Such a regulation *a fortiori* prohibits payments for shoe imports. A second possibility was to read the language as condemning all restrictions—direct or indirect—except those whose purpose was to effect a result considered legitimate within the meaning of the Articles. The emphasis here is on the motive for which the restrictions were imposed. Such an interpretation might permit, for example, a restriction imposed for balance of payments reasons. The third possibility for interpretation is the one that has been adopted. In their decision of June 1, 1960 the Executive Directors indicate that "the guiding principle in

---

[18] For an example of a practice which could amount to a restriction but for the absence of official government action requiring it, see Woodley, *Exchange Measures in Venezuela*, XI STAFF PAPERS 337, 344 (1964).

[19] Gold, *The Code of Conduct,* in II IMF HISTORY 1945–1965, 554 (1969).

ascertaining whether a measure is a restriction on payments and transfers for current transactions . . . is whether it involves a direct governmental limitation on the *availability or use of exchange as such.*" [20] This interpretation is narrower than the first possibility since it prohibits only *direct* restrictions on the use of payments media. And it is both wider and narrower than the second alternative. It is wider in the sense that it prohibits (subject to two minor exceptions to be discussed below) restrictions for whatever *reason* imposed. It is narrower, on the other hand, in that it prohibits only *direct* restrictions.[21]

The Executive Directors' interpretation is based primarily on the history of the Articles of Agreement. For the Fund was to be one of three international institutions which would establish and police an interrelated set of norms for the postwar conduct of international trade and financial relations. The Funds' sister institutions were to be the International Bank for Reconstruction and Development (IBRD) and the International Trade Organization (ITO). The ITO was stillborn but many of its functions have devolved upon GATT. To illustrate the division of responsibility between the IMF and GATT we may revert again to the example of shoe imports. If shoe imports are limited directly, e.g., by quantitative restrictions or tariffs, they fall within the responsibility of the GATT. If, on the other hand, imports are limited by restricting the quantity of exchange made available for such imports they fall within the responsibility of the Fund. There is little question but that this interpretation is the most valid of the alternatives in the light of this history, as well as the language of Article VIII.[22] As we shall

---

[20] Decision 1034–(60/27), reprinted in III IMF HISTORY 1945–1965, 260–261 (1969). (Emphasis added.)

[21] See Gold, *supra* note 15 at 9–11.

[22] This "division of labor" has been termed "shocking" by Professor Robert Mundell. "Switching from one set of trade restrictions to another shifts a country from the jurisdiction of the IMF to that of GATT. . . . Yet these two methods of restricting trade are perfectly equivalent from an analytic point of view." R. MUN-

see, however, the provisions of the GATT itself substantially blur the distinction so that the Fund has, in fact, a major role in the GATT structure. To the extent however that the distinction remains valid in terms of defining the limits of Fund responsibility, it has had important consequences on the rule of law aspects of exchange distribution in developing countries. For present purposes of identifying the limits contained in the Articles of Agreement on the ability of developing countries to establish systems of exchange distribution however, it is important to note only that these apply only to restrictions on payments and not on the underlying import transaction.

In addition to prohibiting direct restrictions on payments, Article VIII, 2(a) forbids restrictions on "transfers." The distinction between a payment and a transfer is that a *payment* is made by a *resident* of the country imposing the restrictions while a transfer is made by the *nonresident recipient* of that payment. To have excluded transfers from Article VIII 2(a) would have meant that a government could have limited the use of its currency (or that of a third country) by a nonresident in another country. To illustrate the interrelationship, take the case of an exporter in country *A* who sells shoes to an importer in country *B*. The prohibition of restrictions on payments means that country *B* must allow the importer to make *payment* to the exporter in a currency acceptable to the exporter (either *B*'s own currency or that of another Fund member). When the exporter in country *A* receives his payment, he may not be limited in using (transferring) the payment by any restriction imposed by country *B*. The dual prohibition of restrictions on payments and transfers thus frees both exporter and importer to trade where they will and in this way promotes the "multilaterism" goal of the Agreement.

Finally, Article VIII, 2(a) prohibits direct restrictions on

DELL and A. SWOBODA (eds.), MONETARY PROBLEMS OF THE INTERNATIONAL ECONOMY 159 (1969).

"current international transactions." This phrase is defined in the Agreement. Article XIX, (i) provides "Payments for current transactions means payments which are not for the purpose of transferring capital and includes, without limitation: (1) All payments due in connection with foreign trade, other current business, including services, and normal short-term banking and credit facilities; (2) Payments due as interest on loans and as net income from other investments; (3) Payments of moderate amount for amortization of loans or for depreciation of direct investments; (4) Moderate remittances for family living expenses."

As is evident from the first sentence of Article XIX, (i) the Articles of Agreement have adopted a fundamental distinction between current and capital transfers. This is reinforced by Article VI, Section 3 which provides that "members may exercise such controls as are necessary to regulate international capital movements." The basis for this distinction is the history of the 1930s, reviewed in chapter 2. In an early draft of the Fund Agreement, prepared by British monetary experts under the leadership of Lord Keynes, it was noted that: "There is no country which can, in the future, safely allow the flight of funds for political reasons or to evade domestic taxation or in anticipation of the owner turning refugee. Equally, there is no country that can safely receive fugitive funds which constitute an unwanted import of capital, cannot safely be used for fixed investment. For these reasons, it is widely held that the control of capital movements, both inward and outward, should be a permanent feature of the post-war system." [23]

These views were shared by the majority at Bretton Woods and were incorporated in a broadly worded provi-

---

[23] II U.S. Department of State, Proceedings and Documents of the United Nations Monetary and Financial Conference, Bretton Woods, New Hampshire, July 1–22, 1944, p. 1566 (Pub. No. 2866). (Reprinting text of a paper containing proposals by British experts for an International Clearing Union.)

sion. That the language and the substantive right were intended to be broad was reaffirmed in a Decision of the Fund's Executive Directors on July 25, 1956, which provides in part: "Members are free to adopt a policy of regulating capital movements *for any reason,* due regard being paid to the general purposes of the Fund, and without prejudice to the provisions of Article VI, Section 1." [24] The decision is even broader than the words used for it; it has been interpreted to mean that members may regulate capital movements *by any means they choose,* an interpretation not necessarily compelled by the language of Article VI, 3.[25] Again, this interpretation appears sound in view of both the text of the·Articles of Agreement and their history. For the Articles not only permit members to maintain controls on capital movements, but actually authorize the Fund to request a member to control such capital movements (Article VI, Section 1(a)) and prohibit the use of the Fund's resources to meet "a large and sustained outflow of capital." In short, the Articles take a dim view of capital outflows and permit, even encourage, members to act promptly by any means to stop them. This gloss is as Keynes intended. The one caveat is that such controls must not interfere with current payments.[26]

In order to effect the distinction in the Articles of Agree-

[24] Decision No. 541–(56/39) of July 25, 1956, reprinted in III IMF HISTORY 1945–1965, 246 (1969). (Emphasis added).

[25] Gold, *The Fund's Concepts of Convertibility* 7 (IMF Pamphlet No. 14, 1971).

[26] A statement in the 1964 Annual Report of the Fund seems to draw back a bit from the carte blanche given members with regard to restrictions on capital movements. At p. 28 the Report notes that with regard to current payments, members are expected to avoid restrictions "to the utmost extent practicable. Restrictions on capital movements may be less objectionable. . . . Because of the difficulties and drawbacks attached to such restrictions, it is, however, preferable to follow, wherever possible, policies aimed at attracting appropriate equilibrating movements of private capital. . . ."

In addition to what a country may do unilaterally to control capital movements, the Executive Directors also specifically approved international arrangements to the same end. This was another of Keynes' ideas. See U.S. Department of State, *supra* note 23 at 1548.

ment between current payments and capital transfers, it was necessary to define current payments. Note that the illustrative definition adopted by Article XIX is not necessarily the definition that would be adopted by economists.[27] Long-term loans, for example, are generally considered capital transfers. Amortization of these loans would therefore be considered a repayment of capital. So, too, sums transferred for depreciation are normally thought of as representing that part of capital which has been "used up." The apparent reason for incorporating those kinds of payments within the meaning of current international transactions was to compromise the views of those who feared capital flight and those who wished to facilitate international investment. But the latter were limited in their achievement by the word "moderate." Only moderate amounts may be repatriated for amortization or depreciation. With regard to depreciation, the Fund has indicated that the measure of moderation begins with the "useful lifespan of any item of plant or equipment." [28] But accountants and economists know that once this is agreed upon there are several choices in depreciation methods. Article XIX is silent on whether moderate depreciation is computed by applying the straight-line method, the "sum-of-the-digits method," or the "declining-balance" method. Since the latter two methods are means of accelerating depreciation and would result in the largest transfers being made immediately after the investment has been completed, it would not be surprising to find capital importing countries taking the position that the straight-line method is that which most accords with moderation.

Current transactions also include "all payments due in connection with . . . normal short-term banking and credit facilities." Any definition which employs the word "normal" is obviously open to considerable interpretation. Some guid-

---

[27] See Gold, *supra* note 15 at 12.   [28] Evans, *supra* note 6 at 34.

ance as to the meaning of this phrase is again given by reference to earlier drafts of the Articles of Agreement. It is clear from this history that "short-term" was intended to mean "within one year." [29] And "normal facility" has been interpreted to mean "the customary practice in the particular trade or business for which the facility is being made available." [30] Of course, "the customary practice" may modify what is "short-term." As a rule, therefore, no restrictions can be placed on repayments of loans of less than one year's duration. Nor may restrictions be placed on repayments of loans of more than one year's duration where the practice in the trade or business indicates that the normal banking or credit facility extends beyond one year.

Aside from the ambiguities that may be present in any illustrative definition like the one used in Article XIX(i), such definitions also leave the special problem of transactions which are not mentioned. As an example of some of the difficulties in classifying transactions, take the case of gifts. A gift is not usually considered the kind of transaction which "establishes a capital position abroad for the donor." [31] From the donor's perspective, therefore, a gift is not a capital transfer. Yet the question may look different from the point of view of the government imposing the exchange restrictions. For it, "current payments" are usually thought of as those for which its residents receive an immediate *quid pro quo* in the form of goods or services.[32] By its very nature, there is no *quid pro quo* for a gift. Some have argued that the question of whether the transaction is current or capital should be determined from yet a third point of view, that of the recipient. But a gift to a foreign university, for example, might fit in either category depending on whether the gift went to meet operating expenses or was added to endowment. Difficulties of this kind provide us

---

[29] *Id.* at 35.   [30] *Ibid.*
[31] See Evans, *supra* note 6 at 34.   [32] *Ibid.*

with some hint of the reason why the Fund has never exercised its power contained in Article XIX(i) [33] to supplement the illustrations of current payments.

Some assistance in resolving the ambiguities and filling in the interstices in Article XIX(i) may be gained from the Fund's *Balance of Payments Manual,* a handbook of instructions on how to prepare the statistical returns required of Fund members.[34] The manual runs nearly 200 pages and consists largely of definitions and explanations of the terms involved in balance of payments accounting. For the present it is sufficient to note that for statistical purposes the Fund has abandoned the use of the term "current" [35] in favor of two categories "goods and services" and "transfers." The goods and services account includes payments for merchandise transactions, freight and insurance on international shipments of goods, transportation other than freight, payments for travel, investment income, and "all other." Transfer payments include payments made "without a *quid pro quo.*" Private transfer payments include inheritances, student grants, "missionary, educational, and benevolent contributions," compensation payments for damages, and remittances by migrants.[36] While the Fund has not definitively interpreted the Article XIX(i) definition of current

---

[33] The power derives from the words "without limitation." See Gold, *supra* note 25 at 5.

[34] See Evans, *supra* note 6 at 30.

[35] INTERNATIONAL MONETARY FUND, BALANCE OF PAYMENTS MANUAL 24 (3d ed. 1961).

[36] Note that it is only the latter category of transaction that is mentioned in Article XIX (i). In fact item (4) in Article XIX (i) "moderate remittances for family living expenses" read, in an earlier draft, "moderate immigrant remittances" for family living expenses. This proposal caused a controversy at Bretton Woods because immigrant remittances looked like one-time transactions and thus would have been difficult to distinguish from capital transfers. A majority thought otherwise, however, and by dropping the word "immigrant," the provision was actually expanded. See Evans, *supra* note 6 at 33. The term "transfer payment" in the *Balance of Payments Manual* does, however, include assets taken out of the country by emigrants, a category of transaction normally considered a capital transfer. For statistical purposes, such transfers are considered transfer payments rather than capital transactions.

transactions to include the types of payments treated as "transfers" in the *Balance of Payments Manual,* one might safely hazard a guess that this is the de facto situation that obtains in the Funds consultations with its members.

Note finally that restrictions on current transactions are not permitted unless *authorized* by the Fund.[37] In their decision of June 1, 1960 the Executive Directors indicated that "the Fund will grant approval only where it is satisfied that the measures are necessary and that their use will be temporary while the member is seeking to eliminate the [balance of payments] need for them." [38] The author is aware of no measure that has ever been found to satisfy these criteria.

To summarize briefly at this point, the Articles of Agreement of the Fund seek to establish a relatively free system of multilateral monetary transfers and payments. Article VIII, 2(a) effectuates this goal by prohibiting restrictions on such transfers and payments to the extent that they can be categorized as "current." The term "current" is fraught with ambiguity and has, in fact, been abandoned by the Fund for statistical purposes. It would appear to be a reasonably safe assumption that "current payments" are generally those referred to in the *Balance of Payments Manual* as "goods and services" and "transfer" payments. Monetary transfers falling outside the ambit of these types of payments are generally considered capital transfers which may be restricted under Article VI(3).[39]

---

[37] This situation is most likely to arise where the country has exhausted its drawing rights under Article V, Section 3 and where the Fund is unwilling to extend credit to the member under Article V, Section 4. The only alternatives to authorization would be deflation or devaluation neither of which is appropriate to meet a temporary balance of payments crisis. See R. TRIFFIN, THE WORLD MONEY MAZE 164 (1966).

[38] Decision No. 1034–(60/27), ¶2, reprinted in III IMF HISTORY 1945–1965, 260 (1969).

[39] The Panel on International Monetary Policy of the American Society of International Law, in its study entitled *Long-Term International Monetary Reform,* recommended the abolition of the distinction between "current" payments and "capital" transfers on two grounds: 1) it is difficult to "segregate capital flows from trade flows" and 2) that the Articles "underestimate the economic benefits of freedom of

To the general prohibition of restrictions on current payments, there are two important exceptions. Fund members are permitted to impose restrictions on current payments and transfers for security reasons. Early in the Fund's history the Executive Directors saw that they could not get into the quagmire of deciding whether restrictions were imposed for such reasons. Nonetheless, without exercising some role in policing such transactions, the Fund would have left the door wide open for wholesale evasion of the requirements of Article VIII, 2(a). In that event, the Directors adopted a policy of requesting notification if a member wished to impose restrictions for security purposes which were not authorized by Article VIII, 2(a). If within 30 days after the Fund receives notice of the restrictions, the Fund does not notify that member that "it is not satisfied that such restrictions are proposed solely to preserve . . . security, the member may assume that the Fund has no objection to the imposition of the restrictions." [40]

There is one other provision of the Articles of Agreement in which the imposition of exchange restrictions on current transactions is permitted. Article VII, Section 3 provides that if the demands made upon the Fund for a particular currency exceed the Fund's ability to supply that currency, the Fund may declare that currency "scarce." Such a delaration "shall operate as an authorization to any member after consultation with the Fund, to limit exchange operations with respect to that currency." This provision was designed by Keynes to meet the postwar "dollar shortage." [41]

international capital movements." *Study* at 34. The Executive Directors of the Fund agree that for these two reasons the distinction "has been only partially observed." See Report by the Executive Directors, International Monetary Fund, *The Role of Exchange Rates in the Adjustment of International Payments* 24 (1970).

[40] Decision No. 144–(52/51) of August 14, 1952, reprinted in III IMF HISTORY 1945–1965, 257 (1969).

[41] Keynes indicated that it would put the United States "on the spot." See GARDNER, *supra* note 4 at 126. The U.S. was considered "the chronic bad actor of the 1930s" for running a persistent balance of payments surplus. See Johnson,

The rationale was that following the war, the United States would run a huge export surplus, in which case the U.S. would be collecting large amounts of foreign currencies and credits while paying out very few of it dollars because there was little available for it to import. IMF members would thus earn few dollars—virtually the only currency universally acceptable—and their demands on the Fund would soon exhaust the Fund's supply of dollars. In the end, the scarcity never developed, because the Marshall Plan and other types of postwar aid provided the dollars necessary to finance reconstruction imports to Europe.[42]

The scarce currency clause has never been invoked and has lately been termed a "dead letter." [43] It was nonetheless an attempt to deal with a real problem not yet resolved by the Fund. If a country runs a payments deficit, it will eventually lose its reserves and must inevitably depreciate its currency. If it runs a surplus however the day of reckoning never comes. Yet a persistent surplus is a sign of an undervalued currency that should be revalued upward. The scarce currency clause was an attempt to discipline a surplus country into revaluing.[44] Events in recent years indicate that the international financial community has yet to agree on the solution to this problem. It does, however, appear to have concluded that the "scarce" currency clause is not the answer.

Aside from these minor exceptions, there is a provision in the Articles of Agreement that modifies de facto the rigid

---

Political Economy Aspects of International Monetary Reform, 2 JR. INT. ECO. 401, 410 (1972).

[42] GARDNER, *supra* note 4 at *ixiv;* Johnson, *The International Monetary System and the Rule of Law*, XX JR. LAW & ECON. 277, 289 (1972).

[43] GARDNER, *supra* note 4 at *lxiv.*

[44] It was for this reason that Randolph Burgess, then President of the American Bankers Association, testifying before the U.S. Senate on the Articles of Agreement of the Fund "called the scarce-currency clause 'an abomination of the wicked' because it put 'the whole burden of responsibility on the creditor.'" Quoted in GARDNER, *supra* note 4 at 131.

prohibition of Article VIII, 2(a). Article XIV permits a member to "maintain and adapt to changing circumstances . . . restrictions on payments and transfers for current international transactions" during "the postwar transitional period." This provision was originally designed to cover the period during which the war-torn economies of Europe were recovering, for at the time the Bretton Woods agreements were negotiated, the war was still raging.[45] The draftsmen were designing a charter for "normal" conditions. They realized that it would be some years after the end of the war before those conditions would prevail and thus provided in the agreement for a transitional period, generally assumed at the time to be about five years, during which the Articles of Agreement would not apply with full force and effect.[46] In fact, the transitional period for the West European countries lasted until the dissolution of the European Payments Union in 1957.

Article XIV has been interpreted to permit developing countries to "maintain and adapt" their restrictions, which existed when they joined the Fund because it was recognized that many were not, upon attaining independence, capable of applying the provisions of the Agreement in toto to their territories.[47] As of April 30, 1974, 85 of the total of 126 Fund members were operating under Article XIV.[48] These coun-

[45] In the Anglo-American Financial Agreement, both parties agreed not to avail themselves of Article XIV. See GARDNER, supra note 4 at 217. The effect of this agreement was a commitment to make sterling convertible for current transactions. Keynes introduced the idea of the transitional period to "allow us to maintain sterling area arrangements and payments agreements." See id. at 120.

[46] In Keynes's view, "not less than five years." Quoted in Madan, Echoes of Bretton Woods, VI FIN. AND DEV. 30, 31 (June 1969). See also EVITT, A MANUAL OF FOREIGN EXCHANGE 224 (1955) (The transition period was to last "three years" or "five years at most.")

[47] The procedure is provided for in Article XIV, Section 3. A new member notifies the Fund "whether it intends to avail itself of the transitional arrangements. . . . or whether it is prepared to accept the obligations of Article VIII . . ." See Gold supra, note 28 at 3.

[48] INTERNATIONAL MONETARY FUND, TWENTY-FIFTH ANNUAL REPORT ON EXCHANGE RESTRICTIONS 64 (1974).

tries, all of whom are developing countries and who constitute over two thirds of the total Fund membership, were thus not obligated to eliminate restrictions on current payments and transfers when they joined the Fund. Moreover, Section 2 of Article XIV provides that these countries "may . . . adapt" their existing restrictions "to changing circumstances." On the other hand, Article XIV does not permit the introduction of *new* restrictions during the transitional period—except for territories occupied by the enemy during World War II, a qualification no longer relevant. Thus, the member operating under Article XIV who wishes to introduce new restrictions is in the same position as one that has accepted Article VIII. That is, it must seek the Fund's approval.

Article XIV permits retention of existing restrictions only for balance of payments reasons. The relevant language provides that "members shall withdraw restrictions maintained . . . as soon as they are satisfied that they will be able, in the absence of such restrictions, to settle their balance of payments in a manner which will not unduly encumber their access to the resources of the Fund." While this provision is drafted in terms of the country's being "satisfied," the "encumber . . . access" language indicates that the restrictions may be retained only so long as, in the opinion of the Fund, they are justified to protect a country from a severe loss of reserves.

Despite these limitations some writers consider Article XIV a gaping loophole in the Agreement. The "transitional period" has been characterized by one economist as "a period of transition between one transition period and another." [49] Moreover, the prohibition on the introduction of new restrictions may be less severe than appears on the surface. For the Fund's General Counsel has indicated that "it is possible that in deciding whether to grant its approval

---

[49] S. ENKE and V. SALERA, INTERNATIONAL ECONOMICS 213 (1957).

[for new restrictions] the Fund may feel less reluctance in the case of an Article XIV member than in the case of an Article VIII member." And it would appear that any modification of a member's exchange restriction could represent an adaptation to changing circumstances. Countries do not as a rule engage in such modifications solely to provide work for their legal draftsmen or to keep their monetary authorities "on their toes." Virtually all modifications in exchange restrictions are reactions to change in the balance of payments position—precisely the kind of "changing circumstances" to which Article XIV refer. As a caveat here, however, it should be noted that the Fund's legal officers maintain that there is a discernible line between the "modification of an existing restriction" and the "introduction" of a new restriction.

Unlike escape clauses in other international agreements, the "gaping loophole" view of Article XIV overlooks the fact that the Fund has a ready means for persuading recalcitrant members that the Fund's view is the correct one. First, it has the formal "authority to make representations to an Article XIV member at any time that conditions are favorable for the withdrawal of any particular restriction, or for the general abandonment of restrictions on the making of payments and transfers to current international transactions." If these representations go unheeded, the Fund has the leverage flowing from the financial assistance it provides to members in balance of payments difficulties. Discussion of sanctions has been deferred until chapter 9 so as not to digress from our immediate purpose, which is to identify the international legal framework within which exchange distribution systems are supposed to operate.

Having worked our way through the relevant sections of the Articles of Agreement of the IMF,[50] it would be well to

---

[50] Other relevant provisions of the Articles of Agreement will be discussed *infra* in the context of particular exchange distribution systems.

briefly summarize the obligations of Fund members with regard to exchange distribution. Fund members may restrict capital transfers in whatever way they deem most suitable. Fund members who have accepted the obligations of Article VIII may not restrict payments for current (roughly noncapital) transactions, except with the approval of the Fund. Members who are operating under the "transitional period" provisions may "maintain and adapt" restrictions on current payments that existed at the time they joined the Fund if their maintenance is justified for balance of payments reasons. Virtually all of the countries whose distribution systems we will examine in this study come within this latter group. Thus for these countries the possibilities for establishing a particular type of exchange distribution system are limited to those which represent adaptations of a system which existed at the time the country became a Fund member or a system of which the Fund approves.

THE GENERAL AGREEMENT ON TARIFFS AND TRADE

Recall that in 1960 the Fund formally concluded its responsibility with regard to merchandise imports and exports— the largest category of international transactions—and the balance of payments accounts was limited to monitoring restrictions on payments. Restrictions on the importation and exportation of the goods themselves were recognized to be the province of the General Agreement on Tariffs and Trade. Like the IMF, the GATT provision that is immediately relevant is an outright prohibition on import restrictions. Article XI:1 provides that "no prohibitions or restrictions other than duties, taxes, or other charges, whether made effective through quotas, import licenses, or other measures shall be instituted or maintained . . . [on] importation . . . of any product." This sweeping provision is qualified in several ways, the most important being paragraph 4(a) of Article XVIII:9 which permits a developing country to utilize quantitative restrictions to "safeguard its external financial position and to ensure a level of reserves adequate for the implementation of its program of economic development." There is thus a certain parallelism between the status of an Article XIV country under the IMF Agreement and an Article XVIII country under the GATT. Under the former, a country may maintain and adapt restrictions on trade payments for balance of payments reasons, while under the latter a country may maintain *as well as* introduce quantitative import restrictions for balance of payments reasons. There is, however, more than parallelism in the relationship of the Articles of Agreement of the IMF and the GATT. For Article XV:2 provides that the GATT members are to "consult fully" with the IMF whenever they consider or deal with problems concerning "monetary reserves, balance of payments or foreign exchange arrangements." [51] More particularly, in reaching decisions concerning Article XVIII:9 the GATT is to accept IMF determinations "as to what constitutes a serious decline in the contracting party's monetary reserves, a very low level of its monetary reserves or a reasonable rate of increase in its monetary reserves and as to the financial aspects of other matters covered in consultation in such cases." [52] The practical effect of this provision has been to delegate to the

[51] Together with the introductory language of Paragraph 1 of Article XV, this language has been interpreted to mean that "the GATT is required . . . to act in collaboration with the Fund . . ." Jones, *The Fund and the GATT*, FIN. AND DEV. (Sept. 1972). "For all practical purposes, quantitative restrictions for balance of payments purposes constitute the principal subject of consultation between the Contracting Parties and the Fund. . ." Hexner, *The General Agreement on Tariffs and Trade and the Monetary Fund*, I STAFF PAPERS 432, 434 (1951).

[52] For an analysis see K. DAM, THE GATT: LAW AND INTERNATIONAL ORGANIZATION 156 (1970). On the special meaning of "findings" and "determinations" see Hexner, *supra* note 51 at 449. A parallel relationship between an individual Contracting Party and the Fund has been established in a "Declaration" proposed by the Committee of the Board of Governors of the International Monetary Fund on

Fund the primary responsibility for determining whether a developing country may impose quantitative restrictions on imports under the GATT.[53] And since quantitative restrictions on imports are the functional equivalent of restrictions in payments for those imports, it is difficult to believe that the Fund would determine that the former are justified where the latter would not be. In short, if under the Fund Agreement a country could restrict payments for imports, the country has the alternative of imposing quantitative restrictions on imports under the GATT.[54] This interplay goes even to the nature of the restrictions which may be imposed. For although Article XVIII:9 of the GATT permits the introduction of quantitative import restrictions, Article XIII requires that those restrictions be maintained on a nondiscriminatory basis.[55] However, a country utilizing Article XVIII:9 may discriminate "in a manner having equivalent effect to restrictions on payments and transfers for current international transactions which that contracting party

---

Reform of the International Monetary System and Related Issues. Paragraph A of the Declaration provides in part that a Fund member subscribing to the Declaration "will not on its own discretionary authority introduce or intensify trade or other current account measures for balance of payments purposes that are subject to the jurisdiction of the GATT . . . without a prior finding by the Fund that there is balance of payments justification for trade or other current measures." III IMF Survey 181 (1974).

[53] See, e.g., K. Dam, *supra* note 52 at 156–157. In reaching their "final decision," the contracting parties are free to rely on information other than the "findings" and "determinations" made by the Fund, although there is little doubt that the Funds' conclusions are "a very weighty element." Hexner, *supra* note 51 at 451. See also G. Curzon, Multilateral Commercial Diplomacy 138 (1965) ("Contracting Parties have always accepted the Funds' views.").

[54] This should perhaps be qualified by noting that a country that could impose payments restrictions under Article VIII of the Fund Agreement could impose import restrictions under GATT Article XVIII: 9. Payments restrictions maintained or adapted under Article XIV of the Fund Agreement, on the other hand, will not necessarily meet the GATT Article XVIII: 9 standard. In practice, however, this possibility is unimportant since it is difficult to believe that the Fund would cause a member to be found in violation of its GATT obligations while being satisfied that restrictions were justified under Article XIV for "balance of payments" reasons.

[55] Restrictions are to "aim at a distribution of trade in such product approaching as closely as possible the shares which the various contracting parties might be expected to obtain in the absence of such restrictions." Article XIII, 2.

may apply under Article VIII or XIV of the Articles of
Agreement of the International Monetary Fund . . ." (Article XIV:1) (emphasis added).[56] Here again, if the restrictions discriminate in a way compatible with the Fund Agreement, they are permissible under the GATT. Finally,
GATT Article XV:9(b) permits the use of quantitative restrictions "to make effective . . . exchange restrictions" that
are imposed in accordance with the Articles of Agreement.

Deference to the Fund on the part of GATT with regard
to quantitative import restrictions is a sound policy.[57] Were
each agency to pursue an independent line, conflicts might
easily result.[58] Moreover, balance of payments problems
and how they should be dealt with are essentially financial
matters. Perhaps more important from a practical point of
view is the fact that the Fund as a provider of resources has
the means to enforce its views, whereas the GATT depends
largely on conciliation procedures which, though generally
effective, are not always so.

From the point of view of a developing country ponder-
ing the question of a choice of a system of exchange distribution, it can be taken as a rule of thumb that what is acceptable to the Fund will be compatible with the GATT.

BILATERAL COMMITMENTS

In addition to the multilateral parameters for decision-making represented by the Articles of Agreement of IMF and

[56] The word "may" has been emphasized to indicate that the restrictions need
not *have been* approved by the Fund, but that they are permissible under the
GATT if they "*would* have been" approved by the Fund. See DAM, *supra* note 52 at
154.

[57] The interplay was apparently the result of efforts by the United States, which
has a larger role in the structure of the Fund than in the ITO (or GATT) See
C. WILCOX, A CHARTER FOR WORLD TRADE 45 (1949).

[58] Conflicts have, in fact, been avoided, possibly because of "a certain passivity
on the part of the GATT." DAM, *supra* note 52 at 157.

GATT are bilateral treaty obligations a developing country may undertake that affect the nature of its exchange distribution system. These have been treated in some detail by the present writer and others.[59] It is sufficient to note here that with regard to quantitative restrictions on imports a country may be under a bilateral obligation (1) not to impose them on particular products or (2) to administer its system of quantitative controls so as to ensure that the other party will receive the same percentage share of the total permitted imports as it enjoyed or would have enjoyed in the absence of such restrictions. For example, Article VI of the Commercial Agreement between the United States and Honduras, *done* at Tegucigalpa, December 18, 1935[60] provides in part that:

If [either Party] establishes or maintains any form of quantitative restriction or control on the importation . . . of any article in which the other country has an interest, . . . the government taking such action will . . . (b) allot to the other for such specified period a share of such total quantity, as originally established or subsequently changed in any manner, equivalent to the proportion of the total importation of such products which such other Party supplied during a previous representative period.[61]

With regard to restrictions on payments, the parallel provision is that the other party receive the same percentage share of total available foreign exchange as it enjoyed prior to the imposition of the restrictions. Article IX of the Commerical Agreement between the United States and Sweden, *done* at Washington, May 25, 1935 [62] provides that:

[59] See G. VERBIT, TRADE AGREEMENTS FOR DEVELOPING COUNTRIES, Chap. 5 (1969); Kewenig, *Exchange Control, The Principle of Nondiscrimination and International Trade*, 16 BUFF. L. REV. 377 (1967).

[60] 167 L.N.T.S. 313, 318 (1939).

[61] For discussion of this provision as well as a general discussion of bilateral treaty provisions dealing with exchange restrictions, see Kewenig, *supra* note 59 at 398–409.

[62] 161 L.N.T.S. 109, 115–117 (1935).

If either Party brings into force any form of control of foreign exchange, it shall administer such control so as to insure that the other Party will be granted a fair and equitable share in the allotment of foreign exchange and in this regard it shall be guided in the administration of its control by the principle that as nearly as may be determined, the proportion of total foreign exchange available for commercial transactions alloted to the other Party shall be no less than that employed for the purchase of products of the other Party in a representative period prior to the entry into force of the control.[63]

The effect of both bilateral and multilateral treaty obligations on the kind of exchange distribution system that a developing country might establish, may be explored by taking the simple case of a country that wishes to reduce its imports of automobiles so that it may increase its imports of wheat. The country may be inhibited from doing so by a bilateral commitment that prohibits it from imposing quantitative restrictions on imports of automobiles. Absent such a commitment, it may be inhibited by a bilateral commitment with regard to exchange restrictions of the kind quoted above if the exporting state has little else to export to it—an unlikely but theoretically possible circumstance. Absent commitments of these types, the standard bilateral commitment on quantitative import controls would require only that it share the new quota for automobile imports pro rata among exporting states.

If the country has no relevant bilateral commitments but is a member of the GATT, it may introduce a new restriction under Article XVIII:9 for balance of payments reasons provided the Fund verifies the bona fides of the country's balance of payments difficulties. If the restriction limits payments for automobile imports—and the country is a member of the IMF and comes within Article XIV—it must

[63] Discussed in Metzger, *supra* note 3 at 315–316.

similarly establish a balance of payments purpose and must further establish that the restriction represents an "adaptation" of the exchange distribution system in force at the time it joined the IMF. If, however, the restriction on imports of automobiles is a "new" restriction, or if the country is an Article VIII country, it must seek permission of the IMF to introduce the restriction.

If a restriction is justified on balance of payments grounds, it makes little difference whether that restriction falls on imports of automobiles or toys or payments for foreign travel. In each case the effect is to decrease the debit side of the balance of payments accounts and so reduce the balance of payments deficit. In particular, GATT does not prevent discrimination between products. Thus a country limiting imports for balance of payments reasons may impose import restrictions on automobiles but not on imports of shoes even though country A may export only automobiles and country B only shoes, although by choosing its products as it did, the country imposing the restrictions affects country A differently than country B. In sum, therefore, neither the GATT nor the Articles of Agreement evidence a concern about which imports or types of current payments are given priority by their contracting parties and members. The respective interests of the two international agencies as evidenced by their constitutive agreements are more in the direction of ameliorating all restrictions than in deciding which goods or payments should be restricted. Thus our discussion of exchange distribution procedures in the next chapter commences at precisely the point where a country's multilateral commitments end—the establishment of priority uses for exchange.

In concluding our introductory discussion on the parameters for exchange distribution systems contained in the GATT and the Articles of Agreement, we might briefly examine those two documents for provisions relevant to our concern with the rule of law. At the outset it can be noted that the very existence of both documents indicate that their members subscribe to the idea that international economic relations ought to be governed by the rule of law. It does not necessarily follow, of course, that the member states of the GATT or the IMF maintain similar views with regard to economic relations with their own nationals. What does appear possible however is that international obligations may carry with them as an externality, to borrow a phrase from economics, de facto consequences for the development of the rule of law with regard to exchange distribution.

Article X of the General Agreement on Tariffs and Trade provides, in part, that

Laws, regulations, judicial decisions and administrative rulings of general application . . . pertaining to . . . requirements, restrictions or prohibitions on imports . . . or on the transfer of payments therefor, shall be published promptly in such a manner as to enable governments and traders to become acquainted with them. . . . The provisions of this paragraph shall not require any contracting party to disclose confidential information which would impede law enforcement or otherwise be contrary to the public interest or would prejudice the legitimate commercial interests of particular enterprises, public or private.

This provision is an almost verbatim restatement of Article IV of the International Convention Relating to the Simplification of Customs Formalities, *done* at Geneva, November 3, 1923.[64] The publication requirement has thus been a part of the public law of international trade for some time. And with good reason. For it is readily apparent that without information on "requirements, restrictions, or prohibitions on imports" international trade would be severely handicapped. The information published with regard to imports is

[64] G.B.T.S. No. 16 of 1925 (Cmd. 2347).

that which is of immediate relevance to exporters. This follows from the nature of the publication obligation. For under Article X a member state commits itself to other member states to publish information of benefit to those other member states and their traders. It is, on the other hand, highly unlikely that a government would undertake an international obligation to publish for the benefit of its own nationals. What this means in practice is that the general terms of import programs, i.e., the nature and quantity of permitted imports, are ordinarily published. What these publications rarely contain is information as to who will be permitted to import the quota of auto parts, raw materials, and so on. This practice indicates that Article X is being interpreted not to require this type of information. The reason for this interpretation would seem to be an assumption that the personality of the importer is irrelevant for export purposes. That is, an exporter of auto parts need only know that a specific quantity or value of auto parts may be imported into country X in planning his marketing strategy. The difficulty with this reasoning is that it ignores the realities of international trade. For, outside the realm of state trading, it is a rare situation where there is only one possible buyer for a particular product. The usual case is that there are several importers dealing in a type of goods, each with traditional ties to one or more exporters. In this situation it matters very much to the exporter which importer receives the greater portion of exchange made available for a particular type of import. For importer A may have his traditional source of supply in country B, while importer X may utilize a source in country C.

Exporting states have long recognized this situation. Only in rare instances however have they attempted to create an international obligation that would prohibit an importing state from regulating its imports in a way that would alter the *composition* of exports from a particular state.[65] Instead, they have occasionally attempted to obtain commitments that the *total volume* of exports, or of exchange, made available for their exports would not be less than that made available in some "previous representative period." The failure of exporting states to insist upon binding commitments with regard to the composition of their exports as opposed to the overall volume of exports might lead to the conclusion that they are little concerned with the former. This would however be a non sequitur. The lack of a binding commitment with regard to the export mix does not mean a lack of interest in the composition of exports. Rather the more likely explanation is that a binding commitment would be vigorously resisted by the importing state as a serious invasion of its sovereignty. Yet the exporting state might very well have a legitimate interest in preferring that its exports be those, for example, with a high local value-added component. A change from exports of this type might have significant affects on domestic employment in an exporting state. Moreover, even if the export mix remained unaffected by an exchange distribution system, an exporting state may have a legitimate interest in which of its export firms is active in trade with a particular country. For example, exporters A and B might each have 50 percent of the market in exports of auto parts from country X to country Y. Exporter A sells to importer A while exporter B sells to importer B. If, due to arbitrariness or corruption in the exchange distribution system of country Y, the entire trade or exchange quota for imports of auto parts is given to importer B, exporter A might be eliminated from the market. Country X might well be concerned about anticompetitive effects of this situation.

[65] See, e.g., Trade Agreement between the United Kingdom and Estonia, *done* at London, July 11, 1934, 152 L.N.T.S. 131 (1934), quoted and discussed in VERBIT, *supra* note 59 at 76–77.

Given then the fact that an exporting state may have a legitimate interest in the personalities involved in its export trade as well as the products which comprise that trade, the issue is whether Article X of the GATT requires the publication of "laws" etc., which affect decisions as to who shall be permitted to import. The resolution of this issue depends upon whether Article X is viewed as dependent or independent. That is to say, is the function of Article X to provide member states with the information needed to determine whether other members are adhering to their substantive obligations under the Agreement, or is Article X a separate substantive obligation? There is no interpretive material that militates in favor of a resolution of this question. The language of Article X does not, however, stand in the way of an interpretation that it is an independent obligation. For it requires publication of "laws . . . pertaining to . . . requirements, restrictions or prohibitions on imports . . . or on the transfer of payments therefore" as opposed to publication of laws, etc., relevant to the rights and obligations incorporated in the Agreement. Moreover, the fact that Article X is a reproduction of Article IV of the 1923 Convention on Customs Formalities is some indication that Article X was not drafted to provide information relevant only to other obligations contained in the GATT. While by no means determinative, these considerations, combined with the legitimate interest of an exporting state in the distributee of exchange for imports, lead to the conclusion that all "laws, regulations, judicial decisions, and administrative rulings of general application" *governing the distribution of exchange among importers* are required to be published by Article X of the GATT.

Unlike the GATT, the Articles of Agreement of the International Monetary Fund do not oblige members to publish information. Article VIII:5 does, however, obligate members "to furnish it [the Fund] with such information as it deems necessary for its operations, including . . . a comprehensive statement of exchange controls in effect at the time of assuming membership in the Fund and details of subsequent changes as they occur. . . ." [66] The Fund has interpreted "exchange controls . . . to designate a broad course of action and an entire apparatus of control" including "exchange restrictions." [67] As we have seen, the Fund has interpreted "exchange restrictions" to exclude restrictions on trade for the purpose of effecting a division of responsibility between the Fund and the GATT. If, however, "exchange controls" means more than "exchange restrictions" it can legitimately be read to incorporate restrictions on trade. And the fact that the *Annual Report on Exchange Restrictions* contains, in its country surveys, a lengthy section on "imports and import payments" provides some evidence that such subjects are covered in the "comprehensive statement." Additional evidence on the point is provided by Decision No. 1034 (60/27) of June 1, 1960 in which the Executive Directors requested that contracting parties to the GATT imposing import restrictions continue "to send information concerning such restrictions to the Fund." As to Fund members who are not parties to the GATT, the decision indicates that the Fund "will seek to obtain such information . . . by agreement with members." Even if, however, the Fund is interested in and receives information on import restrictions, the issue remains as to whether the Fund deems "it necessary for its operations" to inquire into the criteria utilized to distribute exchange for import payments among competing applicants? In response to this point a basic distinction might be made between the code of conduct aspects of the GATT and the Fund. For, as noted

[66] The Fund performs a valuable service by publishing summaries of these statements in its *Annual Report on Exchange Restrictions*. This report is itself kept current by information appearing in the Fund's IMF SURVEY. Needless to say these publications proved the most valuable sources for the present study.

[67] II IMF HISTORY 1945–1965, 217, n. 1 (1969).

above, the GATT is exporter-oriented in the sense that its prohibitions are principally on practices that interfere with other parties trading opportunities. The principal code of conduct provision of the Fund Agreement, on the other hand, is very much importer-oriented. That is, Article VIII, Section 2 prohibits restrictions on current payments and transfers by *residents* of a member country. Its focus is on exchange users and its thrust is that they should have access to and be permitted to use foreign exchange without restriction. This distinction cannot be carried too far as the goal of both codes of conduct is to free international trade from "artificial" restrictions. But the very language of the Fund Agreement admonishes the organization to look at restrictions applied to a member's residents in the first instance. And if that is true with regard to exchange restrictions, and if, as we have argued, the Fund appears also interested in information about import restrictions, it would seem to follow that that interest in import restrictions ought to extend to the manner in which those import restrictions are administered. The point has, I fear, already been belabored. A brief look at *Staff Papers* should serve to convince any skeptic of the Fund's interest in the application of import restrictions.

Finally, we must note the distinction between the obligations of a GATT member to publish regulations, requirements, etc., and the Fund member to inform the Fund of its exchange controls. The possibility, even probability, thus arises that the Fund will know more about the operations of a member state's exchange-distribution system than will a resident of that state. Should the Fund urge members to publish the data and what should be the Fund's attitude if a member objects? The point the present study will attempt to establish is that certain systems of exchange distribution are more susceptible to subversion than are other systems. If an arbitrary or corrupt system threatens "exchange stability," or hampers "the growth of world trade," or increases "disequilibrium in the international balances of payments of members" the Fund has a vital interest in such systems. To the extent that arbitrariness or corruption in exchange distribution may be a cause of a political change in government, a good case could be made that such an event threatens "exchange stability." For it is rare indeed to find exchange stability in a climate of political instability. And even if such drastic consequences do not ensue, can it be said that arbitrariness or corruption in the distribution of foreign exchange does not adversely affect the balance of payments disequilibrium? Either may lead to a squandering of scarce exchange on luxury imports instead of utilization of exchange to develop a viable export sector in the economy. And if the criterion for the use of exchange is the largest bribe, can long-run trade relationships be established? It would seem therefore that a case can be made for the Fund's having an interest in seeing that exchange is distributed in accordance with the rule of law. Thus, while the Articles of Agreement do not contain a requirement of publication of rules concerning exchange distribution, it would appear to be an important prerequisite to the achievement of the Fund's ultimate purposes. In such a situation it would appear legitimate for the Fund to urge member states to publish the data necessary to make their exchange-distribution systems compatible with the rule of law.

Chapter 4

Establishing Exchange Priorities

Having obtained control over the available supply of
foreign exchange, the authorities in a country implementing an exchange distribution system embark on a series of
decisions that "may affect profoundly the whole economic
structure." [1] The primary decisions involve broad distributions between types of overseas payments. Traditionally a
priority category has been that of foreign debt obligations.
Recently, however, the public and private overseas debt obligations of developing countries have become so large in
proportion to the supply of available exchange that these
obligations have become the subject of rescheduling arrangements. Thus one formerly fixed category of overseas
payment has become increasingly flexible. Nonetheless
some provision for repayment of principal and interest on
these obligations is normally the first order of business in
drawing up the list of exchange uses.[2] Thereafter sums are

---

[1] Report on Exchange Control, LEAGUE OF NATIONS, II ECONOMIC AND FINAN-
CIAL, II. A. 10, p. 38 (1938).

[2] See Bhatia, *Import Programing in Ghana 1966–69*, 10 FIN. AND DEV. 20 (March
1973).

apportioned to cover "necessary" imports and "development" imports. At the same time, the planners will examine the present categories of overseas payments to determine whether an "excessive" amount of exchange is being utilized for nonpriority payments. In the early stages of foreign exchange budgeting these efforts are directed at the elimination of luxury imports.[3] The rationale was well stated by the Ghanaian Minister of Trade, Kwasi Amoako-Atta, at a press conference in Accra, July, 6, 1964: "This system of import licensing was introduced therefore to limit the import of luxury goods and nonessential items and thereby save foreign exchange and finance development projects . . . ."[4] Similar views were expressed by a senior Philippine official almost 10 years earlier: "[E]xchange controls . . . for the express purpose of preventing their [exchange resources] being wasted on commodities and services that are not essential for the maintenance of a strong body economic." [5] Difficulties arise, of course, because one man's luxury is another man's necessity. But taken as a whole, there is a remarkable degree of agreement among the developing countries on what constitutes a luxury good. The prohibition of such imports constitutes an immediate foreign exchange saving. And such a policy has another real advantage. One of the principal problems of concern to most developing countries is the "demonstration" effect of consumption by the rich. The wealthy set the material stan-

---

[3] See, e.g., MYRDAL, ASIAN DRAMA 2082 (1968) ("With the prevailing economic stratification in these countries, it could be expected that the demand not only for 'luxury' imports but for all less essential imports would show a particularly high degree of response to an opening up of the market for foreign exchange. *That minimum of planning needed to design import controls to prevent such a disastrous development is simply a necessity. Foreign exchange difficulties are not a temporary exigency but a normal and permanent condition in very poor countries, pressing economic development to the limit set by all the attendant circumstances.*").

[4] Reported in *Ghana Times*, July 7, 1964, p. 4.

[5] Quoted in Banez, *Exchange Control and the Social Interest: A Reconciliation*, 32 PHIL. L. J. 621, 623 (1957).

dards to which the remainder of the citizenry aspire, and when the major components of that standard are luxury consumer goods, there is "continuing and growing pressure for more imports of such goods." To the extent that tastes are a function of availability, by eliminating certain goods from the market, consumers' attention is redirected toward those goods which are available. It has been suggested for India, for example, that "if washing machines, refrigerators, air conditioners, and vacuum cleaners are ruled out from the consumers' horizon, they may end up wanting and getting more servants (who are in elastic supply in an over-populated country)" [6] If, however, a policy of restricting luxury imports is decided upon, planners must face the fact that knowledge concerning the elasticity of demand for particular luxury imports is imprecise at best.[7] Moreover, what seems to be the case is that luxury imports tend to face an inelastic demand curve at the high end of the price scale. Given these considerations it is not surprising that planners will opt for restrictions directly limiting the supply of luxury commodities as opposed to restrictions affecting their cost. The twin attractions of foreign exchange savings and the dampening of the propensity to consume luxury goods thus accounts for one of the initial determinations in planning foreign exchange distributions—the restriction of luxury imports.

Before going on to explore the refinement of this basic determination, however, it would be useful to further analyze the effect of restricting luxury imports. For there is some disagreement among economists as to whether this

[6] Bhagwati, *Indian Balance of Payments Policy and Exchange Auctions,* 14 Ox. Econ. Papers, N.S. 51, 60 (1962). But see NURKSE, PROBLEMS OF CAPITAL FORMATION IN UNDERDEVELOPED COUNTRIES 118 (1953) ("Luxury import restrictionism does not stop this pervasive indirect influence of international discrepancies in consumption levels.").

[7] Schlesinger, *Multiple Exchange Rates and Economic Developments,* 20 (Princeton Studies in International Finance, No. 2, 1952).

decision, without more, will be beneficial to the economy. The clear majority believes that this is not the case. For *A,* now prohibited from importing a Mercedes-Benz automobile, will not necessarily use his foreign exchange to import an electric generator or an automatic lathe or any other type of developmental capital good. *A* could, for instance, bury the foreign exchange in his mattress. Thus it is not usually sufficient that the government prohibits the use of foreign exchange for the importation of luxury goods. Instead, the government will utilize its exchange distribution mechanism by requiring those who hold foreign exchange to turn in their foreign exchange for local currency. The government will then devote that exchange to development imports.

Some development economists believe that the diversion of a portion of the foreign exchange supply from luxury expenditures to development imports is the critical step.[8] Others may take issue with this analysis and argue that without more, the consumer may well utilize his local currency for nondevelopment oriented investment, i.e., luxury apartment and office building, or spend it on locally produced luxury goods.[9] Where the supply of such goods is limited, increased demand may actually call into production luxury goods formerly imported. For these economists the critical factor is a lack of savings in developing countries. Their point is that a reallocation of exchange uses will not increase the savings that are the necessary corollary of productive in-

---

[8] See, e.g., MYINT, THE ECONOMICS OF THE DEVELOPING COUNTRIES 99 (1964).

[9] Schlesinger, *supra* note 7 at 31 ("In many of the underdeveloped countries, the problem of redirection is essentially one of rechanneling investments from real estate ventures to industrial ventures."); Triffin, *Exchange Control and Equilibrium,* in HARRIS (ed.), FOREIGN ECONOMIC POLICY FOR THE UNITED STATES, 413, 416 (1948); NURKSE, *supra* note 6, at 114. This theoretical possibility was the reality in Pakistan, for example, in the early and mid-1950s. See Thomas, *Import Licensing and Import Liberalization in Pakistan,* VI PAK. DEV. REV. 500, 506 (1966). For similar Indian experience see Lal, *Foreign Exchange Constraints in Economic Development: A Geometric Note,* 18 IND. ECO. JR. 33, 44 (1970).

vestment. In fact it has been suggested that import restrictions reduce "the future value of savings and hence the incentive to save."[10] To ensure that the prohibition on importation of luxury consumption goods results in the importation of "development" goods, the government must prohibit the local production of luxury goods or, at a minimum, levy an excise tax on their sale "that would neutralize . . . much of the protective effects of the import controls."[11] The latter course was suggested in the draft outline of the Indian Fourth Five-Year Plan.[12] But such suggestions are rare and their adoption rarer still. Thus for many developing countries a restriction on the distribution of foreign exchange for imports of luxury goods results in the growth of local manufacturing of such goods. And since local manufacturing is, in and of itself, considered "development" in many government circles, this result is viewed as a policy success.

The economists who focus on the foreign exchange saving as opposed to domestic saving believe that there already exists in developing countries a level of savings adequate to provide for the requisite investment. They point to India as the classic case in support of their argument. Because India suffers from such a low ratio of exports to national income, they identify the critical bottleneck for India's development as a shortage of foreign exchange.[13] Both schools of economists agree, however, on the necessity for government intervention in the distribution of exchange for luxury imports, which is the decision of concern for present purposes.

[10] Johnson, *Towards a General Theory of the Balance of Payments,* in COOPER (ed.), INTERNATIONAL FINANCE, 237, 248 (1969).

[11] MYRDAL, *supra* note 3 at 2086.

[12] Planning Commission, Government of India, The Fourth Five-Year Plan: A Draft Outline 87 (1966), quoted in MYRDAL, *supra* note 3 at 2086 n. 2.

[13] See MYINT, *supra* note 8 at 99. See generally BURENSTAM LINDER, TRADE AND TRADE POLICY FOR DEVELOPMENT (1967).

As the corollary of deciding which exchange distributions are luxuries, the planners also identify "necessities" for which exchange must be provided. High on every developing country's list of favored exchange expenditures is the importation of capital goods. Capital goods for social overhead projects and industrialization must be imported since almost by definition the developing countries lack the capacity to produce capital equipment. And to achieve an even modest increase in the rate of growth of the economy, a very considerable rise in the level of capital imports may be required. Without going into the detailed assumptions, a panel of economic experts estimated that in order to raise income per capita in a typical developing country by 2 percent, a modest amount in view of the goals of most developing countries, capital goods imports would have to rise by almost 40 percent.[14] Thus in a country like Colombia, 44 percent of the marginal increment in merchandise export earnings goes for the importation of capital goods.[15] There is no dispute about the fact that those capital goods which are needed must be imported. There is, however, considerable critical comment devoted to the question of which capital goods imports are "needed." The criticism follows from the fact that by favoring exchange distributions for capital goods imports, policy makers make such importations attractive. Such a policy can and often is carried to the point where it is "cheaper" to import capital equipment to perform a task that could be done equally well through the use of a more labor-intensive technology.[16] This gives rise to the anomaly of manufacturing and semimanufacturing in developing countries utilizing the most modern labor-saving

[14] See GATT, TRENDS IN INTERNATIONAL TRADE 49 (1958).

[15] Marwah, *An Econometric Model of Colombia: A Prototype Devaluation View*, 37 ECONOMETRICA 228, 238 (1969).

[16] See, e.g., Steel, *Import Substitution and Excess Capacity in Ghana*, 24 Ox. ECON. PAPERS 212, 222 (1972) ("Licensing and other policies had the effect of encouraging investors to adopt relatively capital-intensive techniques.").

equipment in the midst of societies characterized by wide-scale unemployment and underemployment. In addition, the cost distortions created by favoring exchange distributions for capital goods imports will adversely effect the ability of those enterprises utilizing capital intensive manufacturing processes to eventually compete in world markets.[17]

As we shall now see, the usual exchange distribution plan involves more than the decision to restrict luxury imports and to favor capital goods imports. In refining the categories of permitted foreign exchange use, two principles seem to be operative. The first is that the fewer the categories the more difficult the job of the classifier. The second principle is related to the first. That is, the greater the number of categories, the more precise the control over the import mix. These two principles militate in favor of a proliferation of import categories.[18]

In a simple two-category system, imports are classified as necessary or nonnecessary. Brazil and Iran have had recent experience with two-category systems. In the Brazilian system, which was in force from 1961–67, priority was given to "most ordinary importations" which were classified as General Imports. The second category, Special Imports, included items considered "to be unnecessary importations." These were primarily of two types. The first were "luxury" goods. The second were locally produced items.

The Brazilian system was introduced to replace a very complex system of classification to be discussed later and was designed to lead to the abandonment of administrative exchange distribution. As of March 1, 1967, this came about by the elimination of the special category and the inclusion of virtually all imports in the general category. This ul-

---

[17] For a sophisticated framework for making these sorts of decisions see Bardhan, *Optimum Growth and Allocation of Foreign Exchange,* 39 ECONOMETRICA 955 (1971).

[18] See p. 253 *infra.*

timate simplification of the system came after three successive years of trade and balance of payments surplus and was followed by the adoption of a policy of periodic (sometimes monthly) devaluations.[19]

Iran has also employed a two-category system in which priority was accorded to goods by a similar "process of elimination." Priority imports are termed "authorized" imports and consist of all goods that are not luxury goods and which are not produced in Iran in sufficient quantities to meet domestic requirements. The second category is, naturally enough, "unauthorized" imports, although the term is somewhat misleading as imports of those goods may "occasionally" be permitted "when the supply of the protected local product is considered insufficient."[20] The Iranian two-category system does not appear to have grown out of exchange difficulties so much as in an effort to use exchange distributions as a means of protecting local industry from the competition of imports. This is borne out by experience that indicates that the trend is moving goods from the authorized to the unauthorized list as local production gets started. The Iranian experience of adding to the restricted category reflects the fact that Iran is at a different stage of development than Brazil, with the former making a greater effort to promote and protect local industry, a stage through which Brazil passed in the 1930s to the 1950s.

In one sense, the Brazilian and Iranian systems are not so much two-category systems as three-category systems since they, as other countries, maintain a list of prohibited imports. The prohibitions may be goods from a particular country, e.g., the Union of South Africa, the Peoples Re-

[19] See 21 INTERNATIONAL MONETARY FUND, BALANCE OF PAYMENTS YEARBOOK 6 (1969).
[20] INTERNATIONAL MONETARY FUND, TWENTY-FIRST ANNUAL REPORT ON EXCHANGE RESTRICTIONS 243 (1970).

public of China, Rhodesia, or goods of a particular kind, e.g., gold, narcotics, firearms, etc. Since all countries maintain lists of prohibited imports of this nature, and since the composition of those lists have less to do with exchange distribution than with international and domestic political issues, this category of import classification will not be further discussed.

Colombia and Indonesia have maintained three-category import systems. Imports enjoying the highest priority in Colombia were placed on the "free" list and generally consisted of raw materials and machinery. In Indonesia, "Group I" imports consisted of rice, fertilizers, raw cotton, and government imports. The difference in priorities is fairly evident. The problem in Indonesia was to feed and clothe the population. Colombia, at a more advanced stage of development, and without the problem of importing foodstuffs, was concentrating on developing its manufacturing sector. This was Indonesia's second priority. Its "Group II" imports were primarily raw materials and machinery for export and import substitution industries.[21] Colombia's second category includes all other goods whose importation was not prohibited. Third category imports for both countries were restricted imports. For Colombia these consisted mainly of luxury goods and, according to Article 71 of Decree 444/67 "goods . . . of which the market is sufficiently supplied by domestic production at reasonable prices." The latter were, for example, corn, milk, textiles, and clothing. For Indonesia, such imports were "graduated according to different categories of nonessentially." [22]

Pakistan for some time categorized imports into four main groups. Those considered most essential are on the "free list," which means that they may be imported without

---

[21] Kanesa-Thasan, *Multiple Exchange Rates: The Indonesian Experience,* XIII Staff Papers 354, 358 (1966).
[22] *Ibid.*

import license. When the quadri-partite classification system was first announced, the principal "free list" imports were iron and steel, chemicals, nonferrous metals, dyes, life-saving drugs, medicines, and spare parts.[23] The second priority group of imports are those which are "licensable." This category of imports is the "catch-all" and its content has been established from time to time by moving items *from* it to the other three categories. The third priority of imports is contained on the "cash-cum-bonus" list. Items on this list are mainly industrial raw materials. The final category are those imports available under the Bonus Voucher Scheme.[24] Items on the Bonus Voucher list are mainly consumer goods, raw materials for consumer goods and capital goods.

Yugoslavia has also maintained a four-category import system. Priority is given to imports of raw materials, spare parts, and foodstuffs. These priority items are included in two imports lists—the LB list and the LBO list. The difference between the two is that LB goods can be imported from most countries, whereas LBO goods are imported under bilateral agreements, principally with Eastern European countries.[25] The second category of goods—the GDK list—consists of raw materials used in manufacturing and export, most capital equipment, and most consumer goods. As with Pakistan, the distinction between the LB and GDK lists is that exchange for LB goods is provided at official rates whereas imports under the GDK system generally

---

[23] Thomas, *supra* note 9 at 538. Thomas points out that, at least initially, items on the "free list" could not be freely imported, but were restricted both quantitatively, in terms of the means available to finance them, and as to source. *Id.* at 540. Nonetheless, for present purposes, the "free list" represents the highest priority category of imports.

[24] This system is examined in detail at pp. 178–81 *infra*.

[25] In one sense LBO imports enjoyed a higher priority than those on the LB list. If Yugoslavia has credit balances with bilateral trading partners, which must be used to import goods from those countries, the natural inclination is to use those balances to the extent that they can be used to fill import demands and to reserve free foreign exchange for goods that cannot be supplied by bilateral partners.

must be financed out of the importers own supply of foreign exchange. In contrast with Pakistan, however, the Yugoslav importer must generate his own foreign exchange through exports, whereas his Pakistani counterpart can purchase exchange through the Bonus Voucher Scheme. The next priority are goods whose importation is limited by quota and consists of items that are produced in limited quantities locally, or which are considered of rather limited necessity. The principal components of this list are wheat, sugar, rice, coffee, cigars, cigarettes, salt, and machine tools. The final category consists of goods subject to "ad hoc" licensing. They include gunpowder, ammunition, opium, motor vehicles, tractors, certain textiles fibers and yarns, television sets, railroad rolling stock, and aircraft.[26]

The final exercise in establishing foreign exchange priorities to be noted is the Brazilian system that operated in the mid-1950s. This system utilized six categories of foreign payments. The first, termed "very essential imports," included wheat, petroleum products, newspaper and printers supplies, newspapers, cinematographic films, and books. Thereafter the priorities were roughly grouped as follows: agricultural supplies and raw materials for the pharmaceutical industry, other types of raw materials, industrial equipment, consumer goods, and "all other." This system was abandoned in 1961 as unmanageable.[27]

From these brief illustrations of import priorities, as well as others examined later, certain generalizations can be made. Basic foodstuffs, if permitted to be imported at all,

[26] For a more recent example from Argentina, see the four "lists" announced in Banco Central Circular R.C. No. 446, October 20, 1972 and the accompanying Decrees Nos. 7250 and 7251, summarized in 6 BOLSA 623 (1972).

[27] In the early 1950s Indonesia operated with the following commodity categories: Group A—essentials (base foodstuffs, simple textiles, raw materials and equipment for export industries); Group B1, type one–"semi-necessities," type two–" 'infant-industry' " items, Group B2–"semi-luxuries"; Group C—luxuries; Group D—prohibited imports. See *The Application of Multiple Exchange Rates in Selected Asian Countries*, ECAFE BULL. 19, 28 (1960).

will usually enjoy the highest priority. Despite an announced commitment to rapid economic growth, most developing countries recognize the need to provide basic
foodstuffs for their populations. The amounts of exchange
provided for this category are generally highly volatile, reflecting as they do both local production of foodstuffs and
the availability of food aid. And to a great extent the decision-making apparatus that normally operates in the exchange distribution field is largely removed from dealing
with basic food imports.[28] These are largely decisions of
overwhelming political priority, for the costs of starvation
for some segment of the population cannot be rationally
weighed against the advantages of increased infrastructure
or raw material imports. In nonemergency situations, however, imports of foodstuffs have occasionally played havoc
with domestic food production. The two most oft-cited
cases are the meat industry in Peru and the wheat-flour industry in Ecuador where high priorities given to imports of
those commodities destroyed local production.[29]

Another fact that is apparent from the systems examined
is that materials that tend to promote industrial development are usually given high priority. For a variety of reasons many countries equate development with the growth
of manufacturing or processing capacity. High priority is
generally given to imports of those raw materials and spare
parts necessary to keep existing plants in operation, with a
slightly lower priority given to imports of equipment to expand those facilities. As a corollary to these policy choices,
imports of goods currently being manufactured locally are
generally prohibited or given the lowest priority. This accounts for the sometimes hodge-podge nature of the low-

[28] See, e.g., Marwah, Measurement of Devaluation Impact: Indian Case Study, 17 IND.
ECO. JR. 737, 741 (1970) ("Basically, the imports of good have been 'stress'
imports. Foreign exchange constraint and relative price variable, therefore, become
irrelevant and do not appear in the relationship.").

[29] Bernstein, Some Economic Aspects of Multiple Exchange Rates, I STAFF PAPERS 224,
230–231 (1950).

priority imports category. In addition to the examples here-tofore cited, the case may be illustrated by reference to Legal Notices 15 and 35 of 1967 in Kenya, where the government transferred from the quota sector to specific licensing, a reduction in priority, the following items: shoes, furniture polishes, plastic seats, dry cells for torches and transistor radios. None of these items are as dangerous as arms or opiates, whose importation the government need closely watch or prohibit altogether. And while the point may be argued, shoes and dry cells are not usually considered luxury goods. The explanation for the limited importability of these goods lies solely in the fact that they are being locally manufactured.

A third point to note about exchange distribution priorities is the high standing accorded to imports by the government. This is almost an *a fortiori* class of goods since it is the government itself that establishes the import priorities and it would be a rare government indeed that did not accord to its own needs the very highest priority. In some cases imports by governments are not even included in the list of exchange priorities, as their priority is taken for granted. In the light of the increasing trend in the developing world for government to become involved in commercial activities as entrepreneur and trader, a caveat to the priority for government imports needs to be added. Public sector enterprises do not always enjoy the same high priority as government itself. In Pakistan, for example, goods imported by the Central Government are not subject to formal limitation, while goods on the "free list" may be imported by public sector agencies only with specific authorization to import such goods. While governments may show some favoritism toward public sector enterprise as opposed to the private sector, a claim voiced in Turkey with regard to exchange distributions,[30] generally public enterprise needs

---

[30] USAID/Ankara, The Turkish Import Regime 95 (1968).

are not given the same high status as those of the government in its traditional role.

Since the present study is concerned with the administration of exchange distribution systems, our focus should now properly shift to the question of how these priorities are established and, in particular, the nature of the administrative institutions making the decisions. As an illustration of the process we will take the case of Turkey.

Plans for exchange distribution begin with annual estimates of imports of raw materials, investment goods, and consumer goods developed by the Turkish State Planning Organization. These estimates provide the first guidelines for the future distribution program. The estimates are forwarded to a Central Allocating Committee in the Ministry of Commerce, composed of several representatives of government departments and one representative of the private sector. For it is the Ministry that is charged under the relevant legislation with the task of drawing up the import program.[31] The role of the Planning Organization is advisory only. In addition to the Planning Organization's estimates, the Allocating Committee collects information on requests from individual importers and from the Union of Chambers of Commerce, Industry, and Commodity Exchanges—an organization officially designated to represent the private sector in the planning and distribution process. As well as the "needs of the country," the governing legislation charges that the import programs are to take into consideration "the available sources of foreign exchange" and "the balance of payments and trade with bilateral countries." [32] This information is supplied to the Central Allocating Committee by the Ministry of Finance. With both supply and demand figures in hand, the Committee decides

---

[31] See Article 11, *Decree on the Foreign Trade Policy*, OFFICIAL GAZETTE, Jan. 4, 1966, reprinted in TURKISH ECONOMIC REVIEW 47, 48 (1966) (official trans.).
[32] *Ibid.*

which imports shall be restricted on the "quota list" and which shall be included in the "liberalized list," which shall be financed by free foreign exchange, and which shall come in under bilateral agreement, P.L. 480, or other special import arrangements. The process of "negotiation," by which these decisions are arrived at, employs an "ultimate logic" that observers have described as "not easy to perceive." What appears to happen is that "allocations are determined on the basis of experience of the previous period; changes are incremental." [33] When the Committee reaches its decisions, the results are published each January and July in the Turkish Official Gazette as an annex to the "Decree Concerning the Foreign Trade Regime."

Viewed against the rule of law standard, the norms incorporated in the Decree on Foreign Trade Policy, according to which the Turkish Ministry of Commerce is to determine import priorities, leave something to be desired. Recall that the three norms incorporated in the legislation are 1) "the needs of the country," 2) "the available sources of foreign exchange," and 3) "the balance of payments and trade with bilateral countries." Such vague criteria are not unusual with regard to exchange distribution. When the Foreign Exchange and Trade Control Commission (FETC) was controlling exchange distribution in Taiwan, it was charged with establishing import priorities according to whether or not control was "necessary" for the "proper adjustment in the utilization of foreign exchange," whether "reasons of security, health, education, culture, diplomacy, economy, and monopoly" require control, and whether goods could be produced "in our country, in adequate quantities sufficient to supply the domestic demand." [34]

---

[33] USAID/ANKARA, THE TURKISH IMPORT REGIME 16 (1968). For a detailed examination of a similar process in Ghana, see Bhatia, *supra* note 2 at 20.

[34] Article 3, *Regulations for Classification of Imports and Exports,* summarized in FETC, FOREIGN EXCHANGE AND TRADE HANDBOOK 1966, pp. 49, 51 (Taipei 1965).

In his study of exchange distribution systems in Europe during the 1930s, Dr. Heinrich Heuser observed a similar practice. As an illustration he pointed to Article 3 of the Danish law, which provided that:

The Minister of Trade . . . shall be authorized to take import-regulating measures to secure the ability of the country to pay its foreign obligations and for the promotion of trade-political purposes, to secure and extend the export of the country, to fulfill present and future agreements with foreign countries, and to maintain the re-export and transit trade of the country, besides to maintain and extend the production of this country for export as well as for home consumption through the supply of raw materials . . .[35]

This language, to quote Dr. Heuser, is "exceedingly vague." [36] He noted that "the almost complete lack of published principles according to which . . . institutions allot foreign exchange for imports" illustrates the "arbitrary nature" of such systems. The same lack of published criteria is evident in contemporary exchange distribution systems in Colombia,[37] Ethiopia,[38] and India.[39] And the process by which priority uses for exchange are established has continued to be characterized by knowledgeable observers as "basically a function of administrative discretion." [40]

While the statutes indicate that a high degree of administrative discretion is delegated to the distribution authorities,

[35] *The Redemption of the Notes of the National Bank and Measures for the Safeguarding of the Danish Currency*, quoted in H. Heuser, The Control of International Trade 125 (1939) (official trans.). In practice the Danish exchange office (*Valutakontor*) distributed exchange under the following headings: 1) necessary for the maintainence of exports, 2) necessary for domestic production, 3) necessary, 4) desirable, 5) dispensable.

[36] *Id.* at 124.   [37] See Article 208, Decree 444 of 1967 (unofficial trans.).

[38] See Proclamation No. 211 of 1963, Negarit Gazeta, 25 December 1963, at 47.

[39] See Imports and Exports (Control) Act 1947 and Imports (Control) Order, 1955.

[40] See Schlesinger, *supra* note 7 at 10.

it is doubtful that at this stage in the process one could characterize it as arbitrary. This is true for two reasons. First, there are universal norms operating on decisions of this type. The norm of incremental decision-making that was evident in the Turkish system is characteristic of virtually all exchange distribution systems.[41] Moreover, all systems manifest the "luxury-necessity" dichotomy as we have seen earlier in this chapter. The second and perhaps more important reason why the system is protected against arbitrary decision-making is the fact that the decisions are almost universally published. This means that in the vast majority of cases the norms applied can be discovered inductively.

For members of the GATT, publication is required by Article X. Recall that this Article provides that "Laws, regulations, judicial decisions and administrative rulings of general application, made effective by any contracting party, pertaining to . . . requirements, restrictions, or prohibitions on imports or exports, or on the transfer of payments therefor . . . shall be published promptly in such a manner as to enable governments and traders to become acquainted with them." [42] The GATT requirement has been incorporated in domestic legislation in many countries. Article 12 of the Turkish Decree Concerning the Foreign Trade Regime thus provides that "Imports shall be effected in accordance with lists . . . to be published in the Official Gazette." [43] Article 3 of the Japanese Trade Control Or-

---

[41] See Marshall, *Exchange Controls and Economic Development,* in H. ELLIS, ECONOMIC DEVELOPMENT FOR LATIN AMERICA 430, 435 (1966).

[42] Publication of import programs may also be required by bilateral treaty commitments. For many years the United States incorporated in its bilateral trade treaties a provision requiring that "prior to the entry into force of such quantitative restriction, ["the government taking such action will"] give public notice of the total quantity, or any change therein, of any such product permitted to be imported . . . ." Commercial Agreement between the United States and Honduras, *done* at Tegucigalpa, December 18, 1935, Art. VI, 167 L.N.T.S. 313, 318 (1936), quoted and discussed in G. VERBIT, TRADE AGREEMENTS FOR DEVELOPING COUNTRIES 72–73 (1969).

[43] Article 12, *Decree on the Foreign Trade Policy, supra* note 31 at 48.

der of 1949 provided that "The Minister of International Trade shall stipulate and publish items of goods which are required to receive import allocation . . ."[44] Even in the absence of explicit statutory requirements, details of import programs are almost universally published for the wholly practical reason that local businessmen must be given some idea of what they will be permitted to import if they are to function effectively.

Published data normally consists of two elements. For it is clearly not sufficient that the government publish only the list of items in each priority category. Quantities, either of goods or of exchange to be distributed for the purchase of such goods, must also be made known. For only with that information can importers and exporters adequately plan their transactions. And for our purposes, publication of quantities is required for the foreign exchange user to know whether he is receiving his "fair" share of the exchange available and, if not, thereby to alert him to the possible existence of arbitrary decision-making in the system. In the countries studied the norm was to publish both items categorized by priority and quantities permitted to be imported. Thus in the issue of the Turkish *Official Gazette* of July 4, 1967, the import program for the second half of 1967 provides that commercial importers would be permitted to import "stencils" to a total value of $15,000 (Turkish lira) (item 162), that industrialists could import up to $500,000 worth of articles "for manufacturing wireless sets" (item 402), and up to $700,000 worth of "articles required for manufacturing tires" could be imported (item 411), but that part or all of the costs would be covered by the "A.I.D." account.[45] For the benefit of exporters, im-

[44] Cabinet Order No. 414, reprinted in Foreign Exchange Study Assoc., Japan Laws, Oordinances and Other Regulations Concerning Foreign Exchange and Foreign Trade (B)-67 (1964) (official trans.).

[45] Turkish Official Gazette, No. 12638, July 4, 1967 reprinting Decree No. 6/8452 (unofficial trans.).

port programs are reprinted in detail in publications such as the *Board of Trade Journal.*

The major exception to the observation with regard to publication of quantities is India. On April 1 of each year the Government of India publishes what is undoubtedly the most elaborate statement of "import trade control policy" extant. The policy is incorporated in a volume, known as the "Red Book," of nearly 700 pages and is widely available at dealers in government publications. For commercial importers the Red Book indicates the basis upon which they may calculate their import entitlement. As we shall see in chapter 7 exchange distributions in this area are incremental and the import policy is stated as a percentage of base period imports. For industrialists who import goods for their own use however there is no indication as to the quantities of a particular good that may be imported. For them the only indication given in the Red Book is whether import applications for particular items "will be considered" and if so, how one should proceed with an application. While examination of the distribution process indicates that decisions are, in fact, incremental, based on across-the-board percentage increases or decreases, there is no indication in the Red Book that this is the case. Since the figures for broad categories of imports have been decided when the Red Book is published, there would seem to be no particular handicap in terms of availability to their publication.

Prior to 1965, the Indian import planning mechanism was even more secretive. For it was the practice of the Chief Controller, Imports and Exports (CCI&E) to supplement the Red Book with confidential General Licensing Instructions ("GLI's"). The original purpose of the GLI's was "to clarify either the import policy or the basis for licensing." [46]

[46] Directorate of Commercial Publicity, Ministry of Commerce, Government of India, *Report of the Study Team on Import and Export Control Organisation* 11 (1965).

In fact, the study team that examined the operations of the CCI&E's office found that for the licensing period 1964–65 several of the GLI's "restricted or liberalized the provisions contained in the Red Book." [47] The study team therefore recommended that GLI's be used only to "communicate foreign exchange ceilings and the formula, if any, for calculating the entitlements of various categories of importers, as also such departmental instructions for the guidance of the licensing authorities as the trade and applicants are not normally concerned with." The Government accepted this recommendation.[48] The study team did not indicate why it was not recommending the publication of the foreign exchange "ceilings" and the "formula" although by implication it seems that these were items which the team thought ought properly to be kept confidential. Why this should be the case is not clear. The present study indicates that such information is normally published by countries utilizing administrative exchange distribution procedures and is the kind of information that may be required to be published by prevailing notions of international law. The likely argument that to publish quantitative figures would limit the flexibility of the authorities runs aground on the fact that this is done without great effort in other countries. Virtually every issue of the Turkish *Official Gazette* contains a "Circular Regarding Imports" that modifies the basic import program. The publication vehicle of a gazette is available to the Government of India and there would seem little reason not to utilize it to dispel the fears of importers concerning the fairness of the treatment from the authorizing authority.

In considering the susceptibility to corruption of the process of establishing exchange use priorities, it seems advis-

[47] *Ibid.*
[48] See Ministry of Commerce Resolution, dated 31st March, 1965, containing the decisions of Government on the recommendations of the Study Team, reprinted in Directorate of Commercial Publicity, *supra* note 46 at 105, 106.

able to begin with an identification of the potential source of pressure upon the decision-makers.

The importer seeks to have the products he deals in enjoy the highest priority on the import program. For without merchandise the importer is out of business. Importer pressure on the classification of goods is often intense and has been identified as the primary point in the distribution process heretofore discussed where corruption is liable to creep in.[49]

There is countervailing pressure on some items from manufacturers who favor a limitation on imports so that they can protect their production locally. To the extent there is manufacturer interest in a particular type of goods, that interest will almost inevitably prevail in a developing country. This means that products which can be manufactured locally will generally be relegated to the lowest category on the scale of import priorities. While such pressure will offset importer pressure for high-priority classification in some cases, those cases will be few since the potential range of local manufactures in developing countries is relatively small. On the other hand, there is strong manufacturer pressure for high priority to be accorded to imports of raw materials, spare parts, and capital equipment. And as we have seen, these types of imports are everywhere given high priority. Note, however, that this status may, and probably will, be less the result of manufacturer pressure than a belief on the part of planners that manufacturing is to be encouraged since it is the *sine qua non* of development. The critical pressure on the import classification system is therefore generated by importers of goods that cannot, given present levels of technology, be manufactured domestically.

[49] See Woodley, *Multiple Currency Practices*, 3 FIN. AND DEV. 113, 118 (1966); INTERNATIONAL MONETARY FUND, EIGHTEENTH ANNUAL REPORT ON EXCHANGE RESTRICTIONS 46 (1967). A somewhat different problem results from the fact that importers who fear a downward reclassification may stockpile thus adding to the exchange problem. See Schlesinger, *supra* note 7 at 11.

There are several factors that operate to protect the system from being corrupted by such pressures.

Principal among the institutional prophylactics against corruption is the committee system. Recall that in Turkey the priority decisions are made by the Central Allocating Committee. The role of the Central Allocating Committee is typical of the procedure followed in most of the systems studied. That is to say, the decisions as to which product or payments shall enjoy priority in the exchange distribution procedure are generally made by committees at a senior level of government. In Pakistan, for example, the Foreign Exchange Budget is prepared by a committee of senior civil servants made up of the Finance Secretary, Chairman, the Secretaries of the Ministries of Commerce, Industries, Agriculture, Defense, and Foreign Affairs, and a representative of the Planning Commission. A representative of the State Bank of Pakistan serves as a consultant to the committee.[50] The committee distributes the exchange for public sector use to each ministry, based on the budget request that the ministry has submitted to the committee. These distributions are further broken down into two categories—development and nondevelopmental imports. Exchange for the private sector, roughly two thirds of the total available, is distributed in a lump sum to the Ministry of Commerce based on estimates submitted by the ministry. The decisions reached by the committee are then sent to the Cabinet for approval. Following the process of decision-making with regard to private sector imports, the area with which this study is primarily concerned, the lump sum distributed by the Foreign Exchange Budget Committee to the Ministry of Commerce is then divided by the Chief Controller of Imports and Exports. The Chief Controller is guided in the decision-making process by several committees. The most

---

[50] See Naqvi, *Import Licensing in Pakistan,* in ISLAM (ed.) STUDIES ON COMMERCIAL POLICY AND ECONOMIC GROWTH 89, 90 (1970).

important of these is the Central Ceilings Committee of which the Secretary of the Ministry of Commerce is Chairman. Prior to 1972, this committee consisted of 15 members. In addition to the Chairman and the Chief Controller, the membership consisted of the Controllers of Lahore and Chittagong; the Deputy Controller, in charge, Karachi; the Secretary of Commerce, Labour and Industry, East Pakistan; Directors of Industries, East and West Pakistan; and "representatives from the various ministries of the Central Government." [51] It is apparently this committee that determines basic import priorities. Two other groups also make inputs. The Tariff Commission recommends items whose importation should be banned because the country is "self-sufficient" in a particular good or commodity. And investment imports, primarily machinery, are generally decided upon as a by-product of the annual plans of the Central Permissions Committee of the Ministry of Industries.

The "committee" system pervades decision-making at this level of the exchange distribution process throughout the developing world. In Colombia, the Board of Foreign Commerce (Junta de Comercia Exterior) has the task of making the lists of goods that may be freely imported, those which require a license (licensa previa), and those whose importation is prohibited.[52] The Board is made up of the Ministers of Foreign Affairs, chairman, Finance and Public Credit, Agriculture and Development, the head of the Planning Office, the director of the National Federation of Coffee Producers, and the manager of the Bank of the Republic.[53] In the United Arab Republic an annual foreign exchange budget is drawn up by the Supreme Committee for Foreign Exchange, appointed by the Minister of Economy and Foreign Trade. The budget is then divided in accordance

[51] Naqvi, supra note 50 at 93, n. 4.
[52] See Articles 68 and 208, Decree No. 444 of 1967.
[53] See Article 207, Decree No. 444 of 1967.

with a nine-part sectoral division of the economy, e.g., agricultural, industrial, transportation, and each sector receives a foreign exchange quota. Imports for each sector are then planned by Commodity Boards, which distribute the exchange according to their view of essentiality in their respective sectors.[54] In Yugoslavia the "Federal Executive Council" prescibes the general provisions in respect to foreign trade and exchange transactions."[55] In particular the Council can (a) specify "a foreign exchange quota in round figures," (b) specify "a foreign exchange limit," or (c) specify "a commodity limit of issuing an import permit." In India, as befits the most populous country utilizing exchange distribution, the administrative mechanism at the top reaches the pinnacle of complexity. There are in fact two parallel systems for exchange distribution operating in India. The one we shall consider first is the system of basic exchange distribution for industrial imports. This system is the responsibility of the Directorate General of Technical Development. The Directorate or DGTD is responsible for the planning and development of all industries in India, with the exception of iron and steel, textiles, jute, and sugar. In carrying out that responsibility it distributes the foreign exchange needed by those industries. The process begins with a "consolidated allocation" of exchange for the Ministry of Industry and Supply by the Department of Economic Affairs. The Economic Adviser to the Ministry of Industry and Supply then makes a "notational" distribution under 26 different categories of import.[56] The categories include different types of raw materials, e.g., raw cotton,

[54] See Egyptian Ministerial Decree No. 286 of 1967, INTERNATIONAL MONETARY FUND, TWENTY-FIRST ANNUAL REPORT ON EXCHANGE RESTRICTIONS 510 (1970).

[55] INTERNATIONAL MONETARY FUND, TWENTIETH ANNUAL REPORT ON EXCHANGE RESTRICTIONS 522 (1969).

[56] Department of Supply and Technical Development, Ministry of Industry and Supply, Government of India, Report of the Study Team on Directorate General of Technical Development (Part I) 92 (1965).

raw wool, sulphur, and more general categories, e.g., "components and spare parts," "machine tools." [57] These tentative allocations are then put in final form at a meeting chaired by the Secretary (Industry) and attended by representatives of the Ministries of Finance, Commerce, Petroleum and Chemicals, Mines and Metals, the Planning Commission, Directorate General of Technical Development, and the Chief Controller of Imports and Exports.[58] As to the first 25 categories of exchange use, the distributions are fixed at this meeting.[59] The 26th item, however, involves a "bulk allocation" to the DGTD for the Chemical and Engineering groups. Under this heading the apportionment between industries is carried out by the DGTD staff.

We have some information on how this subdistribution was carried out during the period October 1964–March 1965. As to chemical industries, the suballocation was made by the Deputy Director General (with the approval of the Director and the Secretary, Supply and Technical Development). Since the distribution process at this level, in India and elsewhere, tends to be incremental, the initial possibility was for an across-the-board decrease of 19 percent since exchange available under this heading had been cut 19 percent by the Economic Adviser. However, "certain special aspect [sic] had to be taken into consideration." [60] The Government had decided to give the cement industry a high priority so its share of the available exchange was not cut by the full 19 percent. A new factory for the production of borax had come on stream, which meant that imports of alkali could not be substantially reduced. Finally, users of aromatic chemicals had to be granted an added share of

---

[57] The complete list is given in id. at 90–91.   [58] Id. at 12.

[59] The Economic Adviser actually subdivides exchange under each of these categories into that which is to be utilized by industrial units which are "borne" by D.G.T.D. and those who are the responsibility of other parts of the government. See id. at 12–13.

[60] Id. at 92.

foreign exchange as a Dutch foreign aid allowance that had been expected to finance such imports did not materialize. As to the engineering industries, the distributing official continues to be the Deputy Director General. In this case, however, he set his distributions after consulting with the Industrial Advisers, and within the framework of a tripartite classification of high-, medium-, and low-priority industries. Classification of industries is "effected either under a directive from the administrative ministries or with their approval." [61]

With regard to imports for resale—the other general category of Indian imports—the principal actor is the Chief Controller, Imports and Exports. In establishing his priorities in this area, the Chief Controller "receives suggestions" from Chambers of Commerce, Trade Associations, and the Export-Import Advisory Council.[62] But such consultations are not required by the statute nor are they firmly established in practice. This is therefore the sole significant instance in this study where import priorities are determined by the staff of a particular ministry as opposed to a senior interministerial committee or at the level of the political leadership.

While our data concerning corruption is so fragmentary that it makes generalization difficult, it does seem to be accepted that corrupt decisions are less likely to be made by committees than by individuals. This is probably based on the common-sense notion that it is more expensive and more difficult to bribe a group of officials than it is to bribe just one. And we do have one instance—Taiwan—where experience with corruption within the government prior to 1949 led directly to the conclusion that exchange distribution should be the responsibility of a committee. Also, there

[61] *Id.* at 93.
[62] Directorate of Commercial Publicity, Ministry of Commerce, Government of India, *supra* note 46 at 10.

is evidence that the "committee" system may be preferable, for the same reason, in the eyes of the IMF. The Fund provided technical assistance to the Government of Somalia in drafting legislation regarding the distribution of foreign exchange.[63] An Advisory Commission made up of nine representatives of government ministries, the Somali National Bank, Customs Authority, and Finance Guard is "responsible for the establishment of criteria for the licensing of imports and other foreign transactions and generally for deciding on various exchange and commercial policies." [64] The fact that these committees are made up of senior officials provides additional assurance that their decisions are not likely to be the product of corrupt influence. For the senior decision-makers are both better paid and more in the public eye than are the junior civil servants. The second interesting feature of the Turkish decision-making process with regard to the establishment of priorities for exchange use is the role of the private sector. The formal participation by the private sector evidenced by membership in the Central Allocating Committee is a unique feature of the Turkish system. In many developing countries the private sector has been substantially deprived of its role in the import trade and it is not surprising that it should play little role in establishing import priorities. In the United Arab Republic, for example, all imports are made by publicly owned companies affiliated with the Egyptian General Trade Organization. Even where the private sector is strong however it rarely enjoys the kind of formal participation in decision-making so evident in Turkey. But in historical terms the Turkish case is not unique. After World War I, the Austrian Government established the German-Austrian

---

[63] See Presidential Decree No. 203, Sept. 26, 1964, V. BULLETTINO UFICIALE, Sept. 27, 1964, Supp. No. 6.

[64] *A Note on the New Foreign Exchange and Trade System*, SOMALI NATIONAL BANK BULLETIN 5, 7 (July 1965).

Central Office for the Regulation of Payments in Foreign Countries. The Central Office had the task of "the regulation in accordance with the existing laws, of trade and commerce in foreign means of payments, the disposal of credit balances and the control of trade with foreign countries." (Art. 1) The Central Office was managed by an executive committee of 21 representatives of leading Austrian banks (public and private). The committee was charged with the duty of laying down "the policy of the Central Bill-Broking office along general lines." In the 1930s Denmark's import priorities were established by the Danish Exchange Regulation Council, created by the Law Concerning the Redemption of the Notes of the National Bank and Measures for Safeguarding of the Danish Currency, 1932, 1936–37. The council was "appointed by the Minister of Trade, Industry, and Shipping after consultation with the Minister of Agriculture and Fishery and the Minister of Foreign Affairs, and shall consist of four representatives of the Agricultural Council, two representatives of the Federation of Danish Industries, two of the Collaborating Trade Unions, one of the Joint Representation of Danish Handicraft and Industry, one of the Committee of the Merchants Guild, one of the Provincial Chamber of Commerce, one of the Cooperating Merchants Associations of Denmark, one of the Merchants Council, one of the Collaborating Danish Cooperative Societies, one of the Union of Cooperative Associations in Denmark, one of the Danish Associations for the Promotion of Fishery, one of the Shipping Council, one of the Joint Representation of the Danish Association of Functionaries, one of the Ministry of Trade, Industry and Shipping, one of the Ministry of Finance, one of the Ministry of Agriculture and Fishery, and one of the Ministry of Foreign Affairs." [65] Other West European states involved the private

---

[65] H. HEUSER, *supra* note 35 at 132 n. 5.

sector in import policy planning. On each occasion that the Swiss Government sought to restrict importation of a new commodity it was "obliged" to consult a committee consisting of representatives of "professional interests" (employers and *employees*) and of "consumers." [66]

The participation of the *private sector* in the decision-making process is an additional factor that tends to relieve some of the pressure on the system. A select committee investigating corruption in India found that businessmen in Calcutta and Bombay "almost unanimously pointed out that nonassociation of trade organisations or their representatives in matters like licensing and allocation of scarce commodities encouraged malpractice and corruption to some extent." [67] This evidence must, of course, be discounted because of its self-serving nature. And many would think that to place representatives of the private sector on the committees making exchange policy would surely amount to placing the fox among the chickens. But if one views corruption as in part the result of businessmen driven to the point where they will risk substantial criminal sanctions in order to ensure the survival of their enterprises, it would not appear totally illogical to utilize business representatives as sources of information on the level of restriction that they can tolerate. Moreover, while the businessman is likely to press for the interests of the private sector in general, he is unlikely to be the spokesman for any one industry or group. Finally, the presence of representatives of the business community would assist in detracting from the aura of secrecy that surrounds the deliberations of the intragovernment committees.

A third factor bearing on the safeguarding of the process from corruption is the role of the financial authorities. In

[66] *Id.* at 98.
[67] Ministry of Home Affairs, *Government of India, Report of the Committee on Prevention of Corruption* 42 (1964).

most of the countries studied the role of the financial authorities with regard to trade transactions, which are the largest element in the balance of payments, is, paradoxically, rather limited. The typical input of the Finance Ministry and/or central bank is the overall limit of exchange available for imports. The reason for this rather minor role in the process is the result of the means by which control is exercized over imports. As noted in chapter 3 there are two basic types of systems used to alter the free-market composition of imports. The most common system is to declare that no goods may be imported into the country without an import license. This is the technique employed by the United Kingdom and those countries whose legislation is modeled on it. For example, Clause 3 of the Indian Imports (Control) Order, 1955 provides that:

Save as otherwise provided in this Order, no person shall import any goods of the description specified in Schedule I, except under, and in accordance with, a license or a customs clearance permit granted by the Central Government or by any officer specified in Schedule II.

Once the license has been issued, the exchange to pay for the goods being imported is automatically provided.

The alternative system is to ration the supply of foreign exchange available for imports. The choice between the two appears to be a function of current conceptions as to the nature of the problem being dealt with. In the 1930s, where the problem was initially thought of as capital flight, it was natural enough to place responsibility for regulation with the central bank authorities who were the officials primarily concerned with the government's foreign exchange reserves. After recognizing the importance of "disguised" capital flight, the bank authorities extended their regulation to trade transactions. This accounts for the leading role of the financial authorities in trade regulation in Austria, Bulgaria,

Czechoslovakia, Hungary, Latvia, Lithuania, and Poland in the 1930s.[68] In the postwar era the problem has appeared to be much more one of "development," i.e., to utilize foreign exchange resources for development imports and to limit their use for luxury imports. This shift in emphasis has resulted in decision-making with regard to trade transactions being delegated to officials responsible for industrial development, as in India, or more generally to those responsible for trade. In Taiwan and Brazil, until recently however, the financial authorities were found to play a broader role. Until 1969 policy and program decisions concerning all foreign payments in Taiwan were made by the Foreign Exchange and Trade Control Commission, an executive agency of the Executive Yuan (cabinet). The Commission had as members the Minister of Finance and Economic Affairs, the Secretary General of the Council for International Economic Cooperation and Development, a representative of the Central Bank of China, two representatives of the Taiwan Provincial Government, the Chairman of the Board of Directors of the Bank of Taiwan, and three members appointed by the Executive Yuan. Although it was the final authority for trade policy, the FETC membership was heavily financial. Brazil is also a country that has traditionally regulated its imports by directly controlling distributions of foreign exchange rather than by restriction of imports. Thus the administration of the system has tended to be in the hands of government officials concerned with finance as opposed to those whose primary responsibility is commerce. Prior to 1966 Brazil's exchange system was administered by a branch of the Finance Ministry known as the Superintendency of Money and Credit (SUMOC).[69]

[68] See H. HEUSER, *supra* note 35 at 54.

[69] On April 1, 1966, the system was altered and the primary responsibility for import evaluation was transferred to the *Conselho Nacional do Comercio Exterior* (*Concex*) whose role was, in turn, limited by the abolition of administrative exchange distribution for imports in March 1967.

The National Bank of Ethiopia has similarly been the primary agency in the exchange distribution process in that country.[70]

A substantial involvement of financial institutions in the process of exchange distribution could help to minimize the possibilities for corruption. Central banks everywhere are profit-making institutions almost by definition. In fulfilling their regulatory role they make financial resources available at interest for which they pay nothing themselves. Their "profits" are, of course, artificial in the sense that they do not go to enrich their shareholders. Nonetheless the autonomy that comes with profit-making enables them to pay their staffs more than they would otherwise earn as civil servants of the central government. Better working conditions, plus a sense of being at a power center of the economy, contribute to a sense of élan and professionalism noticeably absent in other civil servants in most developing countries. In part, this is also attributable to the influence of the IMF, which is itself the outstanding example of how financial independence leads to excellent staffing and on whose staff many developing country central bank administrators have been trained. For these reasons instances of corruption among central bank employees have been far less evident than among their colleagues in Ministries of Trade and Commerce.

For these reasons the critical early decision taken by the Fund in interpreting the language of Article VIII, 2(a) is much to be regretted for those interested in the development of the rule of law and the prevention of corruption. There can be no question that the decision was soundly based, given the history of the Bretton Woods negotiations. Yet the result has been to vest in Ministries of Commerce and Trade the decision-making authority over the largest

---

[70] See Proclamation No. 211 of 1963, NEGARIT GAZETA, 25 December 1963, at 47.

component in the balance of payments. A decision that restrictions on trade were encompassed by Article VIII, 2(a)
might well have led to the decision-making authority being
placed in the more stable central banks. While the decision
must stand as correct, the Fund is not precluded, and
should be encouraged to advise in its discussions with
member states, that trade restrictions might be replaced by
payments restrictions so as to place the responsibility for
distributing exchange for imports in the hands of the central banks and at the same time subject the process to the
periodic scrutiny of the Fund. Such a change would help to
insulate exchange distribution systems from corruption.

Finally note should be taken of two special safeguards
against arbitrary or corrupt classification of import priorities. The first is an unusual feature of the Colombian exchange distribution system. At one time Colombia operated
a two-category exchange distribution system in which certain goods were entitled to a preferential exchange rate and
others to the less favorable "intermediate" rate. To
strengthen the hand of the civil service in dealing with importer pressure, the law provided that "Once a commodity
has been included in the list of goods payable at the intermediate rate, the item may not be transferred to the list of
goods at the preferential rate." [71]

The second special safeguard is that contained in international agreements. In general, the multinational agreements
offer little other than the rather significant publication
requirement of GATT Article X. If balance of payments
difficulties justify the existence of an exchange distribution
system under Article XIV of the IMF Articles of Agreement, moving types of goods or payments to a higher or
lower priority is generally permitted as an adaptation of restrictions in the light of changed circumstances. To the ex-

[71] Article 10, Decree 2322 of September 2, 1965.

tent such a change is permitted under Article XIV, it is also permitted by GATT Articles VIII:9 and XIV:1. The principal exception to this general proposition is where the exchange distribution system employed is of the multiple rate type discussed in chapter 6. In that case, the provisions of the Articles of Agreement have been interpreted to exclude changes in multiple rate systems from the adaptation provisions of Article XIV. Thus a country utilizing a multiple exchange rate distribution system cannot move a particular good or type of payment from a higher or lower priority category without the approval of the Fund.[72] Finally, a country may be limited in its freedom to move goods from one priority to another because of bilateral treaty commitments of the type discussed in chapter 3.

[72] See Gold, *The International Monetary Fund and Private Business Transactions* 19 (1965).

Chapter 5

Allocation by Market Forces

In the preceding chapter we discussed the establishment of priority uses for exchange. The next step in exchange distribution—and the critical one for purposes of our study—is the process of getting that exchange into the hands of those who request it. In considering the various methods which have been utilized to accomplish this end, we will view them as points along a continuum, with the poles being distribution by market forces and distribution by administrative decision. Most exchange systems involve elements of both approaches. Our discussion will begin with those closest to the market system. Three types of devices will be considered. The first is that which employs auctions of foreign exchange. This system, the pet scheme of the academic writers on the subject, has been tried with mixed results in several countries of Latin America. The second system to be discussed is the export retention system, which permits an exporter to keep part of the foreign exchange proceeds received from his exports. The third mechanism is the partial free market system.

EXCHANGE AUCTIONS

In October 1953 Brazil became the first country to use auctions as a principal means of distributing its foreign exchange.[1] The system covered all uses of foreign exchange other than "very essential imports" and government imports. (In 1954 these imports were about 50 percent of the total value of imports.) The uses for which exchange was auctioned were grouped into five categories according to "relative essentiality to the Brazilian economy." [2] Successful bidders in the auctions received a *promessa de venda de cambio*, which gave the holder the right (1) to obtain an import license in the amount of the certificate and (2) to purchase the exchange at the official rate.[3]

In organizing the product it had to sell, the officials of the Brazilian central bank had to take into account the fact that while the convertible currencies were, by definition, interchangeable and could therefore be sold in "mixed lots," the inconvertible currencies had to be broken down into individual lots. This might not cause great difficulties today but in 1953, when the Brazilian auction system was introduced, the only externally convertible currency was the U.S. dollar. Thus, in addition to auctions of dollars, separate sales had to be held for the currency of each country with which Brazil had a payments agreement. This meant that up to 20 currencies were sold at any one auction.[4] Since each cate-

---

[1] See Instruction No. 70, October 1953. The system was "ratified" by Law No. 2145 of December 1953 and Law No. 2410 of January 1955. Much of the material describing this system has been drawn from Kafka, *The Brazilian Exchange Auction System*, 38 REV. OF ECON. AND STAT. 308 (1956).

[2] See p. 139 *supra*.

[3] In purchasing exchange, the buyer had to pay a "remittance tax" of 8 percent. See Kafka, *supra* note 1 at 309.

[4] The system was later simplified so that only "free" dollars and "agreement" dollars were sold. Agreement dollars were good for imports from any bilateral payments country. See INTERNATIONAL MONETARY FUND, SIXTEENTH ANNUAL REPORT ON EXCHANGE RESTRICTIONS 68–69 (1965).

gory of goods was allocated a certain percentage of each currency and since auctions were held once a week—the administration of the system became a rather complex affair, with the officials in charge having to make up to 100 decisions a week matching exchange uses with currencies.[5]

The complexity was compounded by the fact that auctions were held weekly at each of Brazil's 19 stock exchanges. Being an extremely large country, some geographical dispersion was necessary if importers living outside of Rio or São Paolo were not to be penalized by being forced to bear the costs of traveling to those cities to bid for exchange or maintaining an agent for that purpose.

Sales of separate currencies in different localities raised two immediate problems. The number of bidders at any given place for a particular currency might be so small that collusion to keep the bids low was possible. And the possible became the real "at once." In addition, even in the absence of collusion, demands for particular currencies varied from place to place and thus a foreign currency would command a different price in different markets. To "prevent the sales of any currency at a price out of line with its effective buying rate," as well as to forestall collusive bidding, Brazilian officials adopted the practice of setting minimum bids for each currency. During the third week in July 1955, for example, the minimum accepted bid on the Rio stock exchange for U.S. dollars for Category II imports was cr. $81. However, since the "buying rate" for dollars was not the same in all locations, the officials established minimum rates for each location. Thus during the same time period, when the rate for dollars was cr. $81 in Rio, the minimum accepted bid in São Paulo was cr. $106.10 and in Porto Allegre cr. $110.70. And within the same city, minimum bids varied from week to week. During May

[5] The Argentine auction system, see note 9 *infra*, featured daily auctions. See V. SALERA, EXCHANGE CONTROL AND THE ARGENTINE MARKET 99 (1941).

1955, the minimum accepted bid on the Rio stock exchange for Category I U.S. dollars was cr. $66.80 the second week, and cr. $62.00 the third week. Then there were the discrepancies between the cross rates for different currencies. During the first week of May 1955, the minimum accepted bids for Category I French francs, Swedish crowns, and Danish crowns showed discounts of 13 percent, 53 percent and 56 percent respectively against the minimum accepted bids for Category I U.S. dollars. For Category II goods during that same week, the French franc minimum accepted bid was at a 7 percent premium compared with the U.S. dollar minimum accepted bid. The minimum bid system also meant that some currencies were not sold. These currencies were all too often those of countries with which Brazil had a payments surplus. If these currencies were not used to purchase goods, Brazil faced the unattractive possibility that those countries would begin to limit their imports from Brazil.

Because the administration of the system was so complex,[6] the authorities attempted to minimize their difficulties by selling *promessas* in lots of a value of $1,000 (U.S.) and limiting bidders to registered importers. These requirements favored the larger importers for reasons that are obvious with regard to minimum lot size and because only firms and not individuals could register. Moreover, since the *promessa* represented the principal cost item with regard to most imports and since it had to be paid for at the time it was awarded, large amounts of working capital were tied up in financing the purchase of *promessas*. This also tended to favor the larger importer. Eventually some steps were taken to limit the advantages enjoyed by the large importers. *Promessas* were sold in $100 (U.S.) and $500 (U.S.) lots and no

---

[6] Schott, *The Evolution of Latin American Exchange-Rate Policies Since World War II*, 18 (Princeton Studies in International Finance, No. 32, 1959) (This system "the outstanding example of extreme rate multiplicity in postwar Latin America.").

single importer was permitted to purchase more than $50,000 (U.S.) in convertible currency and $50,000 (U.S.) in inconvertible currency in any one week.[7] The favoritism of the larger import houses implicit in the system continued, however, possibly as a means of "rationalizing competition in the import business."

It might be considered something of a paradox that a system for distributing exchange of such enormous complexity as has just been described should be championed by its advocates primarily because of its administrative features. The riddle is resolved however if one considers the Brazilian auction system as a complex framework within which exchange is distributed by impersonal market forces. While a major administrative input is necessary to construct the framework, decision as to *who* shall enjoy the benefits of the exchange are not the subject of administrative decision-making. Thus the Brazilian system was hailed by its authoritative commentator as "a vast improvement over its predecessor [distribution by administrative decision], mainly because it limits substantially the administrative discretion existing earlier . . ."[8] This view was confirmed by Brazilian importers who had to cope with the complex system. For them the auction program was one in which they had a *right* to bid for the exchange they needed, instead of the situation that had previously existed, in which they had to *plead* for their exchange. And it was the exchange distribution by market forces that appealed most to the early champion of auctions, Professor Robert Triffin.

Triffin served as Chief of the Latin American section of the Board of Governors of the Federal Reserve System from 1943–46, during which time he was closely involved with the monetary problems of Latin American countries. As a result of this experience he concluded that, given the

---

[7] See INTERNATIONAL MONETARY FUND, *supra* note 4 at 68–69.

[8] Kafka, *supra* note 1 at 321.

necessity to ration exchange existing in those countries, the best way to distribute exchange beyond that needed for "urgent" payments, was via the auction.[9] To be sure, the Triffin plan did not envisage anything as complex as that later adopted in Brazil. Yet even as enacted in Guatemala and applied in Paraguay under his influence, the system was more complex than that proposed in Triffin's original article. Instead of dividing payments into two categories— "urgent" and "nonessential"—the Monetary Law of Guatemala provided for "the creation of more than two categories of commodities and more than two rates (official and auction) . . ."[10] Professor Gottfried Haberler noted that "[t]his is a far cry indeed from the simplicity of the theoretical scheme . . ." The multiplication of import categories, as in Brazil, may have been inevitable since there was the chance that most of the exchange might otherwise be utilized to finance the importation of luxury goods by the wealthy.[11] Triffin foresaw exchange being auctioned in "one or a few" markets, not the 29 that were established in Brazil. But even a recent proposal for the adoption of an auction system in India recognized that "[o]ne important aspect of the whole problem . . . [is] the amount of money that has to be spent by industry and business, by way of employees' travel to Delhi (where they compete during the

[9] Triffin, *National Central Banking and the International Economy*, in HARRIS, INTERNATIONAL MONETARY POLICIES, POST-WAR ECONOMIC STUDIES (No. 7), p. 69 (1947) reprinted in TRIFFIN, THE WORLD MONEY MAZE 142 (1966). The exchange auction system was "invented" by Dr. R. Prebisch when he served as Director of the Argentine Central Bank. See *id.* at 141 n.2.

[10] Haberler, *Comments on "National Central Banking and the International Economy"* in HARRIS, supra note 9 at 93. In fact the law provided for 3 exchange markets, essential (official rate), nonessential (auction rate) and free market. Arts. 55, 62, 70. In addition Art. 66 indicates that the auctions may be broken down "into groups determined upon generally accepted bases, related to the degree of essentiality." This sounds very much like the Brazilian Category system. The law is reprinted in English in 32 FED. RES. BULL., March 1946 at 259–269.

[11] Schlesinger, *Multiple Exchange Rates and Economic Development*, 22 (Princeton Studies in International Finance, No 2, 1952).

tourist season with exchange-spending tourists for expensive hotel accommodations.")[12] Moreover, Triffin noted that "[n]o distinction need be made between the various currencies bid for on any auction market; on the contrary all auction premiums should be uniform, in percentage terms. . . . The exact currency requested need not even be specified until the bidding is over and allocated." [13] In his article Triffin assumed all currencies would be "interconvertible" and did not postulate the kind of international monetary system existing in 1953. Moreover his plan advocated the sale of all exchange available to the auction market "for whatever rate was offered in an open auction." This, however, "assumes a reasonable degree of competition" in the bidding for exchange and not the kind of "oligopistic collusion" which occurred in Brazil, and which is possible in many developing countries due to the concentration of the import trade in only a few hands.[14] And it also assumes no government intervention against broken cross-rates.

Nonetheless Triffin's essential point about the auction system was that "[i]t would eliminate at the root arbitrary and discriminatory allocation of exchange, drastically simplify the administrative machinery, red tape, and delays, and reduce the possibilities of graft or favoritism in the distribution of exchange permits." [15] The point retains substantial force even in the light of the complexity involved in the Brazilian system and is the focal point of our interest in the auction system.[16]

In addition to its great administrative advantages, Triffin noted that the auction system provided the means for the

---

[12] Bhagwati, *Indian Balance of Payments Policy and Exchange Auctions*, 14 Ox. ECON. PAPERS, N.S. 51, 66 (1962).
[13] Triffin, *supra* note 9 at 67 n. 2.   [14] Schlesinger, *supra* note 11 at 22.
[15] Triffin, *supra* note 9 at 166.
[16] The impersonality of the system may be an unattractive feature where improters are principally expatriates. See H. MYINT, THE ECONOMICS OF THE DEVELOPING COUNTRIES 50 (1964).

government recapturing the scarcity profits which went to importers under a system of administrative allocation. Where such profits could not be reached because of the inadequacy of the tax system the auction plan provided a valuable alternative.[17] During 1954 auction premiums provided one third of the Brazilian Government's total revenue. In a proposal to introduce a limited exchange auction system in India, it was estimated that, assuming a modest premium of 20 percent above the official rate, for the fiscal year 1958–59 the Indian Government would have realized about rupees 1.5 billion in auction premiums, an amount then enjoyed by the holders of administratively distributed import licenses.[18]

For a country like India, where a substantial portion of imports consists of raw materials, spare parts, and equipment, auctioning exchange for these uses has the added attraction of basing exchange distribution on the efficiency as opposed to the present system, to be discussed in chapter 7, of distributing exchange on the basis of past imports.[19] This suggestion has been eloquently supported by a leading Indian businessman, who argues that with the present system the importer will pay virtually any price asked for foreign materials and equipment since he does not know if adequate exchange for such a purchase will be alloted *to him* in succeeding years. With an auction system however the "industrialist, assured that he can get a foreign article any time that he wants it, will begin to think twice before agreeing to pay the price asked for it."[20]

Despite its tendency to approach a system of market distribution of exchange, the auction plan still falls short of the ideal monetary system incorporated in the Articles of Agreement of the IMF. Early in its history, the Executive

---

[17] Kafka, *supra* note 1 at 309.
[18] Bhagwati, *supra* note 12 at 66.   [19] *Id.* at 65.
[20] Tata, *Liberalizing Exchange Control,* 20 TATA Q. 1, 26 (1965).

Directors of the Fund established a Committee on Spreads and Multiple Currency Practices, which reported that "the allocation of foreign exchange by auction" was one of a number of multiple currency practices prohibited by Article VIII(3).[21] This was a specific rejection of Triffin's argument (plea) that his auction system at least should not be considered a multiple currency practice. Triffin's argument started with the assumption that some means of exchange distribution is "both basic and inevitable." Given that, Triffin then made two points. First, that the words "multiple currency practice" were intended to cover a situation where a country established different exchange premiums as between different currencies. In his auction system, however, no distinction was allowed between currencies, but only between "different categories of transactions, irrespective of the currencies involved." Secondly, his auction premiums were completely flexible and would not—as would *rigid* multiple rates—"introduce a more restrictive element to exchange transactions than exists by the broader need to allocate foreign exchange." Since under his proposed system the monetary authorities would be forced "to sell fully that quota for whatever rate was offered in an open auction, the rate itself would not in any way constitute an independent or additional restriction." Thus luxury goods, for example, would continue to be imported in the same quantity and at the same price. Under the old system the importer paid the going price and resold the goods on the local market at a high price determined by the limited supply of those goods permitted to be imported. Under the auction system the importer continues to pay the exporter the usual price and sell at a high price. The only difference is that his high profit must now be shared with the government in the form of premiums he must pay for the foreign exchange. Thus

[21] I IMF HISTORY 1945–1965, 177 (1967).

"foreign exports . . . would be in no way influenced by the fact that the exchange rate diverged from the normal." While Triffin's case is persuasive, the reality of auction systems like the one that existed in Brazil seem clearly to fall within the definition of multiple currency practices.

Even if Triffin's argument had succeeded however there seems little chance that any exchange auction system could be reconciled with a Fund member's Article IV obligation to maintain its exchange rate within 1 percent of its par value.[22] The Fund's view of the auction system was summarized in the decision of the Executive Directors' No. 237–2 of December 18, 1947, where it was noted that "the fewer the transactions subject to the auction rate, and the less essential the goods involved, the better." At the same time the Directors seem to have knocked down the argument that the auction system can be a useful device for revenue raising on the part of the government. In commenting on auction systems in general, they noted that "if, as is usually the case where an auction system exists, a reduction of the money supply is desirable, the proceeds of the auction market should be directed toward this end." In other words, the government should bury the money raised via auction premiums and not use it as a source of financing government expenditures.

In introducing the auction system into India, it was proposed to circumvent the IMF restriction by having the government sell the foreign exchange to the State Trading Corporation. The Corporation would then import the goods that it "guessed" traders might want and the Corporation would auction off the goods. The weak point in the system is the guessing to be done by the State Trading Corporation. While it could survey importer sentiment and order goods accordingly, the importers would have no ob-

---

[22] The "bands" were widened by the Smithsonian Agreement of 1971 and are currently the subject of negotiation.

ligation to purchase the goods. If this were resolved by making the importers place firm orders with the State Trading Corporation, the element of an auction would have been lost.

EXPORT RETENTION

As the title suggests, under an export-retention system an exporter is permitted to keep a part of the foreign exchange he earns by exporting. Export retention systems can be classified into two types according to their primary purpose. The simplest and most common type appear to be designed primarily for *administrative convenience,* their purpose being to avoid circular transactions by which an exporter turns in his foreign exchange to the authorities, only to have a portion of it returned to him for the purchase of imported raw materials, spare parts, and equipment needed for further export. In a proposal recommending an export retention system for Turkey, it was thus noted that "the central objective would be simplicity of procedures and avoidance of unnecessary delays and paperwork." [23] Since the total amount of foreign exchange available to the exporter is limited by his export earnings, there can be no foreign exchange "loss" to the country. And by linking exchange distributions to exchange earnings there is some reward for efficiency, in the sense that the exporter who increases sales abroad, i.e., the "efficient" exporter receives an increasing amount of exchange. Finally the hope is that there may be an overall gain by making the business of processing goods for export easier to carry on. The second type of export retention system focuses on this latter point. Here the goal is primarily the encouragement of exports,

[23] USAID/ANKARA, INSTITUTIONAL REFORMS FOR THE DEVELOPMENT OF TURKISH EXPORTS 133 (1968).

and such systems may be termed export *incentive* schemes. Although conventionally analyzed in terms of their "success" in actually promoting exports, our interest in such schemes is that they are a way of distributing foreign exchange that is somewhat automatic.[24]

Typical of the administrative convenience systems is that operated by New Zealand. Most imports are licensed in New Zealand. An exporter, however, is entitled to import certain kinds of goods without regard to whether he would be entitled to import those goods under the normal import-licensing mechanism. There are three types of exporter licenses. Replacement licenses are available where a manufacturer has used in production for export raw materials or components, that were licensed for use on the domestic market. The replacement license permits him to import the type and quantity of raw materials or components so used. Assistance licenses are available to manufacturers who have not previously exported but who hold firm export orders and need imported raw materials or components to fill those orders. Finally, bonus licenses are available to cover raw materials or components of the same kind and to the same value as those used in actual exports.

In the transition from a nonconvertible to a convertible currency system, Yugoslavia has made use of an export retention system. The Decree of Exchange Control of 1954 [25] provided, in Article 3, that "economic organizations have use of the exchange they earn from commercial transactions and services abroad." Despite the sweeping nature of this statement what was intended, as is made clear later in Article 3, is that the organizations would have the use of a

---

[24] The Brazilian auction system described *supra* contained an element of export subsidization in that exporters of products other than coffee received a premium of cr. $10.00 (almost 50 percent at the then official rate of cr. $18.50 to the dollar) per dollar of exports earnings. This premium was apparently financed out of the auction premium revenues.

[25] R.P. No. 475, in effect, Dec. 1, 1954 (unofficial trans.).

part of their foreign exchange earnings. The percentage
was to be determined by the Federal Executive Council "on
the basis of the Federal Social Plan." At first the percentages
that organizations could retain were rather small, ranging
from 20 percent for exporters of films, ships, chemicals, etc.
to 1 percent in the case of exporters of cereals. That portion, which was retained, was "at the free disposal of the
economic organizations." [26] The portion of exchange proceeds permitted to be retained was gradually expanded. In
1967, Article 26 of the Law on Foreign Exchange Regulations provided that "organizations which export most of
their products and certain services may freely pay for imports of raw materials and other reproduction materials for
their own needs in the amount of the foreign exchange
earned by exports . . ." These organizations are "exporters whose exports settled in convertible currency account for more than 51 percent of their total sales proceeds." [27] In addition, Article 16 of the new law provided
that "[w]orking organizations may use some of the foreign
exchange earned . . . to pay for imported equipment for
their own needs, to pay for foreign exchange credits in
Yugoslavia and elsewhere, and for all other payments."
This export retention system applied to the four principal
industrial areas—metal working, shipbuilding, electrical,
and textiles.[28] In sum, the effect of the new law was to permit exporters to retain most of their export earnings, and to
use that exchange for a wide variety of foreign payments,
principally the importation of goods on the GDK list.[29]

An Export-Incentive Licensing Scheme was introduced in

---

[26] § 5, R.P. No. 478, November 27, 1954 (unofficial trans.).

[27] INTERNATIONAL MONETARY FUND, TWENTIETH ANNUAL REPORT ON EXCHANGE
RESTRICTIONS 524 (1969).

[28] *Ibid.* More recent changes permit all exporters to retain a uniform 20 percent
of their export proceeds. See Yugoslav Export, Feb. 1974, p. 3.

[29] See Korosec, *Import Regulations and Management of Foreign Exchange Earnings,*
Feb. 1, 1967, p. 6. On the GDK list, see pp. 138 and 242.

Pakistan in July 1964. Under the Scheme exporters were automatically granted licenses good for the importation of raw materials and spare parts on a sliding scale of up to 50 percent (reduced to 30 percent in 1968) of the f.o.b. value of exports. The relevant percentage for each industry is based on a rough estimate of the import component of exports.[30] Similar systems exist in many developing countries.

Making exchange freely available to exporters on the basis of the value of imported raw materials, spare parts, and occasionally equipment would appear to leave little room for administrative abuse. And this has generally been the case. There is some evidence, however, that even such automatic systems may be vulnerable to corruption. The Santhanam Committee, which investigated corruption in the Indian import program, identified two corrupt practices with regard to import authorizations under the Export Promotion Scheme: (1) the issuance of licenses to exporters on the basis of false or forged orders from foreign suppliers, (2) the issuance of licenses to exporters for articles not required in the preparation of exports.[31] As to the first practice, the wrongdoer would appear to be the applicant rather than the administrator and thus an illegal practice outside the scope of our immediate interest. And both practices represent a clear departure from the established guidelines. As such they would be detectable fairly readily and therefore unlikely to become so widespread as to infect the distribution system in anything more than a *de minimus* way.

Export-retention systems, whose primary purpose is to provide *export incentives*, are more elaborate and for that reason perhaps more interesting than the administrative

[30] See Hecox, *The Export-Performance Licensing Scheme,* X PAK. DEV. REV. 24, 29 (1970).

[31] Ministry of Home Affairs, Government of India, *Report of the Committee on the Prevention of Corruption* 252–253 (1964).

convenience systems. In establishing such a system the policy makers must first decide which exports shall be "encouraged." For the more developed of the developing countries this may be a trying decision. A team of experts called upon to advise the Turkish Government on "Institutional Reforms for the Development of Turkish Exports" found that "an attempt even to correctly define and identify an 'export industry,' 'export firm,' or 'export product' is fraught with insuperable difficulties." [32] For other countries the program is limited to "nontraditional" exports. It is almost tautologous to conclude that the effort to provide incentives for exports in countries wishing to diversify their economies should focus on nontraditional imports. For in our discussion in chapter 2 concerning elasticities of demand for primary products and manufactures, we found that primary products faced a relatively inelastic demand, i.e., the quantity sold was not greatly affected by changes in price. Therefore, there would be little gained by subsidizing exports of primary products. Manufactures, on the other hand, are sensitive to price changes and subsidies for their export would enable their prices to be competitive in world markets. The export subsidies provided by utilizing export incentive-exchange distribution thus have the effect of a devaluation with regard to manufactured exports.[33]

As an illustration of how *export* incentive systems function, we will look at the Pakistan Bonus Export Scheme introduced on January 15, 1959. As is the usual case, exporters of nontraditional items, i.e., goods other than raw jute, raw cotton, rice, and tea, exchange all of their foreign

[32] USAID/ANKARA, *supra* note 23 at 141.

[33] For the view that the premium is not an export subsidy, see Article XI of the General Treaty on Economic Integration, done at Managua, Dec. 30, 1960, reprinted in UNITED NATIONS, MULTILATERAL ECONOMIC COOPERATION IN LATIN AMERICA 5 (1962): "The differentials resulting from the sale of foreign currency on the free market at a rate of exchange higher than the official rate shall *not* normally be deemed to be an export subsidy; if one of the contracting states is in doubt, however, the matter shall be submitted to the Executive Council for its consideration and opinion."

currency receipts for local currency. In addition however
they receive Bonus Entitlement Vouchers of from 20–40
percent of the net f.o.b. value of export earnings surrendered.[34] These Vouchers entitle the holder to import goods
not otherwise licensed for importation and to the exchange
to pay for those goods at the official rate.[35] The vouchers
are freely transferable and are quoted on the Karachi Stock
Exchange.

The value of the Voucher (the "premium") reflects the
demand for the commodities that can be imported with
Bonus Vouchers. In the early years of the program, the
Voucher premium rose as high as Rs. 170, i.e., the price in
the market for a Voucher entitling the holder to purchase
Rs. 100 in foreign exchange to be used for importing goods
on the Bonus Voucher list.[36] The premium over the face
value of the Voucher represented additional proceeds to
the exporter and was his export subsidy.[37]

This scheme was proposed to the Pakistan Government
by Dr. Wilhelm Vocke, a German advisor to the Government. In doing so, Dr. Vocke may have had in mind a retention system that existed in Western Europe from
1950–55. To induce exporters to sell to the U.S. (the dollar

[34] Exporters must apply with their bank for their Bonus Vouchers within one
month of receipt of the export proceeds.

[35] Bonus entitlements could also be used for certain types of invisibles. See Pakistan Foreign Exchange Regulations, § 230, quoted in Q. AHMAD, THE LAW OF
FOREIGN EXCHANGE IN PAKISTAN 121 (1963). (Exporters can use between 2½ percent and 5 percent of their entitlements for business travel.)

[36] Soligo and Stern, *Some Comments on the Export Bonus, Export Promotion and Investment Criteria,* VI PAK. DEV. REV. (Spring 1966), reprinted in ISLAM (ed.), STUDIES
ON COMMERCIAL POLICY AND ECONOMIC GROWTH 359, 360 (1970).

[37] The figure $P'f$ represents the total proceeds received by the exporter in the
formula $P'f = Pf (1 + vr)$ where Pf is the price paid in rupees by the foreign importer, v is the percentage of Pf earned as a voucher and r is the premium expressed as a percentage of the amount of foreign exchange that the voucher en-
titles the holder to purchase. See Bruton and Bose, *The Pakistan Export Bonus
Scheme* 2 (Monographs in the Economics of Development, No. 11, Institute of Development Economics, Karachi, April 1963). See also Hecox, *Effective Exchange
Rates for Exports in Pakistan,* 8 JR. DEV. STUD. 223 (1972).

area), they were permitted to retain a proportion of their earnings of convertible currencies either for sale or for use in importing goods that could be sold profitably, since imports from the dollar area commanded premium prices.[38]

The Pakistan Export Bonus Voucher Scheme has been analyzed chiefly in terms of its effect on exports. An early study of exports of manufactured jute and cotton products indicated that the Scheme had significantly increased Pakistan's foreign exchange earnings from those two products.[39] More recently however there has been some criticism of the Scheme directed principally at its effect on domestic investment. In particular it has been noted that the policy goal of

[38] The retention system was also utilized in post-World War II Europe for a rather special purpose. In prewar Europe there was a good deal of transit trade. That is, goods from country A would be imported into country B and then sold and shipped to country C. The transit trade was severely hampered by the lack of convertibility of the currencies of the West European countries until 1958. Up to that time an importer in country A could not import goods from country B whose currency was convertible for resale to country C whose currency was inconvertible. The control authorities would never permit such a loss of convertible exchange. The reverse transaction, purchasing from the soft-currency for resale in a hard currency area would have been permitted but was unprofitable at the prevailing exchange rates, II IMF HISTORY 1945–1965, 264 (1969). By using retention quotas it was possible to revive transit trade I IMF HISTORY 1945–1965, 315 (1967). This was done by means of "switch transactions." Importers in country A (*in*convertible currency) bought commodities in country B (*in*convertible currency) for sale at a discount in country C (convertible currency). Under the retention system the traders in A were permitted to retain some of their hard currency earnings resulting from the sale of goods in C. These were used to buy goods in C for resale in D, a country with an *in*convertible currency where goods produced in a hard currency country commanded a premium. A gained some foreign exchange (the part not retained by importers in A); B had a loss of hard currency exports; C obtained imports at a discount; D had obtained imports from a hard currency area using only inconvertible currency. B could not sell his product directly in C because A's exporters were selling B's product in C at a discount. A's exporters could do this profitably only because of the retention quota system.

Iran and Colombia utilized certificate systems in the early 1950s and may similarly have served as a model for the Pakistan system. See INTERNATIONAL MONETARY FUND, FOURTH ANNUAL REPORT ON EXCHANGE RESTRICTIONS 47, 49 (1953).

[39] See Ahmad, *The Operation of the Export Bonus Scheme in Pakistan's Jute and Cotton Industries,* VI PAK. DEV. REV. (Spring 1966) reprinted in ISLAM, *supra* note 36 at 381. See also G. PAPANEK, PAKISTAN'S DEVELOPMENT: SOCIAL GOALS AND PRIVATE INCENTIVES 128 (1967).

increasing foreign exchange earnings involves not only making exports more profitable but, in addition, depends on maximizing domestic investment in the export sector. As originally designed and implemented, the Scheme had the perverse effect of making investment in the import substitution sector more attractive than in the export sector because the Government chose to increase the subsidy to exporters by increasing the number of items on the Bonus List as opposed to increasing the percentage of exchange that could be converted into bonus vouchers (the "bonus rate.") [40] The reluctance of the Government to increase the bonus rate was apparently due to its unwillingness to give up "control" of a larger portion of the country's foreign exchange earnings. [41]

For present purposes, however, the critical point about the Scheme is that for those goods on the bonus list, the decision as to *who* shall import is determined by market forces. [42] Market conditions are controlled to a large extent by administrative determinations as to which exports shall be entitled to Bonus Vouchers and which exchange uses will be permitted under the Voucher system. These are, how-

---

[40] The basic analysis is as follows:

$rm = r \, (l + v)$

$re = r \, (l + bv)$

rm is the rate at which the exporter can buy foreign exchange in the bonus voucher market.

re is the rate at which the exporter can sell vouchers.

v is the average rate of premium.

b is the rate of bonus.

If rm is greater than re, the protective effects of the scheme outweigh the subsidiary effects. rm will be greater than re where v is greater than zero and b is less than 100 percent. The Scheme satisfies both these conditions. The object, then, is to reduce the difference between rm and re. This can only be done by increasing b. Government policy, on the other hand, has been to increase v. See Naqvi, *On Optimizing "Gains" from The Export Bonus Scheme*, Research Report No. 77, Pakistan Institute of Development Economics (1968). See also Naqvi, *Devaluation Perspective: An Anatomy of Pakistan's Balance of Payments Problem*, 10 PAK. ECON. AND SOC. REV. 115, 125 (1972); ISLAM, *supra* note 36 at 31.

[41] Naqvi, *supra* note 40 at 16.   [42] See G. PAPANEK, *supra* note 39 at 130.

ever, the kind of high-level decisions that are protected from abuse by the processes described in chapter 4. Within the general framework there is no administrative discretion as to whether importer *A* or importer *B* shall be permitted to import a given commodity.

The automaticity that renders the Voucher Scheme attractive as a device for exchange distribution from the rule of law point of view contains within itself the basis for a critique on related grounds. For it might be argued that the Voucher Scheme works in such a way as to disguise from general view the degree of export subsidization taking place within the society. For export subsidization via the Voucher is less open to public scrutiny than would subsidization based, for example, on annual legislative appropriation.[43] In the latter case the degree of subsidization, which in 1965–66, for example, was above 50 percent for over half of Pakistan's export industries,[44] would be subject to open challenge and debate. This point however is somewhat beyond the scope of our interest. For the present it is important only to note the effect of the Voucher Scheme on the scope for administrative abuse in the distribution of foreign exchange.

On May 5, 1968 Sri Lanka adopted a Foreign Exchange Certificate Entitlement Scheme, which is a slight variation on the Pakistan Scheme. Like the Pakistan Scheme, it applies to nontraditional exports. Unlike the Pakistan Scheme, however, Ceylonese exporters receive certificates equal to the total amount of their foreign exchange earnings. These certificates are used to import "Schedule II" items, mainly

[43] See Kafka, *supra* note 1 at 321 ("In contrast with more overt forms of discrimination between different types of transactions, such as tariffs and subsidies, multiple rates hide to a quite astonishing extent, to the untrained eye, the real cost to the community of different types of imports and different ways of earning exchange.")

[44] See Islam, *Nature and Impact of Export Incentives and Effective Export Subsidy*, p. 27, Research Report No. 86, Pakistan Institute of Development Economics (October 1969).

"less necessary goods" to the limits of "fairly liberal" quotas and "Schedule III" items, mainly industrial raw materials. The latter are generally not limited as to quantity and it was, in fact, one of the main goals of the Scheme to "increase the flow" of these raw materials.[45] The significant variation on the Pakistan Scheme is that in addition to certificates earned by exporters of nontraditional products, additional certificates were supplied to the market by the Central Bank. In fact, the volume of certificates proposed to be sold by the latter, on the basis of weekly tenders, exceeded the supply fed into the market by exporters. Thus the Ceylonese combined exchange distribution by export retention with the exchange auction technique. The latter should have proved more viable than the Brazilian experiment because of Sri Lanka's much smaller size and because of the concentration of international trade in Colombo as well as the convertibility of the world's trading currencies. Nonetheless the sale by weekly tender was abolished at the end of June 1963, after the Scheme had been in operation only two months. Instead the Central Bank began to sell certificates at fixed premium above the official rates.[46]

At this point it may be worthwhile to briefly summarize our observations concerning the systems in Pakistan and Sri Lanka. With regard to Pakistan we noted that within the parameters of the bonus rate and the list of goods which could or must be imported with vouchers, the distribution of exchange to individual importers is determined by market forces. In Sri Lanka exporters of nontraditional products may continue to sell their certificates at the market rate but the Central Bank appears as the major seller of certificates at a fixed price.[47] This limits the amount of the sub-

---

[45] Kurukulasuriya, *The F.E.E. Certificate Scheme*, 8 FIN. TIMES AND NEWS OF CEYLON 149 (1968).

[46] XX I.F.N.S. 234 (1968).

[47] In point of fact the monetary authorities in Pakistan attempted to fix the price of bonus vouchers at approximately 155–160 percent of the official rate of ex-

sidy that exporters will receive but does not affect the distribution of exchange from an administrative point of view. That is to say, exchange is available at a fixed price to whomever wishes to purchase it. While the fixing of the price may eliminate some potential buyers from the market, the distribution mechanism remains impersonal and the chances of administrative abuse *de minimus*.

Information on the reasons why Sri Lanka adopted a fixed-price system for its entitlement certificates is not available to the present writer. Data from an analogous situation in Indonesia, however, appear to provide a clue to the underlying rationale.

In 1957–59 many imports into Indonesia were required to be covered by export inducement certificates that were given to exporters in proportion to their foreign exchange earnings and could be used to pay for imports or resold to registered importers. The market in export inducement certificates was supposed to be free and their price freely determined. What happened in fact was that the monetary authorities (Bank Indonesia) could not resist the temptation to place limits on the exchange certificate price, i.e., to limit the amount of de facto devaluation of the rupiah. This was accomplished by a variety of devices. At times the Bank issued certificates against its own exchange reserves and announced price ceilings at which certificates could be exchanged. In addition, the Bank experimented with limitations on (1) the period of validity of the certificates, (2) transferability of the certificates, (3) the range of goods that could be imported against them, and (4) the issuance of import licenses for such goods. Thus one possible explanation of the fixing of the price for Sri Lanka's certificates was the desire of the Bank to limit the de facto devaluation of the

---

change by altering the composition of the bonus-import list and thereby affecting the demand for bonus vouchers. See Child, *Liberalization of the Foreign Exchange Market*, in ISLAM, *supra* note 36 at 181, 202.

rupee. An alternative rationale may have been an effort to eliminate collusive bidding by exchange users in the weekly tenders, a problem we are familiar with with regard to the Brazilian exchange auctions.

Yet a third variation of exchange distribution via export incentives is illustrated by the Peruvian Foreign Exchange Certificate System in force from 1955–60 and reintroduced by Decree No. 241 of October 5, 1967.[48] The distinction from the systems heretofore discussed is that the Peruvian system apparently applied to all export proceeds and not only to nontraditional exports. The certificates, unlike those of Pakistan and Sri Lanka, are denominated in U.S. dollars. They are freely negotiable and may be used for a wide variety of purposes. Like Sri Lanka, however, the value of the certificates is fixed by the Central Reserve Bank, and the certificates are valid for only 3 days. This short life is apparently to forestall speculative accumulations of certificates.[49] After three days the certificates must be sold to

[48] III INT. TRADE FORUM 45 (Dec. 1967). The regulations concerning the system were consolidated in Decree—Law No. 17710 of June 17, 1969 and the regulations under the latter in Supreme Decree No. 150—69—EF of October 7, 1969. A certificate system was, in fact, first used in December 1948 and substantially reformed in November 1949. That system differed from the more recent one described in the text in that certificates were required for export proceeds of U.S. dollars, sterling, French francs and Argentine pesos and the certificates were freely negotiable at prices determined by the market. In effect the system was the functional equivalent of a "floating rate" for most overseas payments. See Tsiang, *An Experiment with a Flexible Exchange Rate System: The Case of Peru, 1950–54*, V STAFF PAPERS 449 (1957).

[49] Under the certificate system introduced in Korea in March 1965, the life of certificates was limited originally to 15 days to forestall "speculative hoarding." Kanesa-Thasan, *Stabilizing An Economy—A Study of the Republic of Korea*, XVI STAFF PAPERS 1, 16 (1969). Exporters of nontraditional goods in Colombia receive exchange certificates which have a life of from 5–10 days. See INTERNATIONAL MONETARY FUND, TWENTIETH ANNUAL REPORT ON EXCHANGE RESTRICTIONS 114 (1970). Under the Pakistan system bonus vouchers must be used to acquire an import license within 30 days of receipt. See INTERNATIONAL MONETARY FUND, NINE-TEENTH ANNUAL REPORT ON EXCHANGE RESTRICTIONS at 362 (1969). In Triffins' Guatemala Law, the free exchange was distributed in the form of certificates valid for "eight working days." (Art. 72) See FED. RES. BULL., *supra* note 10. When Ceylon

the Bank at a 2 percent discount.[50] Finally, the Bank stands ready to sell additional certificates at a fixed price. It is apparent that such a system is not a bona fide export-incentive system though it is exporter based. What in fact is happening is that a virtual free market in exchange is being established with certificates being utilized instead of exchange for administrative purposes. In terms of distributing exchange, any applicant may obtain exchange for a wide variety of purposes by simply paying the price fixed by the Bank. But trading foreign exchange itself would make possible hoarding and capital flight. In addition, there are some service and other nontrade transactions that the government wishes to discourage by attaching a higher rate of exchange to them. To effectuate this policy and prevent capital flight, exchange trading takes place through the medium of exchange certificates.[51] And it has been suggested that a system like the Peruvian one also serves to keep the exchange distribution organization intact so that if there is a drastic change in the balance of payments position it will be able to respond quickly and effectively.[52]

---

moved to the fixed price certificate system, see text at *supra,* certificates were valid for seven months but were *not* transferable. See INTERNATIONAL MONETARY FUND, NINETEENTH ANNUAL REPORT ON EXCHANGE RESTRICTIONS 82 (1969).

In the Indian study of corruption made by the Santhanam Committee there is an indication that export incentive licenses "are a fruitful source of accumulating unaccounted money and evasion of taxes." Rather than giving such licenses a short duration, the suggestion is there made that export incentives, i.e. subsidies be given "in the shape of cash." Ministry of Home Affairs, Government of India, *supra* note 31 at 254.

[50] In Colombia certificates "must be surrendered to the central bank at 90 percent of the lowest rate quoted by the Bank in the preceding week." INTERNATIONAL MONETARY FUND, TWENTY-FIRST ANNUAL REPORT ON EXCHANGE RESTRICTIONS 114 (1970). See Article 23, Decree No. 444 of March 22, 1967.

[51] See Morse, *The 1967 Peruvian Exchange Crisis: A Note,* 60 AM. ECON. REV. 189, 190 (1970). A similar system was introduced in Korea in March 1965. See Woodley, *Some Institutional Aspects of Exchange Markets in the Less-Developed Countries,* in A. ALIBER, THE INTERNATIONAL MARKET FOR FOREIGN EXCHANGE 177, 188 (1969).

[52] See Child, *Liberalization of the Foreign Exchange Market,* in ISLAM, *supra* note 36 at 181, 197.

From an administrative point of view, our principal concern, exchange distribution through export retention offers the advantage of minimal opportunities for administrative abuse that could lead to corruption. This is so for the rather obvious reason that the exchange earner and the exchange user are one and the same person. The intermediate process by which exchange is collected by a central administering authority, and subsequently distributed to those requesting exchange, is eliminated. In a sense the potential difficulties have been defined away by eliminating the administrative process. Economically such systems permit distribution more in keeping with market performance than do administrative-distribution mechanisms. Legally, however, the device does run afoul of the obligations of a member of the International Monetary Fund. After a detailed study of retention systems in Austria, Denmark, France, Germany, Italy, Japan, the Netherlands, and Sweden completed by the staff in February 1953, the Fund's Directors called upon members to "work toward and achieve as soon as feasible the removal of . . . retention quotas and similar practices." [53] The principal reason for the Fund's objection to such systems is that "they lead to abnormal shifts in trade which cause unnecessary damage to other countries." [54] What the Directors had in mind particularly was the kind of "switching" transaction described in note 38. It would seem, however, that any retention system

[53] I IMF HISTORY 1945–1965, 317 (1967). The decision is No. 201–(53/29), Mar. 4, 1953, reprinted in III IMF HISTORY 1945–1965, 258–259 (1969).

[54] The Fund has also noted that "[r]etention arrangements . . . involved a high degree of administrative discretion . . . ." I IMF HISTORY 1945–1965, 316 (1967). This comment must again be read in context. While retention arrangements do involve exercises in administrative discretion, e.g., the decision to include or drop items from the Bonus Import List in Pakistan, they involve less discretion than do straight administrative allocation systems. See Chapter 7 *infra*. In addition the Fund has noted that the systems are "subject to frequent variation" and thus have "adverse effects on exchange stability." *Ibid.*

utilized as an export subsidy would have the effect of an "abnormal" shift in trade and that systems like those utilized in Pakistan and Sri Lanka would fall within the purview of this condemnation. On the other hand, the Directors indicated that "the Fund does not object to those practices which, by their nature, can be regarded as devices designed solely to simplify the administration of official exchange allocations." The New Zealand, Yugoslavian, and Pakistan export-incentive systems would thus appear compatible with a member's obligations under the Agreement. This would also appear to be true of the Peruvian system. The Fund's attitude must, of course, be read in the context of its general preference for free-market-exchange distribution. Given the choice between administrative distribution and a link between export earnings and exchange distributions, the Fund would probably favor the latter. In introducing its exchange certificate system, for example, Sri Lanka was moving from a system of "severe quantitative restrictions on imports of raw materials and spare parts" to, in the words of an IMF report, a more "relaxed" system.[55]

FREE MARKET ALLOCATION

To this point we have discussed various means by which the authorities attempt to have a portion of their exchange distributed indirectly by market forces. The emphasis here is on the word indirectly, for they employ intermediate administrative mechanisms, i.e., auctions, exchange certificates, in achieving this end. There are, however, occasions when the monetary authorities simply place a portion of their foreign exchange directly in the free market. The

[55] INTERNATIONAL MONETARY FUND, TWENTIETH ANNUAL REPORT ON EXCHANGE RESTRICTIONS 2 (1969).

principal rationale for the existence of a free market is the safety valve theory.[56] The analogy is to a boiler system, which is essentially a closed system but normally is equipped with a release should the pressure within the system prove excessive due to inadvertence or hyperactivity. Were it not for the release there would be danger of the system exploding. An exchange distribution system is likewise a closed system with the exchange earners required to turn in their exchange to the authorities who in turn redistribute it. But the system normally has leaks and there is a point at which the cost of closing them all becomes so great that the entire system—not only the exchange system but, perhaps, even the government itself—would be endangered. Far better then to allow "exchange proceeds from unimportant and practically uncontrollable transactions . . . [to] be freely sold and bought in a free exchange market." [57] Experience with such safety-valve markets indicates that they are relied upon principally to serve the demand for invisibles and capital transactions—two categories with which we have had little concern heretofore. As noted earlier, capital transfers are not normally permitted by developing countries, at least insofar as the transferrers are residents of those countries. Nonetheless such transfers do take place. Countries with safety-valve markets have opted to allow some transfers to take place legally—though at a high price instead of relegating all such transfers to the black market. Another example of the kind of foreign exchange that is virtually "uncon-

[56] See Schott, *The Evolution of Latin American Exchange-Rate Policies Since World War II* 15 (Princeton Studies in International Finance, No. 32, 1959); de Vries, *Multiple Exchange Rates: Expectations and Experiences*, XII STAFF PAPERS 282, 287 (1965). For an official indication that the purpose of allowing a small free market to operate was to provide a safety valve, see 10 ECO. REV. 10 (1934) (Argentina), cited in SALERA, *supra* note 5 at 100.

[57] Triffin, *supra* note 9 at 166. Art. 70 of the Guatemalan Law indicates the free market is to be fed primarily by capital transfers and reparations, "scarce or occasional" exports and the foreign currency salaries of diplomatic personnel. See 32 FED. RES. BULL. 267 (March 1946).

trollable" is that brought into the country by tourists. Rather than have this currency traded in the black market it has been suggested that it be placed in a free market where residents who wish to travel for pleasure or import luxury goods may bid for it.[58]

As an illustration of a partial free market system adopted for safety-valve reasons, we can look to Chile at the time when the government operated two foreign exchange markets—the "free banking market" and the "brokers" market. The "free banking market" was something of a misnomer since this was the market in which exchange was supplied by the Central Bank at the official rate. Transactions in this market were subject to license. Payments "for the cover and immediate remittance of the value of merchandise imports" were made through this market. The "brokers market," on the other hand, was a free exchange market. All foreign exchange not derived from foreign trade and certain invisible transactions could be sold in the brokers market "at the price determined by supply and demand." Exchange purchased on the brokers market could be used for foreign travel, family remittances, purchases of books, magazines, and newspapers.[59] Although the brokers market was a free market in the sense that the price of exchange was set by market forces, individuals could only buy and sell exchange through "the Central Bank of Chile, the commercial banks, or persons or bodies authorized to deal in foreign exchange."

Variations of the partial free market system combining some of the benefits of the auction system have been utilized in Thailand and Laos. In 1947 Thailand adopted a dual rate structure with a fixed rate for government transactions and essential imports and a fluctuating rate for "all other" transactions.[60] The free market was fed partially by the proceeds of rubber and tin exports and partially by gov-

[58] Tata, *supra* note 20 at 27.
[59] 31 Bolsa 541 (1960).   [60] de Vries, *supra* note 56 at 292.

ernment sales in the free market. In the latter case it was the government, not the exporters, which gathered in the scarcity profits. From 1949 to 1952 these sales accounted for 10–18 percent of the government's total revenue.[61] In Laos, upon the recommendation of an IMF advisory group, a Foreign Exchange Operations Fund was established with resources consisting of exchange donated by the United States, the United Kingdom, France, Australia, and Japan.[62] The Laotian Government sold exchange at the official rate for government transactions and essentials. All other transactions were financed out of sales by the Fund at the free market rate. As the FEOF was primarily an antiinflation device, "profits" from the sales of exchange were "sterilized." [63]

The existence of partial free markets has occasionally been used as a transitional step to a totally free market. To stem a heavy capital outflow, the Government of Venezuela enacted exchange legislation which provided that approximately 75 percent of available foreign exchange would be used to cover essential imports under a system of administrative licensing, and 25 percent of available exchange would be transferred to an "official free market." Approximately one year later "all but 20 percent of imports and virtually all capital repatriations" were transferred to the official free market.[64] Exchange distribution was gradually reduced by further transfers to this market.[65] A similar situation occurred in Indonesia. The Government operated two exchange markets, BE (Bonus Export) and *DP* (*Devisa Pelengkap*). The *DP* market was originally fed from export

---

[61] See *id.* at 293.

[62] See Joel, *The Foreign Exchange Operations Fund for Laos: An Interesting Experiment in Monetary Stabilization,* 6 ASIAN SURVEY 134 (1966).

[63] *Id.* at 142.

[64] Decree of April 2, 1962, discussed in Woodley, *Exchange Measures in Venezuela,* XI STAFF PAPERS 337, 344–346 (1964).

[65] See, e.g., Decree of January 18, 1964, discussed in *id.* at 347.

proceeds above posted prices (the difference between the actual price and the posted price being an export subsidy) and later nourished by the proceeds of and used for payments for invisibles and private capital. The price for *DP* was set by trading between banks and exchange brokers without Government intervention. (The Government did intervene to control the rates in the BE market). On April 17, 1970 the two markets were merged, with a new exchange rate set at the previous *DP* rate.[66]

Given the fact that such partial free markets may serve as a safety valve to reduce illegal currency transactions,[67] and given the fact that they are frequently employed as vehicles for the transition to total free-exchange markets, one would have hoped that the IMF would look with favor upon them. Yet in its 1947 decision on multiple-currency practices, the Fund expressed a strong dislike of free markets because they permitted exchange rates to fluctuate. "The objective should be to eliminate the fluctuations in the free market as soon as such action is reasonably practicable. When it is not reasonably practicable to eliminate such fluctuations, the Fund will encourage members to exclude current transactions from the free market to the extent that this would be reasonable in the circumstances of each case." [68]

The three exchange distribution systems discussed in this chapter—auctions, export linking, and partially free markets—are all multiple exchange rate systems in the sense

[66] An added reason for a partial free market is indicated in Joel, *supra* note 62 at 139. Where large quantities of perishable foodstuffs are imported the trade cannot suffer delays in the acquisition of foreign exchange.

[67] In practice the safety-valve feature has been obviated by government intervention in the market in Chile, Colombia, and Afghanistan. See de Vries, *supra* note 56 at 306. The Peruvian certificate market revived in 1967. See text at note 48 *supra*, originally provided for a small safety valve in the form of a "draft" market. The valve was eliminated in May 1970. See Robichek and Sanson, *The Balance of Payments Performance of Latin America and the Caribbean*, 1966–1970, XIX STAFF PAPERS 286, 309 (1972).

[68] Decision No. 237–2 of December 18, 1947, para. 3(a), reprinted in III IMF HISTORY 1945–1965, 263 (1969).

that exchange is made available at different prices for different uses. For easier analysis, however, the discussion of multiple rate systems in general has been reserved for the next chapter. That chapter will focus on the archetype multiple rate system in which the monetary authorities *fix* two or more exchange rates for different exchange uses.

Chapter 6

Multiple Exchange Rates

The international monetary system incorporated in the Articles of Agreement of the IMF envisages that each member shall establish a single par value for its currency and that exchange transactions within its territory between its currency and the currencies of other members shall take place within one percent of that par value.[1] Thus the heart of the IMF system is the unitary-exchange rate. An exchange scheme that permits or requires transactions to take place at two or more exchange rates is by definition a multiple-rate system. The systems discussed in chapter 5 are multiple-rate systems since they fit this definition. The archetype of a multiple-rate system, however, is one in which the authorities fix two or more rates at which exchange transactions take place. The classic illustration is the exchange system employed by Argentina in the 1930s. On the import side, the most favorable rate of five pesos to the U.S. dollar was given to "preferred" imports, principally fuel oil and coal. "Essential" imports, such as foodstuffs, medical supplies,

---

[1] The "bands" were widened by the Smithsonian Agreement of 1971, and are currently the subject of discussion and negotiation.

and industrial raw materials enjoyed an exchange rate of
7.50 pesos to the dollar. Luxury goods could be imported
by paying the free market rate of 15 pesos to the dollar.
The exchange structure for exports was a bit more complicated. Traditional exports earned dollars that could be exchanged at a rate of five pesos to the dollar. Semiprocessed
exports, such as dressed meats or tanned leather, earned
dollars worth 7.50 pesos each.[2] Exports of cheese and butter could be exchanged at an effective rate of 10 pesos to
the dollar. And the export proceeds from woolen and
leather manufacturers could be sold on the free market for
15 pesos to the dollar.

A more recent example of the use of multiple rates is the
system introduced into Colombia by Decree 2322 of September 2, 1965. Article I of this decree announced that
there would, in the future, be two exchange markets—the
preferential and the intermediate.[3] Article II of the decree
authorized the Monetary Board to "periodically" fix the exchange rates for each market. In Resolution No. 32, of the
same date, the Board fixed the rates at nine pesos to the
U.S. dollar in the preferential market and 13.50 pesos to
the dollar in the intermediate market. Transactions subject
to those respective rates were primarily imports of goods
that were allocated either to the "preferential list" or the
"intermediate list" by the Board of Foreign Commerce (Junta
de Comercio Exterior).[4] The preferential list was composed
of 118 items considered "essential," including seeds, phar-

---

[2] At one time Argentine wool exporters received five pesos to the dollar for half
their export earnings and 7.50 pesos to the dollar for the remainder. See R.
MIKESELL, FOREIGN EXCHANGE IN THE POST WAR WORLD 326 (1954). The effective
rate, 6.25 to the dollar, is known as a "mixing rate." Ibid.

[3] The decree left intact a free market for a limited number of transactions. This
market was supplied by exchange earned through the "export" of invisibles and
some capital inflow. It was available for some invisible payments and capital repatriation. See INTERNATIONAL MONETARY FUND, SEVENTEENTH ANNUAL REPORT ON
EXCHANGE RESTRICTIONS 144–145 (1966). This was apparently a "safety valve" market. See p. 191 *supra*.

[4] See p. 137 *supra*.

maceuticals, and basic raw materials for their manufacture; chemical raw materials and fertilizers, components for optics; medicine; dentistry; farming tools; newsprint. The intermediate list covered all other permitted imports. On the export side, proceeds from coffee sales earned 8.50 pesos per U.S. dollar, manufactures where the imported raw material component was more than 50 percent of the export value earned 9 pesos, and all other exports 13.50 pesos.[5]

The Argentine and Colombian examples are classic multiple-exchange rate systems. There are, however, other means to the same result. In 1963 for example, Indonesia maintained a nominally unitary rate of exchange but imports were subject to an "exchange tax" graduated on the basis of the essentiality of the imported goods.[6] This was no innovation, since between 1955 and 1966 Indonesia utilized exchange taxes under the following titles: "import surcharge, retribution tax, price component levy, export promotion tax, PUIM, PUEK, and TPI."[7] Such taxes have also been applied from time to time by Brazil, Colombia, and

[5] *See* INTERNATIONAL MONETARY FUND, SEVENTEENTH ANNUAL REPORT ON EXCHANGE RESTRICTIONS 145 (1966). Exports of crude oil by foreign-owned petroleum companies were subject to a separate regime. On July 26, 1973 Chile adopted a six-rate system "to simplify foreign exchange operations." See 7 BOLSA 447 (1973). The previous system involved eight rates. See *id.* at 346.

[6] Similar in effect to exchange taxes, though generally considered trade measures, are "advance deposits." Here again there may be a nominal unitary rate, but each type of import requires that the importer deposit in local currency in a local bank a stated percentage of the value of the item to be imported. The percentage of value and the date at which the deposit must be made vary with the essentiality of the item. The amount of the exchange tax is thus the loss of income on the sum deposited. Generally deposit systems are found where a country is in a transition stage from a multiple rate system to a unitary system. The utilization of deposits tend to lessen the shock to formerly protected industries and to prevent pressure on rates "resulting from pent-up demands for certain types of goods not manufactured locally." d'A Collings, *Recent Progress in Latin America Toward Eliminating Exchange Restrictions,* VIII STAFF PAPERS 274, 279 (1961). Deposit requirements are then either gradually eliminated or incorporated into the tariff structure. See *id* at 283. See pp. 73–74 *supra.* For the added problems which de facto multiple rate systems may cause, see, e.g., J. BHAGWATI, TRADE, TARIFFS AND GROWTH 53, 58 (1969).

[7] Kanesa-Thasan, *Multiple Exchange Rates: The Indonesian Experience,* XII STAFF PAPERS 354 (1966).

Cuba.[8] An exchange tax paid along with the official "price" for foreign exchange has the obvious effect of altering the exchange rate, and if exchange uses are taxed at different levels it is a multiple-rate system in everything but name.

Like all exchange-distribution systems, a multiple-rate system represents the adoption of a *resistance* strategy to meet balance of payments problems. This can be illustrated by looking at the circumstances that led to the adoption of the Colombian system incorporated in Decree 2322. The critical event was a 30 percent fall in the export price of Colombian coffee in the first half of 1965. This meant that the existing rate at which exchange was sold to importers— nine pesos to the U.S. dollar—could not be maintained.[9] Believing that the situation was one that called for devaluation as opposed to being the reflection of a short-term decline in export proceeds, the authorities were nonetheless reluctant to devalue totally. Instead they chose to depreciate indirectly and selectively in an attempt to avoid some of the negative consequences discussed generally in chapter 2. As applicable to the present situation, the division on the import side reflects an effort on the part of the government to have the effect of the depreciation limited to "less essential imports" and to avoid the domestic consequences of price increases in food and medical services. The limitation on imports of less essential goods, imposed by the higher intermediate exchange rate, may in turn be designed to encourage domestic production of those goods as well as to conserve foreign exchange. Utilizing multiple rates to achieve the former end, however, has generally been considered a fruitless policy, since the ease with which they can be changed—one of their principle advantages—limits their

---

[8] R. MIKESELL, *supra* note 2 at 168.

[9] Exchange was sold at weekly public auctions by the Central Bank. See INTERNATIONAL MONETARY FUND, SIXTEENTH ANNUAL REPORT ON EXCHANGE RESTRICTIONS 135 (1965). The auction feature was, however, nominal as the Bank intervened to peg the rate at 9 pesos to the U.S. dollar. See also p. 161 *supra*.

attraction to the "intelligent investor" [10] as a means of protection. Colombia had difficulty with both aspects of the import policy when it had used multiple rates before. Between 1955 and 1957 Colombia permitted the import of parts and capital goods as preferred exchange uses. The result was that an "excessive" number of assembly industries were set up.[11] Nonetheless the use of multiple rates for protecting domestic industries has been a rationale articulated by the governments of Colombia, Korea, Venezuela, and Yugoslavia.[12]

On the export side the favorable rate is applied to nontraditional exports, so as to render them more competitive. We have seen the same rationale underlying export-retention systems in chapter 5. Multiple-rate systems have been utilized to this end in, *e.g.*, Korea, Pakistan, Venezuela, and Yugoslavia.[13] They were first used for this purpose by Germany in 1934 to increase trade with Germany's bilateral agreement partners, particularly Brazil, Chile, and Peru. The policy was apparently successful for "Brazil's imports from Germany rose from 13 percent of its total imports in 1929 to 25 percent in 1938. . . ." In the same period, Peru's imports from Germany rose from 10 percent to 20 percent of the total.[14]

The proceeds of traditional exports are redeemed at a much lower rate. Several reasons have been offered for this distinction, although all are grounded in the premise that the demand for traditional exports is generally inelastic. In the 1930s the discrimination against traditional exports was

[10] See Schlesinger, *Multiple Exchange Rates and Economic Development* 35 (Princeton Studies in International Finance, No. 2, 1952).

[11] de Vries, *Multiple Exchange Rates: Expectations and Experiences*, XII STAFF PAPERS 282, 305 (1965).

[12] See Woodley, *Multiple Currency Practices—What Does It Mean*, 3 FIN. AND DEV. 113, 115–116 (1966).

[13] See *id.* at 113–116.

[14] See de Vries, *Multiple Exchange Rates*, II IMF HISTORY 1945–1965 122, 123 (1969).

adopted because the lower rate provided the authorities with "cheap" exchange with which to repay the governments external debt.[15] More recently, the rationale has focused on the windfall profits that would accrue to exporters of traditional products from a devaluation and the limited ability of the tax mechanism in most developing countries for recapturing those profits.[16]

It makes little difference to the exporter whether he surrenders each U.S. dollar for 5 pesos or surrenders each dollar for 10 pesos and is then taxed 5 pesos. Either way he has only 5 pesos left. For the government however there are considerable advantages. Since exchange has to be converted in any case it is easier administratively to combine the exchange and tax functions in one transaction. Administration is also facilitated by the fact that the existing banking system can be utilized for revenue raising as opposed to the development of a separate tax administration. Moreover, since they are administratively determined, multiple rates can be changed more easily than tax rates, which usually require legislative approval.[17] The tax administration advantages of multiple rates are, of course, applicable to all export proceeds. Thus it is not surprising to find that in many countries multiple rates are the principal means of taxing foreign companies. In the fiscal year 1953–54 Venezuela utilized a multiple-rate system to tax the export proceeds of foreign oil companies. Revenue from this source amounted to 5 percent of total government revenue in that year.[18] More generally, multiple rate systems produced an average of 25 percent of total government revenues in the Philippines during the early 1950s.[19] For tax reasons mul-

---

[15] See *ibid.*   [16] See de Vries *supra* note 11 at 288.

[17] See Woodley, *supra* note 12 at 115.

[18] The effectiveness of this system may, however, be a mixed blessing. One study shows that multiple rate systems have substantially discouraged overseas investment by American companies. See R. MIKESELI, *supra* note 2 at 172.

[19] See de Vries, *supra* note 11 at 282, 285 citing Sherwood, *Revenue Features of Multiple Exchange Rate Systems: Some Case Studies,* V STAFF PAPERS 74 (1956).

tiple rates have been employed by Argentina, Bolivia, Brazil, Chile, Colombia, Costa Rica, Ecuador, Indonesia, Iran, Nicaragua, Pakistan, Paraguay, Syria, Thailand, Turkey, Uruguay, and Vietnam.

Multiple rates also perform a revenue-raising function on the import side. In exchange distribution systems, characterized by a fixed rate and distribution by administrative decision, scarcity profits go to importers. The income tax system in most developing countries is unlikely to capture these profits. By selling exchange to these importers at a "higher" price, the government, as in the case of exchange auctions, is able to reach these scarcity profits.

While a multiple rate system can offer administrative advantages over more conventional means of taxation, it is important to note that multiple rate systems are not necessarily revenue-raising mechanisms. For when the export rate is depreciated, the government gives the exporter an increased number of units of local currency for each unit of foreign exchange earned. If the import rate remains constant, however, the government is selling foreign exchange at the same price in terms of local currency that it was before the export rate changed. In this case the government is paying out more local currency to buy foreign exchange, but its local currency proceeds from the sale of foreign exchange remain the same. Instead of acting as a revenue-raising device, the multiple rate system becomes a revenue-losing device.[20] In this situation revenue-losing is another way of saying inflationary. And there is substantial evidence that attempts by governments to preserve low import rates while depreciating export rates have been a major cause of inflation in developing countries.

A "notorious" [21] illustration of this phenomenon is Bolivia, where central bank financing of the revenue loss caused by the discrepancy in import and export rates has been

---

[20] See Woodley, *supra* note 12 at 117.   [21] de Vries, *supra* note 11 at 297.

termed the "principal reason" for the inflation that resulted
in a cost-of-living increase in La Páz in 1956 of 480 percent.[22] The inflation was further aggravated by two indirect
consequences of the disjointed rates. They made reexporta-
tion of imported goods a profitable activity, thus decreasing
the supply of goods available for the domestic market. And
because importers knew the situation could not last, they
imported large quantities of goods to be held off the market
until the inevitable devaluation. This accumulation of in-
ventories further added to the inflation.[23] In the light of
this and other similar experiences, even the most ardent
champion of multiple-rate systems would have to agree
that, a priori, the economic consequences of a multiple-rate
system are "difficult to estimate." [24]

Multiple rates do, however, offer a limited political advantage. Where the government is unwilling to face the political consequences of a straightforward devaluation, multiple rates offer a circuitous route to the same end. There
are numerous examples of this strategy in recent economic
history. The dual exchange market of Colombia established
in September 1965 was "consolidated" on August 22, 1966
by moving all transactions that had enjoyed the preferential
rate to the intermediate rate. The effect was a devaluation
of the peso from 9 to 13.50 to the U.S. dollar over the
course of the year. During that year items had gradually
been shifted from the preferential to the intermediate market so that the final move was anticlaimactic. Similar
mergers of controlled and "free" markets for exchange
were discussed in chapter 5. The political "face-saving" consequences of a multiple-rate system are not to be lightly dismissed. This factor undoubtedly accounts for their continued vitality. The caveat that might be offered in this
regard however is that the route to eventual devaluation

[22] d'A Collings, *supra* note 6 at 280.
[23] See de Vries, *supra* note 11 at 297.   [24] *Id.* at 296.

should not be too circuitous, for the greater the elapsed time between the introduction and consolidation of a multiple-rate system the more likely its political advantages will be outweighed by its negative economic consequences.

For our purposes, however, there is more to a multiple-rate system of exchange distribution than its economic or general political effect. Our primary concern is with the administrative features of exchange distribution under a multiple-rate system. In such a system there are two distinct levels of administrative decision-making. The first level of decision is that common to all exchange-distribution systems—the distribution of exchange under broad use categories as discussed in chapter 4. In market-distribution systems administrative decision-making ends at this point, with the actual rate for exchange under each category being determined by market forces. In what we have termed an archetype multiple-rate system, administrative decision-making reaches down to this second level and determines a rate for each category of exchange use. This distinction is somewhat artificial when considered against actual practice since, as we have seen, authorities in Brazil and Indonesia have intervened to control rates in what purport to be market-distribution systems. Moreover, even absent such direct intervention, the very act of distributing a fixed quantity of exchange for a category of uses will substantially determine the rate for that use. In fact, it may well be that the administrative input involved in fixing the *quantity* of exchange available for each category is precisely the same as the fixing of the *price* of exchange available for each category. There are, however, some obvious distinctions.

Where the authorities limit the quantity of exchange and refrain from otherwise intervening in the exchange market, the ensuing rate will be an equilibrium rate, i.e., a rate that matches supply with demand and clears the market. Where on the other hand the authorities fix the price of exchange—unless they are willing to meet whatever demand for exchange there is at that price—the market will not necessarily be cleared and there may be pressure on the rate. This may result in frequent changes in the rate as the authorities seek to find the equilibrium figure.[25] This is a particular problem in the inflationary situation most typical of developing countries. A market system will automatically reflect the consequences of inflation in higher rates paid for exchange. In a multiple-rate system, however, the fixed prices for exchange may lag behind the rate of inflation and make exchange cheaper and cheaper, thus encouraging increased imports. Many states react to this effect by coupling fixed rates with quantitative import restrictions.[26] This will cause a decline in the frequency of rate changes but only at the cost of adding another level of administrative decision-making. These problems involved in utilizing a fixed multiple rate system are a particular reflection of the more general proposition that cost restrictions are not generally effective in an inflationary situation.[27]

Aside from the economic distortions that may result from the selection by the authorities of the "wrong" rate, and/or frequent changes in the rate, the two systems have significantly different consequences in terms of the perception of the exchange user. Where the rate is set by the market, the exchange user sees the situation as one in which exchange is available to him as a "right" provided he is willing to pay the price established by the demand of other exchange users. If the price should prove too high for his purposes, his disappointment is a result of the activity of his competitors for exchange. On the other hand, where the price of the exchange is set by the authorities, the exchange user sees himself in another "take it or leave it" situation. He has no con-

---

[25] See Baer and Hervé, *Multiple Exchange Rates and the Attainment of Multiple Policy Objectives*, 29 ECONOMICA N.S. 176 (1962) (". . . [I]n practice, policy-makers develop a structure of rates by a process of trial and error.").
[26] See Schlesinger, *supra* note 10 at 17.   [27] See *id.* at 12.

trol over the price of exchange, the rate is being set by "them." If the rate is too high, it is "they" who are responsible. And if the rate is subject to frequent change it is "they" who are incompetent. Note that it is not the change of the rate that disturbs the exchange user—for the rate may vary with each transaction in a market-distribution system—but the party perceived as responsible for the change. Frequent changes by market forces are not generally attributed to the "incompetence" of the market, nor do such changes normally evoke the criticism that "it is impossible to do business" in such an environment. The testimony of Brazilian businessmen with regard to the auction system is quite the opposite. Less frequent changes in the rate by the monetary authorities may, on the other hand, be widely attributed to incompetence and corruption and are heard to create an "impossible business climate." In short, one cannot blame the authorities if an exchange rate set by the market is "too high," but one can do so where the rate is set by the authorities.

A second administrative disadvantage of multiple rate systems is a tendency for the categories of exchange uses to proliferate. We noted in chapter 4 that this is a characteristic of all exchange-distribution systems, since the larger the number of categories the easier for the administration to categorize a particular transaction. This prolifteration reaches an extreme in multiple-rate systems. Refinements in multiple-rate systems have led to cases such as Paraguay where there were at one time fifteen different rates that applied to convertible currencies and seven more that applied to other countries. Before the exchange reform of May 1963, Indonesia has "more than 15 separate import rates in operation" as a result of a combination of exchange taxes and export-retention systems.[28] Less severe cases of proliferation occurred in Argentina in 1952–55 and 1956–58, Bolivia

---

[28] Kanesa-Thasan, *supra* note 7 at 362–363 n. 3.

in 1952–53 and 1954–56, Turkey 1956–58 and Spain 1955–59.[29] This increase in the number of categories has been particularly evident where governments have utilized multiple-rate systems to increase the tax yield from exchange transactions.[30]

Despite this tendency toward the proliferation of rates a multiple-rate system would appear less complicated to operate than either an auction system or an administrative-distribution system. While the Triffin auction plan had among its virtues that of simplicity, the only widespread use of auctions as a means of exchange distribution—the case of Brazil—must be considered an administrative nightmare. It is extremely doubtful that another attempt at introducing such a system would meet with more successful results. The administrative complications arise from the conflict inherent in attempting to duplicate the pattern of exchange distribution that would result from the operation of market forces, while at the same time attempting to control the operation of those forces. It is most certainly the latter element-control that has characterized modern attempts at distribution by auctions. And even where the government is willing to allow the auctions to function freely, the degree of organizational effort required in organizing a weekly exchange auction looms large when compared with the relative case by which rates can be set by a small meeting of central bank officials.[31] In short, the weekly meeting is far simpler to arrange than the weekly auction.

On the other hand it is quite clear that posting a price for each category of exchange use, and making the exchange available to anyone who will pay the price, offers substantial administrative advantages over a system in which exchange

---

[29] See d'A Collings, *supra* note 6 at 280 n. 7.

[30] See INTERNATIONAL MONETARY FUND, EIGHTEENTH ANNUAL REPORT ON EXCHANGE RESTRICTIONS 46 (1967).

[31] Advocates of multiple rate systems have argued that they "could be handled by a small group of trained bankers . . ." de Vries, *supra* note 14 at 133.

is apportioned to each user. More important, multiple-rate systems are indifferent as to the personality of the ultimate exchange user. Herein lies their great attraction for purposes of our study. The distribution of exchange to the individual importer is not subject to administrative decision. This relieves the constant political and commercial pressure on the low-level exchange control authorities. It was one of the principal reasons why Pakistan in 1959 and the Philippines in 1961 adopted multiple rates and abandoned their previous individual licensing systems.[32]

The two considerations just noted—the attraction of multiple-rate systems when compared to administrative exchange distribution and their unattractiveness when compared with market-exchange distribution—have dominated IMF policy with regard to multiple-rate systems. We noted in chapter 5 that multiple-rate systems are inconsistent with a member's obligations under the Articles of Agreement of the IMF.

Three areas of the Articles are involved. Multiple rates patently conflict with Article IV obligations with regard to the maintenance of par values and exchange stability. In addition, the Executive Directors have identified multiple rates as a "multiple currency practice" within the meaning of Article VIII of the Agreement [33] and reminded members that Article VIII, Section 3 provides that "no member shall engage in . . . any . . . multiple currency practices except as authorized under this Agreement or approved by the Fund. If such arrangements and practices are engaged in at the date when this Agreement enters into force, the member concerned shall consult with the Fund as to their progressive removal . . ." Finally, it was noted for the benefit of Article XIV members that multiple-rate systems were

[32] See de Vries, *supra* note 11 at 290.
[33] Decision No. 237–2 of December 18, 1947, § D, reprinted in III IMF HISTORY 1945–1965, 261 (1969).

a "restriction" on current payments. Despite the clear language of the Articles, however, multiple-rate systems were in wide use in the early postwar years and it thus became necessary for the Fund to look beyond the language of the Agreement in its consideration of multiple-rate systems. To this end the Board appointed an Ad Hoc Committee on Spreads and Multiple Currency Practices in May 1947. The Committee examined the existing practices and the reasons for them. In sum, what the Committee found was that while multiple-currency practices were in most cases inconsistent with the obligations of members, they were preferable to exchange distribution by administrative decision because they were easier to administer, "less subject to corruption and discrimination," and their revenue-raising aspect could be used for cooling down inflation.[34] Moreover, the committee noted that "for certain countries the only practicable sort of foreign exchange restriction is multiple currency practices." Rather than adopt the probably fruitless and possibly erroneous strategy of calling for strict enforcement of the letter of the Agreement, the Board urged that members should remove multiple currency practices which were "clearly not necessary for balance of payments reasons," that members should work to remedy the causes of their balance of payments difficulties, and that, where this was not possible, that members should eliminate "the most dangerous aspects of their multiple-currency practices." [35] The most dangerous "aspects" appear to have been considered those "which constitute a serious menace to international economic relations." [36] High on the list here would be systems involving broken cross-rates which established discriminatory trade patterns.

The 1947 policy statement was directed primarily at the

[34] See I IMF HISTORY 1945–1965, 177 (1969).
[35] Decision No. 237-2 of December 18, 1947, *supra* note 33.
[36] I IMF HISTORY 1945–1965, 177 (1969).

West European members of the Fund. By the end of 1949 however the Fund's staff began to actively pursue the question of multiple-rate systems with its Latin American members. In informal sessions in January 1950 the Board reconsidered the question of multiple rates. Aside from a general discussion, the Board considered a proposal by one of the executive directors for a model system that employed a separate rate for exports, a separate rate for imports, and a free market for invisibles. While the Board agreed that this would be the "least objectionable" multiple-rate system, several directors took the view that the system incorporated in the Agreement was the one most likely to optimize global welfare. No formal action resulted from these discussions.[37]

In 1956 a staff study indicated that of the 60 member countries 38 were utilizing multiple-currency practices. Clearly the multiple-rate problem was one that would not go away and the staff believed the time was "opportune for a full reconsideration of the subject." [38] The staff memo began by reviewing practice under the 1947 decision. Under that decision the Board "had acquiesed in the use of multiple-currency practices . . . [1] where the only feasible alternative was quantitative restrictions [i.e., administrative distribution] . . . [2] where they permitted a relaxation of quantitative restrictions, or [3] in those [countries] where multiple-currency arrangements offered the only practical way of depreciating an overvalued currency." In view of the still widespread use of such systems, the staff believed "that the Fund should increase its efforts to discourage multiple currency practices." Since the West European members of the Fund were about to assume their full Article VIII obligations, the developing-country members of the Board may well have believed that the tougher policy was directed against them and objected to the "double standard." It is

---

[37] Id. at 271.   [38] Id. at 435.

not surprising, therefore, to note that when the staff report
came before the Board in January 1957, it "provoked an intensive discussion." [39]

The Executive Directors from Latin America were vigorous in pointing out the advantages of multiple rate systems.
Mr. Paranagua (Brazil) urged the Board to focus on the
harmful consequences of the use of multiple-rate systems
rather than the systems themselves. Mr. Sol (El Salvador)
also pointed out that attention should be focused on multiple-rate systems that were discriminatory, and he gave examples of multiple-rate systems in use in Venezuela and
Costa Rica which were not, in his opinion, discriminatory. A
report of the meeting points out that "Executive Directors
representing developed countries were naturally more sym-
pathetic with the viewpoint of the staff paper." [40] In the end
the Board issued its Decision No. 649—(57/33) of June 26,
1957, which begins by reemphasizing that the "unification
of the exchange rates in multiple-rate systems is a basic objective of the Fund." Thereafter there was a slight shift in
emphasis. ". . . In reviewing the experience of the past 10
years . . . the Fund draws special attention to the fact that
complex systems are difficult to administer, and involve
frequent changes, discrimination, export subsidization, a
considerable spread between rates, and undue differentia-
tion between classes of imports." While again pointing out
the evils, the shift was manifested in the use of the word
"complex." It was *complex* systems that were found to evidence these undesirable characteristics. And while the
Board noted its agreement with the "general approach of
the staff paper" and, in particular, the need for "more
rapid progress," the progress was to be in the direction of
"simplifying complex multiple-rate systems." Thus the word
"complex" seems to have been used to indicate a change in

[39] *Id.* at 436.   [40] *Ibid.*

the Fund's approach from outright elimination of multiple-rate systems to an effort to simplify them. By "simplification" the Board "meant more than merely a reduction in the number of existing rates." Emphasis was placed on a total of two or three rates that would be sufficiently realistic to maintain a satisfactory balance of payments with a minimum of restrictions." [41] Finally the Fund announced its readiness to extend to members both technical assistance and "the use of its resources" in their efforts to "simplify and eliminate complex rate systems." In implementing this policy the Fund provided technical and financial assistance to Chile (April 1956), Bolivia (December 1956), Paraguay (August 1957), Argentina (December 1958), and Uruguay (December 1959–September 1960).[42]

By 1967 the Fund was again cautioning its members about multiple rates. In its *Annual Report* for that year the Fund noted, in what must be a classic understatement, that multiple rates "tend to raise doubts about the stability of the currency." [43] In addition, the Fund indicated that it considered multiple rates an attempt to escape from facing up to the problems of inflation and that such systems "do not engender the discipline that a fixed unitary rate does."

In the final chapter of this study, which contains some suggestions for reform, we shall return to the questions of "inflation, discipline, and multiple rates." In particular we shall consider these issues against the background of our study of the rule of law and corruption problems associated with existing systems of administrative exchange distribution. What should be clear at this point is that multiple rates do offer a way of ameliorating the undermining of the rule of law and of the growth of corruption by eliminating the

[41] See de Vries, *The Decline of Multiple Exchange Rates,* 1947–67, 4 FIN. AND DEV. 297, 302 (1967).

[42] See d'A Collings, *supra* note 6 at 274, 276.

[43] INTERNATIONAL MONETARY FUND, EIGHTEENTH ANNUAL REPORT ON EXCHANGE RESTRICTIONS 46 (1967).

vulnerable point of administrative decision-making—the decision as to *whom* shall foreign exchange be awarded. Once we have considered systems that do not eliminate this area of administrative decision-making, as we do in the next chapter, we shall be in a better position to draw up a balance sheet on multiple-rate systems.

Chapter 7

Administrative Distribution

Administrative exchange distribution systems differ from those previously discussed in that they *personalize* the distribution process. Central to these systems is a decision by an administrator that applicant *A* or applicant *B* will receive foreign exchange. Because of this personalization of the process, administrative exchange distribution systems are the most likely to be subject to administrative abuse and corruption. For the exchange user can focus his efforts on benefiting himself alone and the administrator can respond to his blandishments without immediate wider effects. At the outset of this study we examined an extreme example of the corruption of such a system. In this chapter we shall examine administrative distribution systems on a more general basis. We shall focus on two aspects of those systems. Initially our attention will be on the criteria applied by the administrators to decide who is to receive exchange. For it is the substitution of these criteria for the price mechanism that distinguishes administrative distribution systems from the market and multiple-rate systems previously discussed. In some cases these alternative criteria are objective, the most common being a stated percentage of the exchange distributed to the same user during a base period. In other cases the criteria are rather complex and/or vague. Following our discussion of criteria, we shall look closely at the administrative process involved in applying those criteria. In most countries the distributions are made by civil servants acting singly, in others they are made by committee, and in at least one country the distributions are made by private groups to whom the authorities have delegated the responsibility.

In looking at the criteria utilized we shall examine the scope of discretion delegated to the administrators. Our concern with process will focus on the extent to which the exercise of discretion is limited by institutional arrangements. By way of introduction, we will begin our consideration of administrative distribution systems by noting two institutional practices that emphasize the personal nature of these systems.

Many administrative systems require that an importer *register* before he will be considered as a possible exchange recipient. The purpose of such requirements is, in the words of a former Ghana Minister of Trade, "to insure a more effective control over the issue and utilization of [import] licenses . . ."[1] Control is exercised in a variety of ways. Although registration fees are generally nominal, some countries require proof of financial standing. Yugoslavia, for example, requires that all importing organizations register with the district courts. In order to be registered an organization must evidence a specified minimum working capital.[2] Indian importers must satisfy the Registering Authority of their "general background of trading and industrial experience."[3] While importer registration can serve a

[1] Press Conference, July 6, 1964, reported in *Ghana Times*, July 7, 1964, p.4.
[2] See INTERNATIONAL MONETARY FUND, TWENTIETH ANNUAL REPORT ON EXCHANGE RESTRICTIONS 522 (1969).
[3] MINISTRY OF COMMERCE, GOVERNMENT OF INDIA, IMPORT TRADE CONTROL HANDBOOK 73 (1966).

variety of useful purposes, it also presents an opportunity to cut off an applicant from foreign exchange distributions at a preliminary stage in the distribution process.[4]

The personal nature of administrative exchange distribution is emphasized to an even greater extent by the requirement that the exchange permit (or the import license which carries with it the exchange entitlement) may not be transferred. Article 5 of the Somali Law on Foreign Economic Transactions states very bluntly that "[l]icenses are not transferable."[5] The principle is enshrined in the legislation of other countries as well. It was virtually universal among the countries of Europe in the 1930s[6] and was incorporated in Article III of the Convention Relating to the Simplification of Customs Formalities, *done* at Geneva, November 3, 1923. Paragraph (d) of the Protocol states that "the system of issuing licenses shall be such as to prevent the traffic in licenses. With this object, licenses when issued to individuals shall state the name of the holder and shall not be capable of being used by any other person."[7]

There is an economic rationale for this prohibition on transfer of licenses. The theory is that to allow transfer raises the possibility of one importer obtaining so large a proportion of the permissible supply of a particular item as to effect a monopoly.[8] If the point of maximum profit from a monopoly is for a quantity less than that permitted to be imported, it is profitable for the monopolist importer to limit his imports to the smaller quantity. Note, however, that the higher profits are the results of the monopoly rather than of the licensing scheme. That is to say, only to the extent that transfer of licenses makes it easier to obtain

---

[4] Even after import liberalization, the Korean "Ministry of Commerce and Industry continued to exercise a considerable influence over imports indirectly, through a system of registering qualified importers . . . ." Kanesa-Thasan, *Stabilizing An Economy—A Study of the Republic of Korea*, XVI STAFF PAPERS 1, 19 (1969).

[5] Decree No. 12 of Sept. 23, 1964.

[6] See HEUSER, CONTROL OF INTERNATIONAL TRADE 233–34 (1939).

[7] G.B.T.S. No. 16 of 1925 (CMD. 2347).

[8] HEUSER, *supra* note 6 at 159.

a monopoly position that transferability should be condemned.[9] Fears of such monopoly situations are sometimes
justified. In a press conference on July 6, 1964 the Minister of
Trade of Ghana related that Danawi & Sons had obtained
import licenses covering "a large proportion of the total
allocation of butter licenses." The Danawi company utilized
only 25 percent of the licenses, thus creating a shortage of
butter in Ghana and garnering monopoly profits for itself.[10]

The problem is that prohibitions on transferability are
easy to circumvent. Professor Heuser collected several interesting examples of the trade in licenses in Europe during
the 1930s. At a conference of merchants held in Zurich in
1936, for example, the story was told of "[a] young importer of fruit who had not been given an import license
[and, therefore,] paid the owner of a permit from
4,000–6,000 Fr. annually for import rights. The license
holder no longer found it necessary to carry on any trade
himself." [11] When European governments realized that they
could not prevent trade in licenses by prohibition, they
sought to achieve that end by different means. Switzerland
shortened the period of validity of licenses from three
months to two weeks, thus limiting the duration of any possible monopoly and making it much harder to maintain
one. The system must, however, have put considerable
pressure on importers and the licensing authorities with the
former undoubtedly devoting a considerable amount of
their time to obtaining their biweekly licenses. Holland tried
a different approach. License holders who were not able to
use their entire quota during the license period were permitted to exchange their licenses for others rather than
dispose of the unused portion illegally.[12] The present study
did not reveal that either of these practices are currently in
use in the developing world. Instead, the authorities seem
to rely on general prohibitions against transferability. We

[9] *Ibid.*   [10] Note 1 *supra.*
[11] HEUSER, *supra* note 6 at 236.   [12] *Id.* at 235.

do know, however, from official studies that trading in licenses is a major problem in Turkey and India.[13] Informal studies indicate that the practice is widespread in other countries utilizing administrative exchange distribution systems.[14] Although it is a side effect of such a system, it is a good illustration of one kind of "illegal" activity that several developing countries have avoided by utilizing market distribution systems.[15]

But our principle concern is with the process of initial exchange distributions by the authorities and not subsequent illegal activities which subvert those systems. The first aspect of that process we shall examine is the type of criteria used to decide between competitors for exchange. The most widely used criterion is the fixed percentage of a base period exchange distribution.

BASE PERIOD CRITERIA

The distribution of a flat percentage of exchange allocated in a base period has its history in the 1930s. In November 1931, Germany introduced an exchange distribution system with a base period of from July 1, 1930 to June 30, 1931.[16] In the first month of the program firms were allocated 75 percent of the exchange they used during the same month in the base period. The percentage was subsequently re-

[13] J. MONTEIRO, CORRUPTION 33 (Bombay 1966); USAID/ANKARA, THE TURKISH IMPORT REGIME 95 (1968).

[14] See, e.g., Thomas, *Import Licensing and Import Liberalization in Pakistan*, VI. PAK. DEV. REV. 500, 509 (1966) (". . . [M]any . . . [license] holders had actually stopped importing, and were living on the income from the (illegal) sale of their licenses.").

[15] The Santhanam Report indicated that import licenses provide a convenient vehicle for the investment of "black" money, i.e. unreported taxable income. See Ministry of Home Affairs, Government of India, *Report of the Committee on Prevention of Corruption* 254 (1964). From an economic point of view, prohibition on transferability forecloses the possibility of "market-directed shifts" toward more efficient producers. J. BHAGWATI, TRADE, TARIFFS AND GROWTH 56 (1969).

[16] Ellis, *German Exchange Control, 1931–1939*, 54 Q. JR. ECON. 1, 26 (Aug. 1940).

duced to 55 percent and 50 percent as the Depression worsened. A current example of this system is New Zealand. At the end of March each year the Minister for Customs announces the Import Licensing Schedule for the year beginning June 30. On March 26, 1969, for example, the Minister announced that for the year ending June 30, 1970 "basic" licenses would be issued at 105 percent of the value of the 1968–69 licenses. On March 30, 1967, a period when wool sales were weak, the Minister announced that licenses for consumer goods and many industrial raw materials would be reduced by 20 percent for the following year. Administratively this system has much to commend it. Its outstanding feature is its simplicity. Once the monetary authorities have produced their foreign exchange budget, one or at most a few, calculations need be made before the Minister can announce a policy clearly known and easily applied by each importer. The simplicity of the New Zealand system, however, is also its principle drawback as it does not allow precise control over the import mix.

Much more precise and therefore much more complex is the system employed by India for distributing exchange to "Established Importers." Established Importers are "those who have been actually engaged in the import trade of the articles comprised in any serial or sub-serial number of the I.T.C. [Import Trade Control] Schedule during at least one financial year (1st April to 31st March) falling within the basic period specified for the said serial or sub-serial number." [17] If the importer can prove such past imports, he is issued a *quota certificate*. [18] The certificate is evidence of his past imports and gives both a description of the goods and their value. The quota certificate is the document needed to obtain a *quota*

---

[17] HANDBOOK, *supra* note 3 at 15.

[18] Verifications of past imports required "much effort" on the part of Pakistan's CCIE in the 1950s. Thomas, *supra* note 14 at 505 n. 6. Part of the problem was falsification of letters of credit and customs receipts. See *ibid.*

license (import license). "A quota license is given to an established importer as a percentage of the value of imports fixed in the quota certificate in accordance with the Policy Statement in the Import Trade Control Policy Book [Red Book] for the licensing period in question or the relevant public notice." [19] The Red Book gives an illustration of how the system works. "If the quota percentage for an item is 75 and the basic imports in the quota certificate amount to 40,000, the importer's entitlement will work out to . . . $40,000 \times 75/100 = 30,000$." [20]

The established importer applies for his quota license to the regional licensing authority covering the area where his business is located. There are 15 such offices spread around India. For each item a separate application is required. The license is examined by a member of the nongazetted staff who checks to see that it complies with the regulations, and does the calculations illustrated above. The proposal to issue the license "is then put up to an assistant controller (a Gazetted officer)." [21] If within his financial jurisdiction, the assistant controller issues the license. If not, the application goes up the chain of authority.

The Indian system has lost the simplicity that was the most attractive feature of the New Zealand system. A brief comparison of the two systems makes this quite clear. In New Zealand the percentage of permitted imports is an across-the-board one applying to most, if not all, goods. In the Indian scheme each item in the import schedule has a separate percentage specified. In the New Zealand program, the base period is the previous year. In the Indian program, the base periods vary with the type of goods. The *Import Trade Control Policy Book* for 1966–67, for example, provides that "the basic period for the purpose of calculat-

[19] Handbook, *supra* note 3 at 26.   [20] *Ibid.*
[21] Columbia University School of Law, *Legal Controls of Import and Industrial Licensing* 52 (1968).

ing the quota of established importers is from 1st April 1951 to 31st March 1952. The basic period has been extended to 1952–53, 1953–54, 1954–55, 1955–56, 1956–57, 1957–58, 1958–59, 1959–60, 1960–61, 1962–63, and 1964–65 in the case of a large number of items." [22] Moreover, "importers may choose the most favorable year from the basic period for the purpose of obtaining quota certificates." [23] Finally, while the Indian importer requires a separate license for each import item, his New Zealand counterpart may obtain a composite license covering a number of items classified with a specific "Group." Items within the group are treated as interchangeable so that any item or combination of items in the group may be imported up to the total value of the composite license. [24]

The complexity of the Indian system—the result of an effort to obtain closer control over the import mix—has cost that country dearly in administrative talent. To administer the program the Chief Controller of Imports and Exports has roughly 300 gazetted officers and 1,800 nongazetted officers on his staff. [25] In the licensing year 1964–65 they handled 244,489 applications; in 1965–66, 148,016; and for the first ten months of 1966–67, 186,348. A study of the organization indicates that the normal time for disposing of an application is one month. [26] Assuming 20 working days per month, and eleven months per year per employee, each gazetted officer handled four applications per day in 1964–65, 2.5 per day in 1965–66, and 3.5 per day in

[22] MINISTRY OF COMMERCE, GOVERNMENT OF INDIA, IMPORT TRADE CONTROL POLICY 4 (1966).

[23] Id. at 15.

[24] Import Licensing Schedule 1966–67, NEW ZEALAND RESERVE BANK BULL., 55 (May 1966).

[25] In Germany in 1939, 600,000 civil servants were involved in the administration of the exchange distribution system. See Rashba, Foreign Exchange Restrictions and Public Policy in the Conflict of Laws, 41 MICH. L. REV. 777, 810 n. 133 (1943) (citing an estimate by the French economist Laufenburger.) But see ELLIS, EXCHANGE CONTROL IN CENTRAL EUROPE 287 (1939). (36,000 estimate, based on "hearsay.")

[26] Columbia Law School, supra note 21 at 57.

1966–67. And these figures understate the work load some-what since not all of the gazetted officers process applications. While the manpower cost of processing applications may be balanced out by the fact that in a country of massive underemployment any government activity providing work may be considered a social welfare program, the number of people and volume of transactions act as an invitation to chaos and corruption. For isolated deviations from the norm are likely to be lost in the hundreds of thousands of individual licensing transactions.[27]

The invitation to arbitrary and corrupt decision-making offered by the complexity of the system is substantially counterbalanced, however, by the other important feature of the base period distribution system—the fact that the criterion upon which distributions are made is objectively determined. With knowledge of the criterion, i.e., the base period, each applicant for exchange knows exactly the percentage of the total permitted imports he is entitled to receive. That is, the system "for established importers . . . does not confer any discretion on licensing authorities."[28] Given a fixed total of permitted imports of any one item, any attempt on the part of an administrator to give an applicant more than his proper share of that item must result in reduction of another applicant's share and therefore a well-founded protest. It was this objectivity in the base period system that militated in favor of its adoption by Pakistan, where the government sought an exchange distribution system that would involve a "minimum of corruption."[29] But objectivity is purchased at a price. For utilization of the base period criterion results in a freezing of market positions as they were in the base period. The cri-

[27] See also Thomas, *supra* note 14 at 509 ("The basic administrative problem . . . the licensing authorities lacked adequate staff and information to make wise priority decisions and to implement efficiently the decisions reached.").

[28] Jain, *Administrative Discretion in the Issue of Import Licenses*, 10 JR. IND. L. INST. 121, 124 (1968).

[29] Thomas, *supra* note 14 at 505.

terion takes no account of changes in efficiency and it eliminates newcomers from the market. This is no theoretical possibility. The experience with the system in Germany in the 1930s showed that it "prevented the appearance of new import firms, virtually precluded any shifting of the relative outputs of firms from their 1930 basis, and afforded to importers a sheltered position at a time when the deflationary process was imposing a severe struggle for existence on other enterprises." [30] It was to ameliorate this economic effect that India adopted the policy of the shifting base period. Pakistan has experimented with a different system for providing for newcomers to the import trade. In Pakistan there was a pressing political necessity for the experiment since the base period employed in the distribution system—1950–52—discriminated against importers in what was then East Pakistan.[31] In 1961 the government introduced an "open general license" system, which limited the importation of specified goods to new importers. In addition, the scheme provided that no O.G.L. licenses could be issued to importers in Karachi, Lahore, Dacca (where major importers were not Bengali), Narayanganj, and Chittagong.[32]

PRO RATA DISTRIBUTION

Unlike the New Zealand and Indian systems, the Turkish import program is operated on a six-month basis. Every six months the Turkish Council of Ministers issues a "Decree Concerning the Foreign Trade Regime." This decree itemizes the goods that may be imported for the six-month period beginning the following January or July. The decree

---

[30] Ellis, *supra* note 16 at 26, 27.   [31] Thomas, *supra* note 14 at 507.

[32] Naqvi, *Import Licensing in Pakistan*, PAK. DEV. REV. (1964), reprinted in ISLAM (ed.), STUDIES ON COMMERCIAL POLICY AND ECONOMIC GROWTH 89, 98 (1970).

covers imports from convertible currency areas and contains two lists of goods—the Quota List and the Liberalized List. As the name suggests, items in the Quota List may be imported up to a specified maximum total value. The Quota List is then broken down into allocations for "importers" and allocations for "industrialists.

The system for importers is outlined in the regulations implementing Decree 6/5733 of Dec. 30, 1965. Within 30 days after the publication of lists in the *Official Gazette,* a commercial importer must submit his import application to his commercial bank.[33] Within five days, the application must be forwarded to the regional branch of the Central Bank and then on to the Istanbul branch of the Central Bank. It is the Istanbul branch which has the responsibility for distributing the quota's.[34] The criterion employed is that each importer is given a share in the total quota in the same proportion as his application bears to the total applications for that item. In the words of Article 17(c): "The Central Bank . . . shall distribute the quotas among applicants. Should a quota fail to cover the applications the distribution shall be made pro rata applications" (sic).[35]

This method of distribution is an improvement over the more common base-year system. As noted, the base-year system tends to freeze market shares and penalize the efficient and energetic. Under the Turkish system the importer who can sell more goods will get more goods. The potential flaw in the Turkish system is the importer who applies for a disproportionately large share of the total quota for one item in an effort to monopolize that item.[36] The Turkish system recognizes this possibility and guards

[33] Article 17.

[34] USAID/ANKARA, *supra* note 13 at 80.

[35] Pro rata distribution was also used in Honduras from 1937–41. See Vinelli, *The Currency and Exchange System of Honduras,* I STAFF PAPERS 420, 430 (1951).

[36] A study of the Turkish system reveals that this occurs, although the 20 percent rule does limit it. See USAID/ANKARA, *supra* note 13 at 93.

against it by providing that no single importer may apply for more than 20 percent of the quota established for a particular commodity.[37]

Perhaps a greater defect in the Turkish system is that the criterion applied is less accessible to confirmation than the traditional one. In New Zealand, when the government announces that each importer will receive licenses for a flat percentage of his previous year's imports, the importer can readily determine whether he has received his fair share by comparing his license with his previous imports. The same is true in India. The importer has at hand the information necessary to confirm the objective operation of the distribution scheme. In Turkey, on the other hand, the importer has no way of knowing the proportion his license application bore to the total license applications for the totals are not published. He must, therefore, accept on faith that he has received his proper distribution. The weakness is not that the criterion is difficult to apply; it is rather that the data for its application are not available to the importer. Administrative abuse may therefore go undetected since only the administrator, acting illegally, and his "benefactor" will be aware of the malapportionment of the quota.[38]

TIME OF FILING

Exchange for imports on the Liberalized List in Turkey is apparently distributed according to a different criterion. The Liberalized List is itself broken down into two parts. Goods on List I are mainly imports entitled to priority be-

[37] Import Regulations, Art. 17, Decree No. 6/8452, reprinted in Off. Gazette No. 12638 of July 4, 1967 (unoffic. trans.) ("Applications in excess of 20 percent shall be entirely void.").

[38] But see USAID/Ankara, *supra* note 13 at 4 (Pro rata "allocation system is equitable" though "cumbersome, time consuming, expensive and inefficient.").

cause they are required for export production. Goods on List II are primarily raw materials and capital goods for domestic use.[39] To import goods on List II, the importer applies through his bank to the Turkish Central Bank. If exchange is available it is distributed to the applicant. To the extent that the demand for exchange exceeds its supply "requests for liberalized imports are cumulated by date of application in a waiting list until foreign exchange becomes available.[40] If exchange does not become available during one import period, requests are carried over to the next period. The supply of foreign exchange is related seasonally to exports. Since the export "season" runs from September through April, delays are longest in the summer months.[41]

Although this criterion provides an administratively expeditious manner for dealing with exchange requests, its economic rationale is difficult to apprehend. Although the principle of "first in time, first in right" is firmly established in most legal systems, it would appear useful in the present context only to the extent that the delays involved in providing exchange for liberalized imports were a matter of a few days. Where, as seems to be the case,[42] the delays are much greater, the rule places a premium on filing an early application regardless of immediate need. And while the criterion is objective so as to limit administrative discretion,[43] an applicant will not know how he stands vis-à-vis other claimants unless the Bank publicizes data indicating the date of the receipt of all exchange applications.

[39] INTERNATIONAL MONETARY FUND, TWENTIETH ANNUAL REPORT ON EXCHANGE RESTRICTIONS 465 (1969).

[40] See USAID/ANKARA, *supra* note 13 at 14.   [41] *Id.* at 41.

[42] See e.g., XXI I.F.N.S. 383 (1969) (". . . waiting periods of up to eight months . . .").

[43] The Santhanam Committee recommended that import licenses be dealt with in order of priority. See Ministry of Home Affairs, Government of India, *supra* note 15 at 257.

OTHER CRITERIA

The second major category of importers in the Indian foreign exchange distribution system are termed "actual users." Actual users are "those who require raw materials, accessories, machinery, and spare parts for their own use in an industrial manufacturing process." [44] For actual users in India obtaining a license is a chancier affair than is the case with established importers. Not only is the process more complicated, but some of the criteria on which the issuance of licenses are based are neither quantitative nor objective. And there are no announced quotas for such imports.

There are three categories of actual users: "(i) scheduled industries borne on the registers of the Directorate General of Technical Development [DGTD], (ii) scheduled industries not borne on the registers of the Directorate General of Technical Development and non-scheduled industries other than small scale industries and (iii) small scale industries." Each category is subject to separate distribution processes.

An application to import raw materials by an actual user in a *scheduled industry* is sent by mail to the DGTD. There it is sorted in the control receipts and issues section. From there it is sent to the Coordination Directorate, where the details contained in the license application are transcribed in a register. The license application is then sent on to an Industrial Group Directorate. There are 33 such directorates, e.g., The Paper and Pulp Directorate and the Heavy Electricals Directorate, organized along final product lines. When the relevant Directorate receives the application it is again recorded and the applicant is notified that his application has been received by the DGTD. An officer within the Directorate then pulls the files on the applicant to deter-

[44] See HANDBOOK, *supra* note 13 at 39.

mine whether his past performance will support the present request. In looking at "past performance," however, the officer is not only checking the previous level of imports as in the case of established importers. Since actual users are by and large importing raw materials and equipment for manufacturing purposes, the officer is primarily concerned with seeing how imported goods have been utilized. According to the DGTD's *Annual Report for 1964–65*, the applications are scrutinized "from the point of essentiality and/or indigenous non-availability." [45] The *Import Trade Control Handbook* supplies a bit more detail and indicates that the decision is to be based on "(i) foreign exchange availability or availability of other monetary ceilings, (ii) availability of goods applied for from indigenous sources or other commercial channels, (iii) essentiality of the goods applied for, (iv) stocks in hand and expected arrivals, (v) past imports and past consumption of the item(s) in question by the applicant, (vi) actual production during the preceding year, (vii) estimated production, and (viii) any other factor considered relevant and necessary." [46] With a complicated set of criteria, including open-ended criterion number (viii), it is not surprising to find that a study of the DGTD in 1964 revealed that "the decision rules by which the various directorates assign specific amounts to each firm vary from directorate to directorate." [47] In part this is due to the amount and quality of information available. In

[45] DIRECTORATE GENERAL OF TECHNICAL DEVELOPMENT, GOVERNMENT OF INDIA, ANNUAL REPORT 1964–65, p. 1 (1966).

[46] See HANDBOOK, *supra* note 3 at 42. The "substitutability" provision, item (ii), was utilized in Argentina in the 1930s. It drew the following comment from an astute observer: "One can readily imagine the degree of expertness involved in the essentially layman's judgment of substitutability upon which Exchange Control Office decisions in this period were based." V. SALERA, EXCHANGE CONTROL AND THE ARGENTINE MARKET 212 (1941).

[47] USAID/INDIA, *An Advance Study of the Information System Requirements of the Director General of Technical Development (GOI) with Special Attention to Import Licensing and Related Functions* 28 (Nov. 16, 1964).

part it must also be due to the capacity and ability of the individual civil servant handling an application. And a critical factor is the work load of the DGTD, which must process many thousands of applications each year. The necessity for a convenient means of determining authorizations is readily apparent when one considers that for the fiscal year 1964–65, the DGTD "scrutinized" 58,366 import applications.[48] At this time the gazetted staff numbered 300.[49] The study found that regardless of the criteria detailed in the *Handbook,* "one decision rule is to give each firm what it got last year, increased (or decreased) by the proportion of increase or decrease in the directorate's total allocation of foreign exchange." We are thus back to distribution by percentage of a given base period. In fact, an observer of import licensing in Pakistan has suggested that the base-period criterion is the only one that can be used where the administering authority must deal with thousands of applications.[50] There is no assurance however that this criterion will be utilized in each transaction. The difficulty with regard to actual users in India is that, because of the complex criteria by which applications are supposed to be considered and given the limitations noted above, it is a safe conclusion that there is "ample scope for exercise of arbitrary discretion." [51] And there is some evidence that this possibility has often been converted to a reality.

In the report of the Santhanam Committee, which investigated the work of the DGTD, 43 opportunities for corruption were identified. Many of these arose from the personal contact with the administrative officials considered neces-

[48] In addition to its "normal" workload, the DGTD is the licensing authority for machine tools and in this capacity issued 4088 licenses itself in 1964–65. See ANNUAL REPORT, *supra* note 45 at 73.

[49] See *id.* at 3–4.

[50] G. PAPANEK, PAKISTAN'S DEVELOPMENT SOCIAL GOALS AND PRIVATE INCENTIVES 121–122 (1967).

[51] DEPARTMENT OF SUPPLY AND TECHNICAL DEVELOPMENT, MINISTRY OF INDUSTRY AND SUPPLY, GOVERNMENT OF INDIA, REPORT OF THE STUDY TEAM ON THE DIRECTORATE GENERAL OF TECHNICAL DEVELOPMENT (Part I) 109 (1965).

sary to resolve unanswered questions or to supply missing data. "It is well known that the presentation of any application is followed by visits and letters to the applicant with the offer of 'fixing up' the license for prices depending on the nature of the application." [52]

After the DGTD has made its decisions, it will forward its recommendations to the Chief Controller of Imports and Exports (CCI&E). The DGTD also sends a copy of its recommendations to the applicant. The CCI&E will then check to see that the procedural requirements of the Import Trade Control Rules and Regulations have been followed and, if so, will issue or refuse the license, "as the case may be, based on the recommendations of the Directorate General of Technical Development." [53] The CCI&E has been termed "recommendation-oriented" and "most important licenses are issued on the basis of recommendations which originate outside the organisation." [54]

For actual users, which are scheduled industries but not borne on the register of the DGTD, and for nonscheduled industries (other than small scale) the license application procedure is somewhat different. Two agencies play a major role in determining the import distribution. In this case the applications go to a "sponsoring authority" (listed in Appendix 10 of the Red Book). It is apparently the task of the "sponsoring authority" to determine the applicant's *need* ("certified requirements for 12 months") for the goods

[52] J. MONTEIRO, *supra* note 13 at 33. Despite the possibility for "fixing up," provision for applicants to visit with exchange officials to discuss applications are the norm. See, e.g., Tarr, *The Administration of Foreign Exchange Control in Canada,* XXVII CAN. BAR. REV. 625, 643 (1949).

[53] HANDBOOK, *supra* note 13 at 42. "Where the licensing authority does not, for any reason, accept the advice/recommendation of the Directorate General of Technical Development in its entirety, the necessary intimation to this effect will be given to the DGTD." *Id.* at 43.

[54] DIRECTORATE OF COMMERCIAL PUBLICITY, MINISTRY OF COMMERCE, GOVERNMENT OF INDIA, REPORT OF THE STUDY TEAM ON IMPORT AND EXPORT TRADE CONTROL ORGANISATION 3 (1965).

requested. The actual distributions, however, are made in the offices of the CCI&E. According to the Red Book, "The licensing authority [CCI&E] will (with regard to licenses haveing been found to be in order) proceed to consider the case on merits on the basis of the certified requirements for 12 months as recommended by the sponsoring authority having regard to the following: "(i) availability of foreign exchange or other monetary ceilings; (ii) the stocks held and expected arrivals against the licenses in hand as on the first day of the licensing period concerned, i.e., 1st April; (iii) the quantity of goods or its substitutes likely to be made available through indigenous sources or other commercial channels; (iv) past imports/past consumption of the item in question by the applicant; (v) the actual production during the past licensing period and the estimated production for the period in question; and (vi) any fall in production on account of circumstances, such as breakdown of machinery, labour relations, want of funds, etc." The criteria are virtually identical with those supposed to be applied by the DGTD except for the catchall provision in the DGTD list (item viii) and (item vi) above concerning breakdowns, strikes, etc. There is no apparent reason for this distinction. Nor is it likely to be significant. One can guess that, as we have seen with regard to the DGTD, the CCI&E civil servants tend to use only the criterion that is most convenient and which may not, of course, be the same one in every case.

In India a separate exchange distribution system has been established for small-scale industries. Here again there is a system of sponsoring authorities, each with its own foreign exchange budget. General directions are given by the Development Commissioner, Small-Scale Industries (DC, SSI). The criteria to be applied by the sponsoring authority are precisely the same as those applied for nonscheduled actual users noted above. The sponsoring authority prepares a recommendation for the licensing authority, with a copy to the applicant. The liscensing authority is to issue licenses where the recommendation of the sponsoring authorities "are in concurrence with the policy/procedure in force . . ." The sponsoring authorities are units of the *state* governments (State Director of Industry); and the licensing authority is the *regional* one in whose jurisdiction the user's factory is located. This system was described to the author as "pretty chaotic." As a result, a new system was introduced in 1965 for 59 industries in which small-scale industries were to receive three times their previous exchange distribution directly from the CCI&E, thereby eliminating the State officials concerned.

The Government of Colombia has had extensive experience with several types of exchange systems including administrative distribution. A composite picture of the latter is provided by an examination of Law No. 1 of 1959 as amended by Decree No. 444 of 1967. Under the system established by that legislation, imports may be designated by the Board of Foreign Commerce as requiring a previous license (*licensa previa*). The list of such items is then published in the government gazette, *Diario Official*. Once the list is published, an importer makes application for a license to the License Section of the Board of Importations (Junta de Importaciones) of the Department of Foreign Commerce (Superintendencia de Comercio Exterior).[55] In his application for a license the importer must state: (a) his total approved imports in dollars for the past three years and in the current year, (b) the income taxes paid for the last three years by the importer or importing organization, (c) annual total of minor (other than coffee) exports for the past three years and the current year, (d) description of the goods desired

---

[55] DECREE 444, Article 70 ("The importation of goods included in the list requiring a previous license requires the authorization of the Board of Importations, which may approve totally or partially, or postpone or reject it") (unofficial trans.).

and their value in U.S. dollars, (e) total number of employees and monthly compensation, and (f) a "brief memo-
randum" explaining succinctly the need to import the
requested goods.[56]

In considering an application for permission to import
goods on the previous license list both statutes have been
quite specific in requiring the Superintendencia to apply a set
of criteria provided for in the statute. Regulations issued
under Law No. 1 of 1959 provided that import applications
will be "approved or rejected in accordance with a strict
scale of priorities." [57] Decree 444 was even more specific in
providing that the Superintendencia "must" take into consideration the criteria laid down in the statute.[58] As enumerated in Law No. 1, the criteria were as follows: "a) if
there is a national production which is normally supplying
the demand at equitable prices in the region for which merchandise is intended; b) if dealing with articles which are
not produced in the country, the degree of shortage in the
market, and their price as compared with the cost of importation and nationalization (sic); c) the volume of stock in the
hands of the importer as compared with the previous movement of his business; d) the value of licenses for the same
article requested by the same importer in a given period, as
compared with previous periods; e) the degree of importance that the article has to cover the necessities of popular
consumption and the maintenance of employment level."
To these five criteria, Article 77 of Decree Law 444 adds
three more: (1) "Their [the goods to be imported] contribu-
tion to the development and diversification of exports and
the favorable effect of the latter on the balance of payments
of the country," (2) "The net savings in foreign exchange

[56] See Art. 19, Board Resolution 15, October 17, 1967.
[57] REVISTA DEL BANCO DE LA REPUBLICA, June 1965, p. 717, 727.
[58] Article 77.

which is obtained by the substitution of imports," and (3) "The urgency of attending to the development of industries located in zones economically depressed, with imports of raw materials or goods, even though the goods imported are produced in the country." Article 77 then goes on to emphasize, as did the previous legislation, that consideration of the volume of stock in the importer's hands (criterion (c) above), and the value of licenses previously applied for (criterion (d) above), "does not authorize the Superintendencia to establish individual quotas with respect to the importation of a determined article. They are taken into consideration only to avoid immoderate increases in stocks of the importer for the normal development of his business.[59]

There is no official data available concerning the operation of this system. Given the complexity of the multivariable analysis required by the statute, however, and the data available from the analogous attempts of the DGTD staff in India to apply similarly complex criteria to applications for imports, it would seem a safe conclusion that practice is a good deal simpler then suggested by the statute. Although the volume of applications is far smaller than those handled by the Indian authorities, primarily because the number of items subject to the previous license system is much lower, several of the factors which "must" be considered by the Superintendencia when studying each application call for a fair amount of analysis. A familiarity with the Colombian bureaucracy, as with bureaucracies everywhere, would lead to the conclusion that the authorities probably place most of

[59] The idea that importers stocks should be kept at a minimum was given more emphasis in Article 4 of Law 1 of 1959 where it was noted that applications should be approved only with a view to "maintaining stocks no greater at anytime than the minimum amount compatible with economical operation of his enterprise or business." (Article 26, Resolution of the Board of Foreign Commerce, No. 9 of June 14, 1965.) REVISTA DEL BANCO DE LA REPUBLICA, (June 1965) 727.

their emphasis on the objective criteria, i.e., stock in hand, volume of previous licenses. This view is supported by the kind of data required in the import application. Aside from data on minor exports, the only correlation between the information that an applicant must supply and the criteria specified in the statute is the applicant's import volume. It would appear therefore to be a fair conclusion that despite the elaborate statutory scheme most decisions are made on the criterion of an increment over a base year.

But the system is distinguishable from the base-year systems of New Zealand and India. For in those systems the base-year criterion was identified as the critical factor and any deviation from the easily calculable entitlement would be readily apparent to the applicant. While the result may be the same under the Colombian system, the applicant is in a far worse position from the point of view of detecting possible administrative abuse. His application may be approved, postponed, rejected, or reduced depending upon such factors as "scarcity of the item" and "degree of importance for the satisfaction of the necessities of popular consumption." Even if the authorities have developed formulas for weighting these factors, which is questionable, the applicant will not know them. Nor does the statute require that an applicant be given the reasons for the rejection or modivication of his application. The only safeguard provided by the statute is the requirement that the details of all import licenses granted by the Superintendencia shall be published weekly.[60] The published information indicates the name of the importer and the nature, quantity, and value of the goods for which a license has been issued. From this an importer could make a guess as to whether a competitor has received more favorable treatment if he knew a good deal

---

[60] DECREE 444, Article 75.

about his competitor's business. Since he is unlikely to have the kinds of information required by the import application and the statutory criteria, this safeguard would operate only in the most extreme cases of maladministration. In sum, the Colombian system creates a situation in which an applicant has little basis for understanding any discrepancy between his application and his resulting license, and even less for determining why his competitor may have received permission to import a greater quantity of goods. An easy explanation, widely heard, is that the discrepencies are the results of bribery. While this may not be the case, there is no way to dispel the rumors under the present system.

In distributing foreign exchange to assembly industries, Turkey also uses a multiple variable criteria but with the major difference of providing weights that will be accorded to each variable. Article II of Turkish Decree No. 6/2905 of April 14, 1964 provided that each branch of the assembly industry would be awarded foreign exchange on the basis of three factors: (a) portion of invested capital "corresponding to the product" (as indicated in the balance sheets), (b) foreign exchange savings per unit,[61] and (c) labor force employed (taken from the monthly statement filed with the Labor Insurance Office.) In determining the total award, the figure for invested capital is given a weight of 35 percent, foreign exchange savings 50 percent, and labor force 15 percent. With these figures in hand, each applicant can judge for himself the foreign exchange to which he is entitled. The Turkish experience thus indicates that it is possible to utilize a multiple variable system that will avoid the kind of abuse to which the Indian and Colombian systems are potentially subject.

---

[61] The "rate of foreign exchange savings" is designated in the decree. For trucks and delivery vans, for example, the rate for 1964 was 20 percent. See DECREE 6/2905, Chap. IV, ¶ 2, reprinted in TURKISH ECON. REV. 46, 48 (1964).

PROCESS SAFEGUARDS AGAINST
ADMINISTRATIVE ABUSE

The exchange distribution systems we shall now describe also employ multiple variable criteria and would, if examined solely on a criteria basis, be subject to many of the comments noted above. What distinguishes them is that the process by which the criteria are applied seems to offer more in the way of protection against administrative abuse than do the criteria themselves. The most important of these systems are those in which individual licensing decisions are made by committees.

COMMITTEES

One of the principle reasons for the Nationalist Government's loss of mainland China was the endemic corruption which robbed the government of popular support. In reestablishing their government in Taiwan, the leaders of Nationalist China sought to establish an administration free of corruption. One of the innovations fashioned with this end in view was a unique committee system for distributing foreign exchange. Exchange policy under this system was made by the Foreign Exchange and Trade Commission (FETC) whose composition was discussed in chapter 4. Every two months an Import Commodity Budget was announced by the FETC together with specific dates for accepting applications for import licenses. Where applications exceeded the amount of exchange available, they were to be dealt with in accordance with the following priorities (1955): "(1) the currencies requested in the import allocation having the largest balance in the exchange budget, (2) those applications giving the lowest import cost or lowest domestic wholesale price compatible with quality, (3) applications of importers having commodities (sic), and (4) the applications for import having the earliest filing date." In addition, the FETC could take into consideration the applicant's wholesale price in the domestic market for the item to be imported.[62]

Applications were considered at weekly meetings by two of the seven committees of the FETC, the general import screening committee and the special import screening committee. Members of each committee are "experts" appointed by the FETC.[63] The committees disposed of all "ordinary" import applications. Final decision on "important ones" was referred to the FETC itself.[64]

The committee system of exchange distribution has been adopted in several other developing countries. Pakistan combined a base-period distribution criterion with the committee system in its licensing of commercial imports. Each importer of goods during the period July 1950–December 1952 was assigned a "category" for each type of goods he imported.[65] Thereafter licenses were issued to him on a percentage of his category value for that type of goods. The percentages were determined by, and the licenses issued by, one of three (at that time) regional licensing Boards. The Karachi Board was composed of the Chief Controller of Imports and Exports, representatives of the Ministries of Industries and Finance, and the Director of Industries, West Pakistan. The Lahore and Chittagong Boards were composed of the Regional Controllers, and representatives of the Provincial Ministries of Finance, Commerce, and Industries.

---

[62] See *Procedure Governing Settlement of Foreign Exchange and Application for Exchange Allocation*, March 6, 1955, FOR. TRD. QUART. 10 (April 1964).

[63] *Id.* at 12.

[64] The FETC was dissolved on January 1, 1969 and its functions split among the Central Bank of China, the Ministry of Economic Affairs and the Ministry of Finance. Licensing of import applications is now handled by the Application Receipt and Dispatch Center of the Board of Foreign Trade. According to the Board "most" applications are completed and returned the day following their filing. The Center processes about 1,200 applications per day, or over 300,000 a year.

[65] Naqvi, *supra* note 32 at 96.

Several African states employ the committee system of import license distribution. In Mali an allocation commission established quotas for each importer on the basis of his turnover and the number of his employees. A similar system operates in Cameroon, where each importer receives a "personal import quota from the Technical Committee for Import Distribution [Comité Technique de Répartition des Importateurs (CTRI)] headed by the Directors of Commerce and Foreign Economic Relations." The other members of the committee are nine importers and one representative of industry. The Director of Customs, the Director of Exchange and International Settlement, and the President of the Chamber of Commerce serve as consultants to the committee. Allocations are made on the basis of the value of annual imports,[66] and in "accordance with . . . exchange needs." [67] There is not much data available on how this system works. We do know, however, that where a similar import licensing committee operated in Senegal, all the private importers were members of the French Chamber of Commerce, and they licensed only imports from France unless their cost exceeded the cost of supplies from alternative sources by more than 10 percent.

The exchange distribution system operating in Somalia at the time of this study is interesting for several reasons. First, it is the most formalized committee system. Second, the criteria by which decisions are made regarding applications are secret. Finally, and perhaps most significantly, the Somali legislation was drafted with technical advice from the IMF.[68] From this we may surmise that the Somali system represents the kind of system the IMF would prefer to see in those developing countries which are constrained to ra-

[66] INTERNATIONAL MONETARY FUND, SIXTEENTH ANNUAL REPORT ON EXCHANGE RESTRICTIONS 97 (1965).
[67] INTERNATIONAL MONETARY FUND, SIXTEENTH ANNUAL REPORT ON EXCHANGE RESTRICTIONS 98 (1965).
[68] SOMALI NATIONAL BANK BULLETIN 12 (July 1965).

tion their foreign exchange. The Somali Law on Foreign Economic Transactions (Presidential Decree No. 203 of Sept. 26, 1964) created a Commission on Foreign Economic Transactions which "is responsible for the establishment of criteria for the licensing of imports and other foreign transactions and generally for deciding on various exchange and commercial policies." [69] The Advisory Commission makes known its criteria in the form of "directives" issued to the Licensing Committee. The Licensing Committee, created by Article 8 of the Law, is to "decide on applications for licenses for transactions in goods, services, and capital." Its six members are the Head of the Trade and Foreign Exchange Department of the Ministry of Industry and Commerce and a representative of that Ministry, and representatives of the Ministry of Finance, the Finance Guard, the Customs Authority, and the Somali National Bank. Paragraph 5 of Article 8 provides that "[t]he Licensing Committee . . . shall be guided in their decisions by the . . . directives of the Advisory Commission . . ." What the legislation does not say is that these directives are secret. They are known only to the Licensing Committee and not to the individual applicant. This study did turn up one such directive and its contents are illuminating. On May 30, 1965 the Advisory Commission issued a directive to the Somali National Bank which incorporated within it the criteria covering "those cases where . . . decisions are to be made by the Licensing Committees" with regard to service transactions specified in paragraph *C* of the directive. The directive notes that the "Licensing Committees are given more flexibility [than the National Bank, which "shall adhere to" criteria] regarding decisions and *shall generally consider each application on its merits.*" The criteria are then enumerated and are worth reprinting in full.

---

[69] *Id.* at 7. See p. 155 *supra.*

"1. Foreign Travel: All residents wishing to travel abroad shall be required to submit valid passports with the application for the license.

(a) *Business Travel:* Business correspondence with parties abroad and any other documentary evidence deemed necessary to establish the genuineness of the transaction should be required.

(b) *Tourism:* Applications up to limits specified in paragraph *C* may be granted on an annual basis.

(c) *Health reasons:* A certificate should be required from a qualified medical practitioner to the effect that the kind of treatment required by the applicant is not available in Somalia.

(d) *Education abroad:* A distinction has to be drawn between students undergoing training abroad at their own expenses (sic) and those on scholarship/fellowship . . ."

The interesting thing about these criteria are that they are not criteria at all. Criteria of the sort we are concerned with provide standards by which administrators decide between bona fide claims to foreign exchange. The so-called criteria contained in directive 5 are really requirements to establish the claimant's bona fides. According to the criteria, anyone wishing to go abroad for business purposes need only "establish the genuineness of the transaction." This is a rather loose standard and may well reflect the fact that there was neither great pressure on the Somali balance of payments nor many requests for business travel distributions at the time directive 5 was issued. Or it may be evidence that the real decision-making is by the Licensing Committee, exercising its power to "consider each application on its merits." The interesting and distinctive feature here, however, is that each application is considered by the Committee as opposed to an individual civil servant. Since the applicant has no way to verify whether he has received his fair share of exchange, he must rely on the process of committee decision for protection against administrative abuse. This is not the place for an extended discussion of group dynamics or the various ways in which committees have been found to behave. Committees can be "captured" by a faction or can come under the domination of their chairman or even a strong personality. From the point of view of potential for arbitrary action or corruptibility, however, decision by committee seems to offer an attractive alternative to decision by a lone civil servant.

CLAIMANT PARTICIPATION

A second type of process safeguard against administrative abuse in the distribution of foreign exchange is participation in the process by representatives of exchange users. The import screening committees of the FETC in Taiwan had as members representatives of trade associations involved in the import business. Nowhere, however, is participation of the private sector so significant nor so institutionalized as in Turkey.

The Turkish system for distributing exchange to industrial users employs multiple criteria. But its unique feature is the role of the private sector in the distribution procedure. In the Quota List, which is published semiannually, there are separate quotas established for importers and industrial users. Within 30 days following the announcement of the new import program, a Turkish industrialist submits his import application to his regional chamber of commerce. (All industrial firms employing 10 or more workers must belong to a local branch of the chamber of commerce.) [70] The application is then incorporated in a summary of all applications from that region and sent on to the national Union of Chambers of Commerce, Industry, and

[70] USAID/ANKARA, *supra* note 13 at 75.

Commodity Exchanges of Turkey, in Ankara. At a general meeting in which all regions are represented, usually two and a half months after the beginning of the import program, a distribution of foreign exchange is made to each region for each quota item. Each regional chamber then "subdivides its total for each quota among the various applicants on the basis of plant capacity ratios and recent production levels." [71] After the calculations have been completed, the applicants receive a "requirement certificate" or "certificate of need" authorizing them to apply for a specified amount of foreign exchange.[72] The certificate and application is filed with a commercial bank within three months of its issuance and not later than one month from the end of the six-month period. The bank then forwards the certificate and application to the regional branch of the Central Bank, which sends the requirement certificate to the regional Union of Chambers for signature. After the certificate has been countersigned and returned, the regional Central Bank issues the import permit. This is usually about four and a half months since the beginning of the six-month Import Program. In a survey taken in 1966 however Turkish manufacturers indicated that it took up to six months from application to receipt of licenses for imports originating in Europe and up to twelve months for U.S. imports. This is in part due to the fact that the Central Bank holds up applications when there are shortages of foreign exchange. But it is also due in part to the volume of paperwork and administrative detail involved in processing each application. As if the system described were not cumbersome enough, a large number of import items require permission from other agencies as well—e.g., pharmaceutical imports must be approved of by the Ministry of Health.

[71] *Id.* at 76. In 1967 the Istanbul Chamber introduced income tax payments as an additional criteria with a weight of 10 percent. See *ibid.*

[72] Art. 18, Decree No. 6/8452, *supra* note 37.

The Turkish system is almost the exact duplicate of one used in Greece in the 1930s. Under the import licensing system introduced in May 1932, quotas were adopted for individual items. The quotas were then divided among geographic regions on the basis of size and "activity" of their populations. Within the regions licenses were distributed by the chambers of commerce. Under this system, licenses were "distributed according to (a) capital value of the firm, (b) amount of taxes paid, (c) rent payable on the firm's premises, (d) size of staff, or (e) number of proprietors, and only lastly, (f) imports in former years." [73] To prevent older firms from being frozen out of the import trade because their imports were small during the base period 1929–31, they were permitted the alternative base period of 1924–29. Importers of more than one commodity could substitute among those for which they were granted licenses.

The involvement of private parties in exchange distribution goes back even further than this. A Spanish Royal Order of October 29, 1919 provided for the establishment in Madrid and in other capitals of provinces, and towns of "Exchange Boards" whose function was "to receive applications for the issue of bills payable in foreign money," and to approve or disapprove such requests based on the "needs of the petitioner" and the nature of the goods to be purchased. The Boards were composed of three members each, nominated by the bankers' associations and appointed by the Minister of Finance.[74]

In the post-Nkrumah era in Ghana, the Government introduced the idea of private distribution of import licenses for small importers. All small importers were to form into groups, which would in turn "elect an executive to scrutinise claims of its members regarding registration and import licenses . . ." The Ministry was then to issue a block of

[73] HEUSER, *supra* note 6 at 104.
[74] Documents of International Financial Conference (London) at 75 (1923).

licenses to each group for distribution to the members "in proportion to the capital of each prospective importer, in relation to the sum total of the group's capital." [75]

Yugoslavia has on occasion utilized a system of exchange distribution by exchange users. During 1967, exchange for goods subject to global quotas (GDK), mainly raw materials and semimanufactures, was distributed according to a program "worked out by the enterprises themselves under the aegis of the Federal Economic Chamber and submitted for approval to the Federal Secretariat for Foreign Trade." [76] In 1968 exchange for goods subject to individual quotas (RK and DK) was distributed according to "negotiations among the economic organizations" concerned.[77]

The participation of exchange users in the exchange distribution process may be explained on several bases. Historically the import trade has been a private sector activity and it was natural in the early part of this century for the authorities to consider that in a matter so vitally affecting the trade the participants should have a large role. Moreover, where the private sector is well established it would be politically difficult not to include its representatives in the decision-making process. In many of the developing countries, however, the import trade has been in the hands of the nonindigenous population. Most of the countries where this has been the case have acted to alter this situation, either by instituting state trading or confining the import trade to the indigenous population. In such circumstances it is not surprising that exchange user participation in the distribution system is not prominent. The Ghanaian small-importer scheme is no exception since the purpose of that scheme was to encourage collaboration among indigenous im-

---

[75] AFR. RES. BULL. 836 (1967).

[76] 192 BRD. OF TRADE JR. 610 (1967). See Yugoslavia Export, Jan. 1975, p. 4.

[77] INTERNATIONAL MONETARY FUND, TWENTIETH ANNUAL REPORT ON EXCHANGE RESTRICTIONS 524 (1969).

porters with a long-run view to their merger into several large import firms to compete with those owned by non-Ghanaians. While the trade authorities might have acted directly by granting the bulk of the licenses to Ghanaian importers, the possible abuses inherent in this alternative, brought to light by the Ollennu Commission, probably discouraged it. As well as instilling a cooperative spirit among Ghanaian importers, one of the attractions of this system may well have been the fear of a corrupt alternative.

The idea that participation by the private sector could ameliorate corruption was pointedly made in testimony before the Santhanam Committee in India. The Committee found that businessmen in Calcutta and Bombay "almost unanimously pointed out that nonassociation of trade organisations or their representative in matters like licensing and allocation of scarce commodities encouraged malpractice and corruption to some extent." [78] As a result, the Committee recommended that membership in a trade organization be made a prerequisite for obtaining a license. It saw the role of the organization as screening "the capacity of the applicants, their past performance and conduct."

The participation of exchange users in the distribution process is not itself free from potential abuse. Larger members of a trade association may so dominate it as to be able to garner most of the exchange for themselves. Or the association may serve as a convenient vehicle for monopolization of the trade in particular goods. On the other hand the trade association members are competitors and while they may share common interest vis-à-vis the government, their interests in the distribution of exchange *inter se* are in natural conflict. This would give some basis for assuming that in the distribution of exchange those who believed that they were unfairly treated would be vigorous in protesting.

---

[78] MINISTRY OF HOME AFFAIRS, GOVERNMENT OF INDIA, *supra* note 15 at 42.

This attitude is not so evident where the object of the protest is the government. Perhaps more important is that criticism of whatever abuse does arise in such a system will be directed at nongovernmental participants. It was precisely for this reason—"to relieve the relevant government department . . . of the obligation of making innumerable decisions liable to call forth charges of favoritism"—that the general practice in Europe in the 1930s was to have exchange distribution in the hands of "professional bodies." [79] This is not to say that the government may not be held ultimately responsible for the equitable operation of the system. But it will not provide the incentive to contact the individual civil servant in the hope that one's distribution can be increased. Without such an incentive, the chances for corrupting the system are substantially decreased.

CENTRAL BANKS

We noted in chapter 4 that some exchange distribution systems operate primarily through the medium of central banks as opposed to government ministries. While this process alternative is rare with regard to the distribution of exchange for trade payments, we do have a case study of such a system available from Tunisia. More frequently, central banks are the critical agency with regard to the distribution of exchange for invisible payments. For many categories of such payments the criteria utilized by the central banks in deciding upon exchange applications are either so vague as to place wide discretion in the hands of the administering officials or are known only to the administrators. In either case the applicant is in a precarious position with respect to the outcome of his application. What protection he has against administrative abuse is based in the quality of the personnel administering the system.

---

[79] HEUSER, *supra* note 6 at 96.

An interesting case study gives us some insight into the leading role of the Central Bank in Tunisia. As in all distribution systems, exchange is made available on the basis of priorities. Unlike most other systems, however, the priorities are not published in a formal way. Instead, an official of the Central Bank holds a weekly conference with representatives of trade associations and importers "to discuss priorities of import requests submitted or controlled by them." [80] As a result of these conferences certain high-priority uses have been established. Where an importer seeks goods which do not fall within these well-established categories, his request may be delayed for periods up to one year. Requests are rarely rejected although this may be a formal distinction only, since to delay an import request is often to deny it. Delaying action on "nonpriority" requests as opposed to denying them outright has certain undesirable consequences. Since the importer's request remains alive, he resorts to "hounding" bank officials or utilizing an intermediary ("friends in high places") to the same end.[81]

In most developing countries distribution of exchange for *business travel* is subject to approval in each case. In Morocco the only criterion is that the "Exchange office . . . considers each case on its merits." [82] The Pakistan regulations state merely that applications are referred to the State Bank for consideration.[83] Along with the application, which states the nature and purpose of the trip, forwarding commercial banks are to include "a confidential report on the financial means and status of the applicant." Presumably this confidential data represents information relevant to some decisional criteria. In India no criteria are published. The criteria are, however, contained in a confidential circular.[84] In

---

[80] Columbia Law School, *supra* note 21 at 94.   [81] *Ibid.*

[82] INTERNATIONAL MONETARY FUND, TWENTIETH ANNUAL REPORT ON EXCHANGE RESTRICTIONS 328 (1969).

[83] Q. AHMAD, THE LAW OF FOREIGN EXCHANGE IN PAKISTAN 121 (1963).

[84] MONTEIRO, *supra* note 13 at 61.

interviews conducted by the author, it was indicated that the criteria employed were whether the travel is "necessary and bona fide." Other types of invisible payments considered on an ad hoc basis by central banks include expenditures for overseas medical treatment, exporters' commissions to selling agents abroad, patents, royalties, and pensions.

In all of these cases and many more the exchange user is forced to rely on the bona fides of the administrator. This reliance may be well grounded. For the staffs of central banks in developing countries are distinguishable in several ways from civil servants attached to operating ministries of the government. Staffs of central banks are usually better paid than their equivalent levels in the civil service. This is undoubtedly due to the fact that central banks tend to be self-financing and thus somewhat independent of budget constraints that may be imposed by legislatures or the executive. In addition, a member of a central bank staff works in a more "professional" and less "political" atmosphere. Even where a Minister is nominally responsible for central bank operations, banks are managed by full-time directors whose prestige tends to guarantee substantial autonomy. These better working conditions are primarily the result of the reliance upon monetary policy as the key means of economic regulation in most developing countries. In a way therefore the central bank is self-strengthening. The importance of monetary policy requires an outstanding staff. And the presence of that staff makes monetary policy a more attractive means of economic control. These internal considerations are reinforced in several ways by the IMF. Many senior central bank officials have served an apprenticeship with the Fund. And the Fund has provided advisers and major technical assistance to help "modernize" the central banks of several developing countries. This has helped transform the staffs of central banks into a "transnational elite" whose professional norms are more a function of their counterparts in other countries than a reflection of local attitudes concerning the propriety of "informal" arrangements between themselves and exchange applicants,[85] but evidence to support this speculation is limited. The Tunisian case indicates, however, that although its Central Bank deals with exchange distributions for imports on a virtually ad hoc basis, most observers and importers believe that no bribery ("baksheesh") occurs in the process.[86]

Having introduced the IMF into our discussion at this point, a few words should be said about the Fund's attitude toward administrative exchange distribution in general. At the formal level, systems of administrative distribution are in basic conflict with the Agreement's prohibitions against restrictions on current payments. That having been noted, the de facto situation appears to the outside observer a bit more ambivalent. While most commentary by the Fund's staff ritualistically recites that quantitative restrictions on imports are the ultimate evil and have been so recognized since the 1930s, one cannot escape the feeling—and it is no more than that—that it might perhaps be better to have a country maintain a nominal fixed rate of exchange, with quantitative restrictions, than to let it slip into an alternative system involving multiple or fluctuating rates. This "feeling" may well be the erroneous conclusion drawn from the fact that so much of the Fund's critical commentary is devoted to multiple-rate systems and so little to quantitative restrictions. There is, of course, good reason for this malapportionment. What needed to be said about the evils of quantitative restrictions was said adequately in the 1930s. Nonetheless, one senses a real dilemma on the part of the Fund's staff when considering the alternatives of a fixed

[85] See GARDNER, STERLING-DOLLAR DIPLOMACY xxix (2d. ed. 1969). See generally KROC, *Management Strategy of a Central Bank in a Developing Country,* 9 FIN. AND DEV. 42 (June 1972).

[86] Columbia Law School, *supra* note 21 at 95. See also König, *Multiple Exchange Rate Policies in Latin America,* 10 JR. INTER-AMER. STUD. 35, 48 (1968) ("Central banks, however, assure, in most cases, a more rational and efficient interference because of their strong and independent position and the availability of a well-trained staff.").

rate and quantitative restrictions versus multiple or fluctuating rates. For the norm to which Fund members are committed is a fixed rate without restrictions, and it is no easy choice to decide which of two unattractive alternatives is more likely to move a country toward the norm. On occasion each route has been successful. The dilemma is undoubtedly compounded by the fact that most of the Fund's Article VIII countries continue to employ some quantitative trade restrictions, which are the functional equivalent of restrictions on current payments. And this area of restriction becomes larger if one considers "voluntary" export quotas in their true light. If, therefore, to be an Article VIII country means that some quantitative restrictions may be retained, the natural course for the Fund might be to emphasize a narrowing of developing-country quantitative restrictions to some "tolerable" level—as opposed to encouraging them to taste the headier wine of fluctuating or multiple rates. Better to have the developing countries adhere to half the norm rather than not at all. To do so, however, may be to promote the institutional objectives above the long-term interests of the members, if by interests we include a corruption-free administration.

By focusing on criteria and process as possible deterrents to arbitrary action and corruption in the administrative distribution of exchange, we should not lose sight of the fact that the critical factor tending to undermine administrative distribution is the large and easy profits available to the exchange recipients. Wherever supplies of goods—or the exchange to buy those goods—are restricted quantitatively, there are quota profits to be realized. These profits go to the government under exchange auction systems and to the exporter under export retention systems. They are partially recaptured by the government under multiple rate systems. But they go to the exchange recipient—generally an importer—under administrative distribution systems. And the profits are large. In India it has been estimated that in

1958–59 the profit margin on goods permitted to be imported by established importers was 100 percent.[87] Profits of this magnitude place enormous pressure on the system and its administrators. We have examined criteria and process as potential means for protecting the system against corruption resulting from this pressure; we will next consider more general institutional practices at the national level which would go even further to protect it from abuse.[88]

[87] Bhagwati, *Indian Balance of Payments Policy and Exchange Auctions,* 14 Ox. Econ. Papers N.S. 51, 66 (1962). See also, e.g., Durrani, *The Pattern of Private Industrial Development in Pakistan During the Second Five-Year Plan* 9 (Pak. Inst. Dev. 1966). (Resale's of imported yarn commanded "300 percent to 400 percent" premium.)

[88] At the outset of this chapter note was made of the fact that the primary characteristic of administrative systems for present purposes was their *personalization* of the exchange distribution process. In these systems the administrators must consider the claim for exchange on the part of a specific applicant. There is however a variation of administration distribution which eliminates the personal element. This would be the case where the authority announces that a specific sum which will be granted to each applicant for a particular exchange use. The system is most often used in distributing exchange for invisibles.

One of the major categories for which specific amounts are made available is expenses for students studying abroad. Taiwan provided full expenses for the first year of study, with a limit of $2400 (U.S.) in subsequent years. For Tanzania the amount was 14,000/- (approx. $1900 U.S.) per year for "entrance registration fees, tuition, maintenance, and other expenses incidental to education . . ." Another important category is tourist travel. In 1965, Senegal permitted tourists to go outside the French franc area and spend up to CFAF 75,000 per person per year. Turkey allows up to U.S. $200 per year. In 1965, Tanzania allowed 5000/- "per person for adults and children" during "any one travel year, i.e., 1st November–31st October." Circular to Banks No. 103, The Treasury, June 11, 1965. This was later amended to reduce allowances for children of less than three years to zero and children three to less than 12 to 2500/-. Circular to Banks No. 144, Bank of Tanzania, July 4, 1966. The Banco Central of Chile allowed travelers up to U.S. $60 for travel within 500 kilometers of the Chilean frontier, up to U.S. $200 for travel to other Latin American states, up to U.S. $480 for journeys to North America and up to U.S. $720 for all other countries. See *Banco Central* Circular No. 1499, April 6, 1971, summarized in 5 Bolsa 288 (1971).

Other examples of flat sum criteria include subscriptions to foreign periodicals, for which Pakistan, for example, makes available exchange up to a value of Rs. 150/- per calendar year per person. See Q. Ahmad, *supra* note 83 at 114. In the application for exchange the user must state the name of the magazine or periodical. While relevant to verify the bona fides of the applicant, control of exchange with regard to this type of transaction raises rather unpleasant possibilities.

Chapter 8

The Rule of Law
and Exchange Distribution
at the National Level

The purpose of this study has been to explore the effect of exchange distribution systems on the rule of law in developing countries. The hypothesis, based upon experience with such systems in the interwar period, was that exchange distribution can have an undermining effect on the efforts of a developing country to establish a governmental system based on the rule of law. While it is not maintained that the case has been conclusively proved, there is sufficient evidence of abuse and potential for abuse to give some cause for concern. Perhaps more important is the fact that we have identified systems and parts of systems, some of which tend to undermine the rule of law more than others. On the other hand, we have seen that the process of exchange distribution need not, in and of itself, operate against the rule of law. In this chapter we shall explore the features of various systems which can serve to reinforce the rule of law. These will focus upon aspects of administrative decision-making in the distribution process since it should go without saying at this point that rule of law problems tend to be minimized where distribution systems are governed by market forces.

At a minimum the rule of law requires that norms, which form the basis for administrative decision-making, be articulated and communicated to those whom they are intended to affect and that these norms shall be applied in the same way in similar cases.[1] Implicit in this requirement is that the norms shall not only be applied equally in similar cases but that they *be seen* to be applied equally. At the heart, therefore, of a system based on law is publicity.[2]

To conform to the rule of law what is it that the exchange user needs to know? The answer will depend on the criteria utilized to distribute exchange. In a system where exchange availability is dependent on market prices, or where the government has obligated itself to meet the demand for exchange at a fixed price, all relevant information is freely available to the exchange applicant. This, however, is a rare situation in most developing countries. Where other than price criteria are used to distribute exchange, the exchange user will need to know (a) what those criteria are, and (b) how they have been applied in fact. These requirements present no special problem where *base-period* criteria are used. As we have seen, to be effective the system requires the public identification of both the relevant base period and the percentage of base-period exchange use which will be permitted. The criteria are objective and each applicant

[1] Kjellin, *Legislative Control, Supervision by the Ombudsman and the Obligation to Produce Documents*, in UNITED NATIONS, REMEDIES AGAINST THE ABUSE OF ADMINISTRATIVE AUTHORITY 102, 103 (1964).

[2] "Publicity is the very soul of justice. It is the keenest spur to exertion and the surest of all guards against improbity." Bentham, quoted in Braibanti, *Reflections on Bureaucratic Corruption*, PUB. AD. 357, 369 (Winter 1962).

can easily determine for himself whether the norms have been adhered to in his case. In the case where exchange is distributed on a pro rata basis, the criterion is equally objective but is not in and of itself sufficient to inform the applicant of the fairness of his result. For he needs to know either the pro-rating coefficient [3] for each exchange use or the data utilized in arriving at that coefficient. The latter would include both the volume of requested imports of the item and the total amount of exchange made available for that exchange use. And where exchange is distributed on a *chronological* basis, the third of our single variable administrative systems, the applicant needs to know where he stands vis-à-vis other applicants. At a minimum this system makes it incumbent on the administration to identify each exchange application chronologically and make such identifications available to all exchange applicants.

Where multiple-variable criteria are utilized, the problem increases in complexity. For although criteria are often published, the extent of their actual use in the decision-making process is open to question. This may be so because they call for data that is not easily available to the administrator. Or, if available, their nature may be such as to be too complex to apply to individual cases. Or, if applied, the applicant has little idea of the weight attached to each variable. In short, it is a rare case where the applicant can determine the basis on which exchange has been distributed based on a multiple-variable criterion. It is, however, possible to fashion a system that would meet the requirements of the rule of law. For we have seen with regard to assembly industries in Turkey, exchange is distributed on a multiple-variable basis where the criteria are quantifiable and the weights given to each criterion are made known in the legislation. In a system like the Turkish one, the exchange user would be in a

---

[3] See pp. 221–22 *supra*.

similar situation to his counterpart facing a base period distribution system. Given the relevant quantitative criteria and the weights accorded to each, he could determine for himself the amount of exchange entitlement.

If one looks at the kind of information generally published by developing-country governments with regard to exchange distribution one is struck by the absence of data necessary to determine that "similar cases have been judged alike." It is only where base period distribution is utilized that this is not a problem. For the other administrative distribution systems an examination of what is published establishes what is missing. All governments distributing exchange publish categories of permitted use. Where imports are involved, the lists are ordinarily found in the official gazette. This is the kind of information discussed in chapter 4. With regard to matters within the jurisdiction of the central banks, the information is ordinarily contained in manuals and periodicals published by the banks. But to know the permitted uses and overall quantitative limitations is of limited value to the importer where exchange is distributed *pro rate, chronologically,* or on the basis of *multiple variables.* On occasion governments publish the applications for import licenses. *El Peruano,* the daily official gazette of Peru, publishes applications for import licenses. In the issue of April 1, 1971, for example, licenses filed from March 17 to March 31 were published. The information given includes the name of the firm requesting the imports, the commercial name and technical description of the products, the quantity requested, and the customs identification number. While the Peruvian authorities do not deal with the same volume of import requests that is handled in India, or even Taiwan, publication of this data would offer some reassurance to exchange users as to the probity of the system. And data of this sort are absolutely critical if the government utilizes a pro rata distribution system.

Publication of the results of license applications is a somewhat more common occurrence. Infrequently this is required by statute. For example, Article 19 of Resolution 9 of 1965 of the Board of Foreign Trade of Colombia provides that "The Department of Foreign Trade will arrange to publish at its Bogotá and regional offices, the list of applications approved or rejected by the Imports Board, on the day following the Board's meeting." [4] This policy was continued under the new system introduced by Decree 444. Article 75 of that decree requires the Board of Foreign Commerce "to publish weekly, in numerical order, the registrations and licenses granted, indicating the name of the importer and the nature, quantity, and value of the goods." Even when not required by statute, the usual practice is evidenced by Ghana. The *Commercial and Industrial Bulletin,* published every Friday, is the vehicle through which importers are informed of government policies and programs. In addition, the *Bulletin* publishes the list of import licenses issued. In *Bulletin* No. 24, published on June 9, 1967, there are listed 11 new licenses issued since the previous week's publication. For each license are indicated the name and address of the importer, the import license number, a description of the goods, and their value in new cedis.

Publication of this type of information will have some chilling effect on extreme cases of administrative abuse. Since businessmen ordinarily have some general notions about the volume of their competitors' trade, substantial maldistributions will be readily apparent.[5] Within these broad parameters, however, information about licenses granted to others is of limited value. It would have more significance if published in conjunction with information concerning import applications—something done neither in

---

[4] See Revista del Banco de la Republica 727 (June 1965).

[5] The Peruvian system invites anyone with "pertinent objections" to the granting of an import license to file them with the Ministry of Commerce within five days.

Colombia nor Ghana—but even that would be insufficient to meet a rule of law standard. For absent publicized quantifiable criteria no applicant can know why his competitor received more or less exchange than he did. And that is precisely the data which is not published.

In exploring the issue of the kinds of data which must be made available to the applicant in an exchange distribution system meeting rule of law standards, it is necessary to deal with three objections to such publication. The first and most frequently heard is that publication of the kind of data being discussed here will in some way act to limit the administrative flexibility that attracts planners to exchange distribution as opposed to more cumbersome monetary, fiscal, and trade instruments.[6] Secondly, there is the problem of adding publication to the already crushing burden of paper work involved in administering an exchange distribution system. Finally, one must consider the exchange users who may object to publication of data about their business activities.

There is no question that the administration of an exchange distribution system requires flexibility so that the administrators can correlate programs with rapidly changing, even volatile, payments flows. Nonetheless, the supposed conflict between publicity and flexibility is, upon analysis, more apparent than real. To illustrate we can take a rather simple example. Assume that the annual program for country A provides for the importation of automobile spare parts to a total value of $50,000. Three months following publication of this figure, trade officials realize that exports are not bringing in the amount of exchange projected in the program and some reductions on the import side will be necessary. A decision is made to reduce exchange for the import of spare parts to $25,000. An announcement to this

[6] See e.g., Djojhadikusumo, *Fiscal Policy, Foreign Exchange Control and Economic Development,* VII Ekonomi dan Kevangan Indonesia 211, 219 (1954).

effect is published in the *Official Gazette*. The fact that originally the published import program figure was $50,000 has
not meant that it could not be modified to reflect changing
circumstances. Exposure to the citizenry does not render
programs or policies immutable. Would the administration
of the system really have been more flexible if, instead of
announcing a figure of $50,000 in the import program, the
government had indicated that exchange for the importation of auto parts would be provided "in the light of available supplies of foreign exchange"? The affirmative case
must be that by announcing an initial figure of $50,000 and
then reducing it to $25,000, importers will be disappointed
in their expectations. But what of their expectations where
no figures are published? One can reasonably expect that
the disappointment suffered with a reduction in an overall
quota is minimal compared to the anxiety generated where
the authorities indicate that exchange will be provided for
imports of auto parts "if available." But there is another
aspect of changes in an announced program to be considered. A reduction in import quotas may serve to embarrass
those officials who draw up the import program by reveal-
ing the inaccuracy of their work. Embarrassment is a state
administrators wish to avoid. Thus they may feel less free to
reduce the quota if no announcement concerning the availability of exchange for spare parts is made. There can be
little doubt that this presents a real dilemma for the policy-
maker. For he must choose between a government program
that gives the appearance of smooth operation and a program that would serve to strengthen the rule of law. From
the viewpoint of this study, however, the choice is not a difficult one. And the potential embarrassment of the civil servants would have, from the writers point of view, the wholly
salutary effect of encouraging them to sharpen their planning techniques.

For proof that concern for flexibility, which supposedly

follows from lack of publication, is not a mere academic point, one can look to the contrasting positions of actual users and established importers in India when an exchange shortfall becomes apparent during the licensing year. Because exchange distributions to established importers are based on their past performance, established importers have in the Red Book all the information necessary to determine the amount of goods they will be permitted to import. If a changed situation necessitates a change in policy, the established importer is informed of the change via announcements in the newspapers and notices in the *Gazette of India*. Experience has shown that this technique works satisfactorily. The volume of imports to be permitted an actual user, however, is unknown to him. It will be decided by taking into consideration "(i) foreign exchange availability or other monetary ceilings, (ii) availability of goods applied for from indigenous sources or other commercial channels, (iii) essentiality of the goods applied for, (iv) stocks in hand and expected arrivals, (v) past imports and past consumption of the items in question . . . (vi) actual production during the preceding year, (vii) estimated production, and (viii) any other factor considered relevant and necessary." This flexible set of criteria has already anticipated the possibility of a foreign exchange shortfall. Thus, "the issue of licenses can be adjusted to meet the new situation . . . without a formal change in the policy." [7]

The key word here is *formal*. For the real basis on which licenses to actual users are being issued has altered to take into account the foreign exchange shortfall. Moreover, this alteration will be communicated to the licensing officer by means of confidential licensing instructions. Thus, the flexibility to deal with changed circumstances which the civil servants retain with regard to actual users amounts to nothing

[7] Jain, *Administrative Discretion in the Issue of Import Licenses*, 10 JR. IND. LAW INST. 121, 137 n. 65 (1968).

more than their ability to alter policy secretly. For in re-
sponding to an exchange shortfall the administrators perform the identical task with regard to established importers
and actual users. In both cases a foreign exchange shortfall
necessitates a reduction in permitted imports. In both cases
this decision is communicated. In the case of established importers, it is communicated through the newspapers and
the *Gazette* to the applicants. In the case of actual users it is
communicated by confidential licensing instructions to the
administrators. Wherein, then, lies the added flexibility of
the system applied to actual users? There is, thus, little reason to believe that the degree of flexibility necessary to enable an exchange distribution system to respond to changed
circumstances cannot be preserved without concurrently
providing the applicant with sufficient information for him
to be satisfied in his own mind that he is being treated
fairly.[8]

The second objection to publication is the mechanics involved. But here again experience shows that the task of
publishing license applications and awards is not so overwhelming that it cannot be done. While every developing
country does not have access to a daily, widely distributed
official publication like *El Peruano,* each does publish an official gazette. And where the volume of trade is large, a specialized publication like the Ghana *Commercial and Financial
Bulletin* is available. So the problem should not be the availability of a vehicle for publication. Moreover the preparation of material for publication need not be an overwhelming concern. The addition of another copy to the already
innumerable copies of exchange applications presently

[8] See USAID/INDIA, *An Advance Study of the Information System Requirements of the
Director General of Technical Development (GOI) with Special Attention to Import Licensing and Related Functions* 6 (Nov. 16, 1964) ("To would-be importers the final outcome of their applications for import licenses is a grim uncertainty often fraught
with serious delays, bickerings, and feelings of deep frustration and helpless-
ness.").

required could be termed the "publication" copy. Unless one is willing to concede that civil servants in Peru have an extraordinary capability in preparing data for publication, the task is one that could be reasonably carried out in most developing countries.[9]

The rule of law need not however require formal publication in terms of a printed notification of wide circulation. For some time now the Swedish Government has been operating under a law which requires that "all government documents must be made available for inspection by any member of the public who wants to see them . . ."[10] The obligation extends to the keeping of an index of such documents to be made available to the inquirer. The sweeping provisions of this law go a good bit further than would be needed in the exchange distribution context. Making applications available to the public at the office of the controlling authority could be affected by the simple expedient of having each applicant file an extra copy of his application; this would be termed the "public copy." The experience in Sweden, with public documents in general, is that the principal audience for examining such documents is the press. "Every day, in the great offices in Stockholm, for instance, documents which have been received are brought to a room where representatives of the newspapers are welcome to see them. A representative of the leading press agencies will never fail to appear, and through him, a flood of news will go to the newspapers and to the general public . . ."[11]

An even less formal publication system, which could satisfy rule of law requirements, is the Tunisian system of the

[9] Note should be made here of the extensive technical assistance program of the International Monetary Fund's Bureau of Statistics "for the establishment and improvement of central bank bulletins." As is evident in the present study these bulletins serve as major vehicles for the publication of information on exchange distribution programs. As of 1972 members of the Bureau had lent assistance to 59 countries. See II IMF SURVEY 154–155 (1973).

[10] Shonfeld, *What Space for Freedom?* 25 ENCOUNTER 20, 22 (Oct. 1965).

[11] *Id.* at 22, quoting Herlitz.

weekly Central Bank conference. To the extent that the information provided is reasonably specific, i.e., "priority imports are. . . . importers will receive exchange according to the following formula. . . ." the exchange applicant would be presented with an opportunity to determine where he stands with regard to exchange distributions. And while it would not be feasible to have every exchange applicant attend such conferences, opening them to the press and/or governments undertaking to publish a transcript or summary of the weekly conference would make the information generally available.

But carrying this concept one step further, as some systems do, by providing for individual conferences seems unacceptable. Paragraph 237 of the *Import Trade Control Handbook* provides that "Ordinarily all matters should be settled by correspondence. However, in cases where importers consider it necessary to discuss in person matters relating to general policy and principles of Import Trade Control . . . or they desire to present their case in person in respect of any application for license . . . they may book an interview with the officer concerned." [12] This opportunity for gaining such an interview has even been identified as a "procedural safeguard." [13] A study of import licensing in Brazil also indicates that the normal course for "solving problems" is for the applicant to "get in touch with" the civil servant handling his application.[14] "The personal contacts between the importer, or his representatives, and the technical staff of CACEX (Carteira de Comercio Exterior) provide a non-bureaucratic way of handling problems that contributes to expediting licensing." While providing an opportunity for resolution of misunderstandings and errors, granting an

[12] MINISTRY OF COMMERCE, GOVERNMENT OF INDIA, IMPORT TRADE CONTROL HANDBOOK 137–138 (1966).

[13] Jain, *supra* note 7 at 133.

[14] SCHOOL OF LAW, COLUMBIA UNIVERSITY, *Legal Control of Import and Industrial Licensing* 13 (1968).

applicant an interview with the civil servant dealing with his application presents an unparalleled invitation to corrupt dealing. The applicant inclined toward bribery is directed to precisely the man he needs to influence. This is given implied recognition in the *Trade Control Handbook,* which provides that interviews should "be booked in advance at the Enquiry Office." Such a procedure permits recordation of the fact that an interview took place and will serve to give some pause to those attracted to corrupt practices. Other possible safeguards could include recordation of the minutes of all interviews and the presence at each interview of two or more officials.

Personal interviews with responsible officials and the rule of law are concepts that are fundamentally incompatible. One need only look at the legislation and regulations of a particular system to determine a priori whether interviews play a significant part in the decision-making process. The less specific the articulated norms, the wider the discretion accorded to the civil servant, the more one finds long lines of petitioners in the anterooms of the distributing authority. It is usually pointed out to the visiting scholar that this "personal" style of administration is in contrast to the "cold, bureaucratic" style that characterizes other government administrations. And it must be conceded that there is a warm, more humane element in a system that grants to administrators discretion of such breadth that they can decide issues on the basis of "just" solutions and recognizes, for example, the natural obligations flowing from extended family concepts. But that such systems are subversive of the rule of law and more susceptible to corruption cannot be denied. And given the sums of money involved in most exchange distribution transactions the temptations are very great. If the society is dedicated to nurturing the rule of law and recognizes such corruption as an evil, it would do well to depersonalize administration so that decisions are made by "faceless men" on the basis of quantitative data contained within the files before them.

The third objection to publication would emanate from applicants themselves who might be unwilling to reveal the nature and volume of their trade to competitors. A system in which an applicant could himself determine what his share of exchange should be under existing policy should result in a belief on the part of an applicant that he had a "right" to that volume of exchange. This would be a welcome change for many exchange users from their present position as supplicants pleading for exchange. At the other extreme would be those businessmen with a vested interest in the present scheme, particularly those who thrive on quota profits. Objections emanating from this group of exchange users need not detain us. Finally there may well be a middle group who, although uneasy about the present system, prefer its risks to those incurred in disclosing the nature and volume of their business. But the interest of the applicant is not the sole measure to be used in determining whether or not to publish license applications and awards. The government also has an interest in maintaining the integrity of the system. By providing applicants with the information necessary to detect deviations from the equal treatment standard, governments can enlist the self-interest of applicants in calling to the government's attention deviations from policy. From the government's point of view the benefits to be gained from this course must surely outweigh the burdens of publishing the information and the inconvenience to applicants of having their business transactions opened to public scrutiny.

There is a possible means of satisfying both the applicant's desire for confidentiality and the requirements of the rule of law, although it places a heavy burden on the administrators. This would involve the administration giving a written explanation to the applicant for any discrepancy between the amount of exchange provided for and the amount eventually distributed to him. The process of attempting to formulate and articulate reasons for a decision is one of the most effective checks against arbitrary action on the part of government officials. "It is no longer to be debated that the duty to give reasons is a cornerstone in the proper administration of the laws and a fundamental safeguard of the rule of law in administrative acts." [15] It is for this reason that the Government of Israel adopted the Administrative Procedure Amendment (Statement of Reasons) Act, 1958. The operative section of the Act, Section 2, provides that "where application has been made in writing to a public servant to exercise any power conferred on him by law and he refuses the application, he shall notify the applicant in writing, of the reasons for the refusal." In a system such as that in India where several hundred thousand applications are processed each year, a requirement of an opinion detailing the reasons for the decision on each application seems inconceivable. Yet the problem, even for that system, appears upon closer examination to be not totally intractable. Many license applications are presently refused because they are incomplete or do not conform to statutory requirements. In a study of 243 applications in the Bombay office of the Joint Chief Controller of Imports and Exports done in 1965, 174 were found to be incomplete when filed.[16] In those types of cases all systems provide for notification of the applicant, informing him of the deficiency in his application and providing him with an opportunity to amend his application or to file a new one. So statement of reasons legislation would impose no added burdens in this area. The new requirement would cover only applications rejected on the merits. And if the volume of these should

[15] Pelley-Karp, Comments, 12 AM. JR. COMP. LAW 72 (1963).

[16] Directorate of Commercial Publicity, Ministry of Commerce, Government of India, *Report of the Study Team on Import and Export Control Organisation* 86 (1965).

prove an enormous burden, it must be considered that the applicants are not being properly informed of the criteria by which the decisions are made. For applicants seek to file successful applications and therefore they orient their applications as closely as possible to the criteria of which they are informed. If too many applications are coming in wide of the mark, it can only be because the criteria are not properly understood. As the criteria are refined, the statement of reasons will become easier both because the applicants will have a keener sense of what is required and because specific criteria permit the use of standardized forms for response. Thus, if instead of "past import performance" we substitute as a criterion "applications must not exceed in quantity 110 percent of imports for the period January to December 1972," and the application does not satisfy this requirement, the administrators need only place a mark on a preprinted response form indicating that "application did not satisfy past import requirement." [17]

That the statement of reasons is an important safeguard against corruption was recognized by the Santhanam Committee. The Committee recommended that in every appeal from a decision of a licensing authority in the office of the Chief Controller of Imports and Exports, the appellant should be given "reasons for the rejection or acceptance of the appeal." [18] The Committee did not, however, go so far as to recommend that the licensing officer provide the ap-

[17] Having strongly urged the adoption of a statement of reasons requirement, it is sad to report that the Israeli Act itself does not apply to refusals to grant import licenses. The Act provides that Section 2 will not apply "if the law which vests the power in him [the civil servant] provided that he is authorized to exercise it at his discretion or without giving reasons." And the Licensing of Imports Order, 1939, provides in Section 6 that ". . . the Director of Customs, Excise and Trade shall have the power to refuse to issue any license for the importing of any goods without assigning any reasons for such refusal." Quoted in Pelley-Karp, *supra* note 15 at 7. One can only hope that this provision will be promptly recognized as a relic of the colonial era which is at war with the rule of law.

[18] Ministry of Home Affairs, Government of India, *Report of the Committee on the Prevention of Corruption* 256 (1964).

plicant with a statement of reasons for rejecting the application in the first instance.[19]

DELAY

Secrecy and delay are the handmaidens of corruption in systems for distributing foreign exchange. The volume of paper work involved in administrative distribution systems make some delay almost inevitable. In India, for example, a study done in 1965 indicated that applications filed by actual users in May would not normally be dealt with until the middle of October. Even more startling is the fact that over 4,000 applications filed during the licensing year April 1964–March 1965 had not been dealt with by February 15, 1965.[20]

That delay in the processing of applications for imports and other trade payments is detrimental to international trade is readily apparent. It is for this reason that the Contracting Parties to the GATT drew up a Code of Standard Practices for Import and Export Restrictions and Exchange Controls. (December 27, 1950).[21] Paragraph 4 of that Code provided, in part, that "[t]he administrative formalities in connection with the issuance of import and export licenses or exchange permits should be designed to allow action upon applications within a reasonably short period."

Of more immediate concern to our study is the effect of delay in the processing of exchange applications at the na-

[19] In Tunisia, an applicant "usually, but not always" is notified of the reasons why his import license application has been refused. See Columbia Law School, *supra* note 14 at 95. With regard to the Small-Scale Industry Section in India, prior to the reform of 1966, there was a requirement that if the licensing authority rejected the recommendations of the technical advisers, the reasons for the rejection had to be communicated to the applicants.

[20] See Directorate of Commercial Publicity, *supra* note 16 at 35.

[21] GATT, "Standard Practices for Import and Export Restriction and Exchange Controls" (Pamphlet 1950).

tion–state level. The Santhanam Committee in India found that "[d]elay in the disposal of applications for licenses provides considerable scope for corruption in this organization [the import control organization]." [22]

Several countries whose exchange distribution systems have been the subject of this study have attempted to deal with the problem of delay by incorporating explicit time requirements in their laws or regulations. The Indian *Import Trade Control Handbook* provides: "If an application for an import license is not disposed of within one month from the date of its receipt in the licensing section, the licensing authority will issue an interim reply to the applicant. If an applicant does not receive an interim reply even after this time limit, he can bring the matter to the notice of the Public Relations Officer in the import trade control office concerned or book an interview with the officer concerned through the Enquiry Office in order to know the reasons for the delay in the disposal of his application." [23] The Committee on the Prevention of Corruption sought to strengthen this provision by recommending that "if at any stage the file is held up for a longer period than laid down in the schedule the officer concerned should send it to the next higher officer with his explanation for delay." [24]

In Somalia the time constraints are much more severe. For applications for exchange for foreign travel, including business travel, tourism, health reasons, and education abroad, applications are submitted to the Somali National

[22] See Ministry of Home Affairs, Government of India, *supra* note 18 at 254. In addition to bureaucratic delays are those that may be caused by the participants themselves. Importers, for example, may use the existence of an exchange distribution system as an excuse for delaying payments to their overseas suppliers. And it was found in Venezuela that some of the banks were delaying submission of applications for exchange to the control authorities so that they could utilize the local currency received with the applications for working capital. See Woodley, *Exchange Measures in Venezuela*, XI STAFF PAPERS 337, 344 (1964).

[23] HANDBOOK, *supra* note 12 at 137.

[24] See Ministry of Home Affairs, Government of India, *supra* note 18 at 257.

Bank. Within *three business days* of receipt, these applications must be forwarded to the Licensing Committee concerned. The Committee "shall decide . . . *within seven working days from the date of receipt.* They shall be returned, after decision, to the Somali National Bank, within a period not exceeding *ten working days* from the date of receipt. In respect of those applications decided on favorably by the Licensing Committee concerned, the Somali National Bank shall grant the licenses *within two business days* from the date of receipt from the Licensing Committee.

"In respect of those applications decided on favorably by the Somali National Bank without prior reference to the Licensing Committees, *the Bank shall grant the licenses within three business days from the receipt* of the application." [25] (Emphasis added.)

Other suggestions for speeding processing have included creation of a special unit within the distribution office whose sole task it is to keep track of applications and notify the responsible officials if they are "not disposed of in time." [26]

While these requirements and suggestions are meritorious in themselves, they focus on the symptom rather than the disease. Except for the cases where the processing of applications is held up solely to extort a payment from the applicant, delay results from the nature of the distribution process itself. It has been repeatedly pointed out that one of the great advantages of the base period criterion for exchange distribution is that it enables administrators to begin issuing licenses "a few days" after import policy is announced. Where multiple variable criteria are utilized, on the other hand, the "working out" of each entitlement is

[25] Resolution No. 5 of 30 May 1965, Advisory Commission on Foreign Economic Transactions, ¶ D.

[26] Department of Supply and Technical Development, Ministry of Industry and Supply, Government of India, *Report of the Study Team on Directorate General of Technical Development* (Part I) 31 (1965).

very time consuming. Thus the lack of specificity, which is itself the object of criticism, engenders the further evil of delay in the administration of the system. The answer is not a hollow admonition to speed up the work. It lies, rather, in the direction of simplifying the work so that the administrative task is reduced to a formal examination to determine whether the specific requirements of the exchange program have been satisfied.[27]

REVIEW

The traditional, and most widely acknowledged, means of attempting to ensure that the discretion granted to government officials is not abused, is by review of the administrative action either within or outside the system. Data on the availability of opportunities for review of exchange distribution decisions was one of the most difficult parts of the research for the current study. In a few cases, the legislation or policy statements concerning exchange distribution explicitly provided for review. Even here, however, there were differences as to what was reviewable. In other cases review was specifically excluded. In general, the legislation said nothing one way or the other about review. In all countries there were law courts or administrative courts whose jurisdiction encompassed the possibility of review of exchange distribution decisions but the instances of attempts to review this kind of decision were rare indeed, if not altogether absent. Where proceedings are not widely reported nor decisions published, it is, of course, extremely difficult to deter-

---

[27] Another possible safeguard to the integrity of the system was the suggestion by the Santhanam Committee that the staff dealing with import licensing be shifted every three years. See Ministry of Home Affairs, Government of India, *supra* note 18 at 256.

mine whether such challenges in fact occurred. But it is more likely than not that the lack of challenges brought to the researcher's attention reflects a situation where there are in fact few challenges. This is due to the nature of the decisions being challenged. The bulk of exchange distributions are made for trade transactions which are in their nature repetitive. That is, the importer must return to the authorities every six months or every year for approval to import the goods he needs. In such a situation it is unlikely that he will seek to alienate the authorities with a formal challenge of their decisions. As Myrdal noted with regard to India in *Asian Drama*, "the officials in charge of the discretionary controls are so powerful that the individual private entrepreneur is seldom tempted to challenge the system; since he knows that he will repeatedly have to seek their favor; he is even loath to protest a particular decision." [28] Gellhorn came to the same conclusion in Japan: "After all, the top administrators who act on the appeal are the very same people who hand down the policy the junior administrators simply obeyed when they made the decisions complained about, so of course the top men are going to uphold the results." [29] There is no reason to think that these attitudes are peculiarly Asian. And certainly, in the developing

---

[28] P. 928.

[29] Gellhorn, *Settling Disagreements with Officials in Japan*, 79 Harv. L. Rev. 685, 692–3 (1966). The Foreign Exchange and Foreign Trade Control Law of Japan (Law No. 228 of December 1, 1949) reprinted in Foreign Exchange Study Assoc., Japan Laws, Ordinances and Other Regulations Concerning Foreign Exchange and Foreign Trade A-1 (1964) (official trans.) provides for administrative appeals in Article 56. That article provides in general terms that "Any competent Minister, upon receiving" a "petition for investigation regarding disposition made under the provisions of this Law or Orders issued thereunder, shall afford to the . . . petitioner an opportunity for public hearing after reasonable advance notice." In the 10-year period from 1956–66, when Japanese import officials were handling roughly 11,000 applications per month, there were only "two or three cases of appeal." Columbia Law School, *supra* note 14 at 68. There was, however, a major *cause célèbre*—"the Banana scandal" in September 1966. *Ibid.*

world, review of administrative decisions is unlikely to be encouraged and may not even be tolerated. As Professor Gellhorn has observed: ". . . efforts to contest decisions may be viewed as challenges to authority itself." [30]

When external review is possible, the kind of review of administrative action available in the exchange distribution area has tended to reflect a country's wider legal tradition. Thus, those developing countries strongly influenced by the French model emphasize specialized administrative review bodies, while those where British influence has been greatest rely on judicial review in the ordinary law courts. With regard to opportunities for review within the system, no such characterization can be made.

The need for internal administrative review is most apparent in large countries where exchange distributions are made from scattered government offices or within different parts of the same government office. The extreme case in point is India. In a sample of 154 cases of license applications considered by various directorates of the DGTD in 1965, 106 were passed on by officers at two levels of the organization. Of these, in nearly 15 percent of the cases "the higher levels differed from the course of action suggested at lower levels." [31]

Where the distribution of exchange is centralized, however, the availability of internal review was an infrequent occurrence. Under the import system obtaining in Brazil in 1966, import licenses (*Guia de Importacao*) were issued by the Foreign Trade Department (Carteira de Comercio Exterior) (CACEX) of the National Foreign Trade Council (Con selho Nacional de Comercio Exterior). If CACEX rejected an application there was no appeal.[32] In Colombia, the decisions

---

[30] Gellhorn, *Protecting Citizens Against Administrators in Poland,* 65 COLUM. L. REV. 1133 (1965).

[31] Department of Supply and Technical Development, *supra* note 26 at 108.

[32] See Columbia Law School, *supra* note 14 at 13.

concerning the distribution of import licenses are made by a Committee for Imports.[33] There is no appeal from the decisions of the committee.[34]

Several systems examined did, on the other hand, provide for administrative appeals. One of the eight committees of the FETC in Taiwan was the Committee on Administrative Appeals. Among its tasks was hearing appeals from orders of the other committees denying requests for foreign exchange. The scope of review is limited to the application of FETC policies to individual cases. The policies themselves may not be challenged.[35] In interviews conducted in Taipei in 1966, the author was led to believe that the Committee delved rather deeply into the merits of the cases appealed. And although screened by the Committee, most appeals were eventually discussed by the full Commission, which issued a written decision to the appellant. At the time of the interviews, the Committee on Administrative Appeals was hearing four to six cases a month. Officials of the FETC indicated that the Appeals Committee had been established as a "democratic gesture."

The Indian *Import Trade Control Handbook* provides that "when a person is not satisfied with the decision of a licensing authority, he may make an appeal against such decision." [36] "In respect of an application for import license, an appeal, in the first instance, will lie with the head of the office in which the application was dealt with." In fact, the appeals are usually dealt with by "separate officers meant for this purpose in the ITC offices." [37] "If the appellant is not

---

[33] Pp. 229–32 *supra*.

[34] Columbia Law School, *supra* note 14 at 104. No appeal lies from the rejection of an import application in Tunisia. See *id.* at 95.

[35] FETC Foreign Exchange and Trade Handbook, 1966, p. 268–69 (Taipei, 1965) ("in case any action or measure relating to foreign exchange is taken by FETC pursuant to its authority and not in respect to a particular subject, administrative appeal may not be filed against such action or measure which does not fall within the scope of appeal.").

[36] P. 112.   [37] Ministry of Home Affairs, *supra* note 18 at 255.

satisfied with the decision . . . he may make a second appeal to the Chief Controller of Imports and Exports, New
Delhi (Appeals Wing)." [38] If the appellant remains unsat-
isfied at the second level, he may, thereafter, appeal directly to the Chief Controller of Imports and Exports in
New Delhi. The appellant has the right to be heard in person at all levels in the appeals procedure.[39]

In a 1965 study of 243 applications from the Small-Scale
Industries sector in the office of the Joint Chief Controller
of Imports, Bombay, 1965, it was found that 48 applicants
appealed against the initial decision. In 21 of those cases the
original order was modified. In five cases a second appeal
was taken, none of which resulted in any change. The first
level appeals were dealt with in average of 48 days, the second level in 80 days.[40] In the same office, 203 applications
from Scheduled Industries were also studied. Only nine appeals were taken, of which four resulted in modification.
Average time to deal with the appeal was 65 days.[41] In total
1,181 appeals against initial decisions were taken in
1964–65 and 1,792 in 1965–66.[42]

While review within the system can provide some protection against abuse of administrative discretion and corruption, many writers believe the independent judicial review
of administrative action is an essential requirement of the
rule of law.[43] As noted in chapter 1, this position emanates
from Dicey, who believed that independent judicial review
was implicit in the definition of the rule of law. It is currently the view of those schooled in the Anglo-American
legal tradition. But the results of our study seem to indicate
that where judicial review of administrative action is available, it is unlikely to be utilized to challenge the decisions of

[38] HANDBOOK, *supra* note 12 at 112.   [39] *Ibid.*
[40] DIRECTORATE OF COMMERCIAL PUBLICITY, *supra* note 16 at 87.
[41] *Id.* at 90.   [42] See Columbia Law School, *supra* note 14 at 58.
[43] INTERNATIONAL COMMISSION OF JURISTS, EXECUTIVE ACTION AND THE RULE OF
LAW 8 (1962).

the exchange authority. In part this flows from a reluctance to challenge officials with whom the petitioner must continue to have an ongoing relationship. And in part it stems from the fact that the exchange distributing administrators have been given broad discretionary authority and the judiciary is reluctant to review the exercise of such discretion.

In common law countries, the appeal would be to the law courts. In the absence of special legislation, however, the scope of review is limited. The traditional distinction is that the courts do not enquire into the reasons that led officials to exercise administrative discretion granted to them by law. What is subject to review is abuse of discretion and failure to follow clear statutory directions. Although the parameters of what is reviewable will vary with the particular legislation, as well as the attitude of the courts, the distinction can be illustrated by posing two hypothetical cases. If the Chief Controller of Imports and Exports in India refused to grant an import license to an applicant solely because the applicant was a member of the Congress Party—and this could be proved—the law courts would overrule the decision on the grounds of abuse of discretion.[44] If, on the other hand, the license was refused because the Chief Controller of Imports and Exports believed the requested imports were not essential or the applicants past production was "unsatisfactory," the basis for reaching that conclusion would not be inquired into by a law court. The scope of review by the law courts is thus rather narrow and unlikely to provide a remedy for any except the most blatant form of abuse. Although the particular reasons for this narrow scope of review will vary from country to country, in general it has been said that the law courts deal with administrative matters only on occasion and if they did not exercise a rigid self-control they "might be inclined to disregard the

---

[44] But see the case of *Haji Sattar* v. *Joint Controller of Imports*, p. 277 *infra*.

routine and the habits generally accepted within the administrative agency, and instead more radically to satisfy the individuals claims for protection of his interests." [45]

In addition to judicial diffidence about delving into the exercise of administrative discretion, the unhappy situation of the petitioner is compounded by the fact that regulatory legislation, such as that dealing with exchange distribution, traditionally grants the broadest sort of discretion to the administrators. In Ghana, for example, the principal legislation governing the control of imports is the Imports and Exports (Restriction) Order, 1948. The entire order is six sentences long; the complete statement of the legislation concerning imports is as follows: "The importation into the Gold Coast of any article is hereby prohibited except under license granted by the Controller of Imports and Exports and subject to such terms and conditions as may be contained therein." It would be difficult to imagine a wider grant of discretion or one in which actual decisions are less subject to review. The Exchange Control Act (No. 71 of 1961) presents a similar wide grant. Section 5 of the Act provides that "Except in such cases as may be prescribed, no person shall . . . in Ghana . . . make a payment to, or for the credit of, an external resident. . . . No Ghana resident shall make any payment outside Ghana to or for the credit of an external resident." Section 38 provides that "The Minister may by legislative instrument make regulations prescribing anything that is to be prescribed under this Act . . ." Similar broad grants of discretionary authority are present in other Commonwealth countries. The New Zealand Import Control Regulations (No. 47 of 1964) provide, in Article 3 "The importation into New Zealand of any goods is hereby prohibited except (a) importation pursuant to a written license granted by the Minister as hereinafter

[45] Kjellin, *supra* note 1, at 104.

provided; (b) importation pursuant to an exemption granted by the Minister under regulation 16 hereof; (c) importation authorized whether before or after importation of the goods by a written permit granted by the Minister as hereinafter provided." Article 9 (1) provides that "The Minister may in his discretion grant a license or permit in respect of all the goods included in any application or in respect of part only of such goods or may decline to grant any such application." And Article 12 provides that "The Minister may grant any license or permit subject to such conditions as he thinks fit."

The limited utility of judicial review where legislation grants such wide discretion to the administering officials can be illustrated by a closer examination of the Indian system for distributing exchange for imports. The Indian Imports and Exports (Control) Act of 1947 confers power on the Central Government to "make provisions for prohibiting, restricting, or otherwise controlling . . . the import, export . . . of goods. . . ." [46] The carte blanche granted to the Central Government by the Act has been narrowed somewhat by the Imports (Control) Order, 1955. The Order begins by repeating the general prohibition on imports: "Save as otherwise provided in this Order, no person shall import any goods of the description specified in Schedule I except under, and in accordance with, a license or a customs clearance permit granted by the Central Government. . . ." As of May 30, 1966 Schedule I ran 33 printed pages and included virtually all products that could conceivably have been imported. The Order nowhere states criteria to be applied in determining whether a license shall be issued. It does, however, in Section 6, state the conditions under which a license may be refused. Although 16 grounds for refusal are stated, many are procedural and do

[46] Section 3.

not go to the merits of the application. For example, ground for refusal (b) is an application containing "any false or fraudulent or misleading statement" and ground (ccc) permits refusal "if the applicant has, on any occasion, committed breach of any law (including any rule, order, or regulation) relating to customs or foreign exchange." The sole ground for refusal dealing with the substance of potential applications is ground (cc), which permits refusal "if the licensing authority considers that the grant of the license will not be in the interest of conserving foreign exchange." One Indian legal scholar has characterized this "limitation" as "nothing more than telling the authority to do what it thinks best." [47] This broad basis for refusal places little limitation on the discretion of the licensing authorities and substantially limits the scope of possible judicial review of a refusal to issue a license.

There are, however, other criteria offering the possibility of judicial review—those contained in the Red Book. Yet the legal status of the Red Book is much in controversy in India. The High Courts of Punjab and Calcutta have termed its content "mere departmental instructions," which indicate policy, but are not to be considered binding on the government.[48] On the other hand, the Bombay High Court has held that the Red Book has "the force of law." [49] The Supreme Court has not yet passed on the question, although in an analogous case the Court ruled that the Government was estopped to deny the legal force of regulations laid down where petitioner had relied on those regulations to his detriment.[50] If the view of the Bombay High Court is eventually accepted, the scope for review will be widened considerably in that the government would then have to establish adherence to the criteria laid down in the Red Book.

[47] Jain, *supra* note 7 at 142.   [48] *Id.* at 135.   [49] *Ibid.*
[50] See *Union of India* v. *Indo-Afghan Agencies, Ltd.*, Nov. 22, 1967, cited and discussed in Jain, *supra* note 7 at 134.

This could result in a refinement of those criteria through court decision. The attempt to sustain the view of the Bombay High Court must, however, deal with Section 7 of the Act, which provides that no order made under the Act "shall be called into question in any Court and no suit, prosecution, or other legal proceeding shall be against any person for anything in good faith done or intended to be done under this Act or any order made or deemed to have been made thereunder." This provision would appear on its face to preclude virtually all opportunity for judicial review of decisions taken by the exchange distributing authority. The sole possibility would appear to be an allegation that a decision was not taken in "good faith." [51]

Even if the Indian Supreme Court were to sustain the view that the CCI&E and the DGTD were bound by the criteria published in the Red Book, they could apparently be changed at will by the Chief Controller. For the High Court in Calcutta has held that the issuance of an import license is a privilege conferred by the Government, not a right to which petitioners were entitled. In *Haji Sattar* v. *Joint Controller of Imports*,[52] the licensing authority had taken an irrelevant consideration into account (the fact that the petitioner was an evacuee with regard to his property in Lucknow) in rejecting the application for an import license. The Calcutta High Court refused to interfere on the ground that "no one was entitled to the grant of a license as a right." [53] This position has been called into question by the decision of the Supreme Court in *Dwarka Prasad* v. *State of U.P.*[54] That case dealt with an appeal by one who had been refused a license to deal in coal by the Coal Controller of the State of Uttar Pradesh. The statute gave the controller absolute discretion

---

[51] It has been suggested that such a narrow interpretation would conflict with the provisions of Article 14 of the Constitution of India. See Krishna, *India's Foreign Trade*, I JR. WORLD TRD. LAW 338, 344 (1967).

[52] A.I.R. 1953 Cal. 591.

[53] Jain, *supra* note 7 at 139.   [54] A.I.R. 1954 S.C. 224.

to grant or deny a license. The Supreme Court held that the grant was unconstitutional absent provision for an appeal to a higher authority. Since the theory adopted in *Haji Sattar* that a license was a privilege effectively precludes scope for an appeal, it has been argued that this "approach is not correct" and that *Dwarka Prasad* effectively overrules the *Haji Sattar* case.[55]

In countries that follow the French model, the administrative courts have a broader scope for review than is true of common law jurisdictions. In particular, administrative courts are specifically authorized to review the exercise of discretion on the part of administrative officials. To refer back to our hypothetical Indian case, an administrative official of the type serving in the *section du contentieux* of the French Conseil d'Etat could, in a case involving refusal to issue an import license on the ground of "nonessentiality," examine the data the administrator had before him to determine whether they support his conclusion of "nonessentiality." This ability to deal with matters considered within the sole jurisdiction of the executive in common law countries stems from the fact that the Conseil d'Etat is formally, as the name implies, and in fact, part of the executive. In the course of time the Conseil has evolved a set of "standards of due and proper administration" (*principes généraux du droit*). Their content may be summarized in the proposition that administrative decisions must be based on reason. Even if

---

[55] See also *Chandralcant* v. *Jasjit Singh*, A.I.R. 1962 S.C. 204; *Mannalal Jain* v. *State of Assam*, A.I.R. 1962 S.C. 386.

The Canadian Foreign Exchange Control Act, c. 53 of 1946, contained a provision for appeals to the Minister from refusals of the Foreign Exchange Control Board to grant exchange permits. Section 37. "The final decision on these matters necessarily depends on foreign exchange policy at the time and, since this is a question for day-to-day determination by the Government, there does not appear to be any basis on which a court would be able to review the Minister's decision. In any event, no attempt to do so has been made up to the present time." Tarr, *The Administration of Foreign Exchange Control in Canada*, XXVII Can. Bar. Rev. 625, 645 (1949).

the civil servant is found to be acting within the scope of his discretionary authority, his action must conform to the general principles of reason.[56] While action is initiated in the *section du contentieux* by the individual complainant, once the complainant has made out a *prima facie* case he becomes very much a spectator as the case becomes a contest between the Conseil as defender of sound administration and the defendant government department. In its work the *section* may ask the government to state the grounds on which its decision is based or may go even further and ask for the file on which the government based its decision. Failure to produce will most probably result in the *section du contentieux* quashing the order of the government. Lest one gain the wrong impression, however, the contest is a friendly one and the individual civil servant sees the Conseil as his protector. This is in sharp contrast to the attitude of civil servants toward the law courts.

Because its scope of review is so much greater than that of the ordinary law courts functioning in common law jurisdictions, institutions modeled on the Conseil d'Etat could provide more effective safeguards for applicants for foreign exchange who are dissatisfied with decisions of the allocating authorities. But at the time of this writing the advantages remain largely theoretical since, in the two jurisdictions that maintain institutions closely modeled on the French Conseil d'Etat, the author could not find an instance in which those institutions had been called upon to deal with a challenge to a decision of the exchange authorities.

Colombia has a system of administrative courts, with one trial level court of three judges located in each department. Appeals from this court can be made to the Conejo de Estado. There is no evidence to indicate that these courts have ever been utilized to challenge decisions of the exchange au-

[56] Hamson, *Judicial and other Remedies Against The Illegal Exercise or Abuse of Administrative Authority*, in UNITED NATIONS, *supra* note 1 at 29.

thorities. Turkey also has a Council of State (Devlet Surasi), which is "closely patterned" after the Conseil d'Etat.[57] "The Council has 31 members elected by the Turkish parliament from a panel of [distinguished and high-ranking] civil servants nominated by the prime minister."[58] Under the constitution any citizen may "secure a judgment as to the legality and the equity of any administrative act."[59] Again there is no evidence that the Council has ever dealt with issues of exchange distribution.

Applicants who were dissatisfied with appeals taken within the FETC structure in Taiwan were also free to pursue appeals through the administrative court system. The author was not able to locate an instance in which a decision of the FETC was pursued in the court system, although this is not surprising given the extensive provisions for appeals within the system itself.

For countries without a system of administrative courts and where ordinary law courts by tradition confine the scope of review of administrative decisions within very narrow limits, a possible alternative offering the opportunity for independent review is the institution of the Ombudsman. This is a Swedish term that has entered universal application to identify an official who serves as a "watchdog" on the bureaucracy. The role and powers of the Ombudsman vary from country to country. In Sweden the Ombudsman's activities are confined to "acts of maladministration . . . where the complaint is that an official has failed to act in accordance with some specific law—and not with complaints about the exercise of administrative discretion."[60] Since, as we have seen, exchange distribution is an area

[57] WORLD PEACE THROUGH WORLD LAW CENTER, LAW AND JUDICIAL SYSTEMS OF NATIONS, *Turkey* 6 (1965).

[58] Prestus, *Statistical Analysis in Comparative Administration, The Turkish Conseil d'Etat* at 4 (Cornell Studies in Policy and Administration 1958).

[59] *Id.* at 4.   [60] Shonfeld, *supra* note 10 at 28.

where wide discretion is typically conferred on administrators, the Swedish Ombudsman would not be a perfect model for use in this area. The Ombudsman would be more relevant to exchange issues if the wide areas of discretion currently obtaining in many of the systems were narrowed by the publication of legally binding criteria upon which distributions must be based. This would enable an Ombudsman to function effectively in reviewing exchange distributions from a jurisdictional point of view. There is however another difficulty. The success of the Swedish Ombudsman is due in no small measure to the fact that there also exists in Sweden an effective administrative court system. This system functions in much the same manner as the Conseil d'Etat in reviewing abuses of discretion on the part of civil servants. The existence of this system of administrative courts is one of the reasons that the case load of the Swedish Ombudsman is kept to proportions so small that it can be handled without the large bureaucracy that would suffocate the Ombudsman concept. Another factor, which works to keep the Ombudsman's case load small, is that the concept has only been utilized in countries with small, highly sophisticated populations where the civil service has extremely high standards of personal integrity and where low-level corruption is virtually nonexistent. A third characteristic of the Ombudsman system that may not find appeal in some developing countries is the atmosphere of publicity that surrounds the work of the Ombudsman. The Swedish Ombudsman does not have the power to overrule or modify administrative decisions. Instead his weapons are publicity and the persuasive powers that are enhanced by his personal prestige in the society. The publicity aspect of his work is effected through the public reports that he issues, usually on an annual basis. In addition, in Sweden, "Every day at 11 A.M. a representative of the Swedish Press Bureau calls at the Ombudsman's office to examine the complaints and the decisions of the previous day. The files are laid out on a table ready for the Pressman's inspection and contain all the inward and outward correspondence and any reports pertaining to the particular complaint or decision." [61] If the society is such that the government will tolerate this form of "unfavorable publicity," and if the number of cases can be kept within manageable limits, the Ombudsman device, like other systems of administrative review, offers two advantages to the government. First, it ensures that deviations from policy will be brought to light so as to ensure sounder, more uniform administration. Secondly, it assures that the citizen will have a chance to air his grievance. As Professor Gellhorn has pointed out with regard to the Swedish Ombudsman, "By finding no fault in ninety percent of the cases about which complaint has been made, he sets at rest what might otherwise be continuing rumors of wrongdoing." [62] In the one country examined that has both an exchange distribution system and an Ombudsman—New Zealand— decisions concerning exchange are not within the jurisdiction of the Ombudsman.[63]

The role of Ombudsman is sometimes played by nongovernmental officials. In Poland, for example, the newspapers play a leading role in dealing with complaints against the administration. A survey of 41 major newspapers in Poland found that 37 of those papers "have a staff lawyer who answers readers' letters and receives personal callers." [64] The Polish Code of Administrative Procedure recognizes the role of journalists and provides that "suggestions forwarded to officials by editorial offices are to be considered and disposed of in the same manner as those

[61] J. MONTEIRO, CORRUPTION 197 (Bombay, 1966).
[62] Gellhorn, *The Swedish Justititieiombudsman,* 75 YALE L.J. 1, 53 (1965).
[63] Gellhorn, *The Ombudsman in New Zealand,* 53 CAL. L.R. 1155, 1192 (1965).
[64] Gellhorn, *Protecting Citizens Against Administrators in Poland,* 65 COL. L. REV. 1133, 1157 (1965).

that come directly from affected parties; and upon the editors' request, information must be promptly given about the action taken." [65]

For a developing country which desires that aberrations from policy be brought to the attention of the government, but not necessarily through the medium of the press, another possible mode is the Permanent Commission of Enquiry which has been established in Tanzania. The Commission has the broad duty to hear complaints of maladministration by citizens against the government. Its proceedings are, however, secret and it reports only to the President.[66]

The necessity for institutional safeguards to protect the rule of law in the system for distributing foreign exchange is directly related to the nature of the system itself. Where exchange is distributed according to market criteria, or where exchange is offered to all applicants at a specified price or in specified quantities, rule of law problems are minimized. Movement away from these systems toward those involving more administrative discretion begin to raise rule of law issues. Where criteria are objective and quantifiable publication of the relevant information would seem to serve as an adequate safeguard. Moreover, criteria of this type would ameliorate the delays attached to many systems of exchange distribution. Where, however, criteria remain complex and/or vague, the rule of law must depend on the rather unsatisfactory safeguard of review. Internal review seems unlikely to work since the repetitive nature of exchange distribution transactions make applicants reluctant to challenge the administration. External review possibilities suffer from the same disability. In addition, in common law jurisdictions the courts have been traditionally reluctant to deal with exchange distribution problems in a manner that would satisfy those interested in the develop-

---

[65] Art. 175, quoted in *id* at 1154.
[66] 3 AFR. RES. BULL. 469–470 (1966).

ment of the rule of law. In this chapter we have focused on the kinds of institutional action which can be taken at the national level to preserve and strengthen the rule of law in the exchange distribution process. In the final chapter we shall look at the role of international law and international institutions to the same end.

Chapter 9

International Reforms to Strengthen the Rule of Law

In chapters 4 through 8 we have measured national systems of exchange distribution against the rule of law and anticorruption criteria. We have observed that systems would more closely conform to these criteria to the extent that, *inter alia,* they permit market forces to distribute exchange between applicants, that maximum publicity is accorded to the decision-making process and that some provision is made to review administrative decisions. We noted in chapter 3 that international norms do not generally reach that part of the exchange distribution process where decisions are made between competing applicants. The caveat that needs to be added to this statement is that certain provisions of the IMF Articles of Agreement as interpreted explicitly discourage limited market distribution systems of the kind described in chapters 5 and 6. In general, we have recognized that international norms do not extend to that stage of the distribution process with which we have been immediately concerned.

In this final chapter we shall move back along the continuum of the exchange distribution process and reexamine issues covered in chapters 2 and 3. In particular, we shall examine the crucial role of the IMF and the norms incorporated in the Articles of Agreement in dealing with balance of payments difficulties. Recall from chapter 2 that the principal reason for the use of exchange distribution by developing countries is a decrease in their foreign exchange reserves and an unwillingness to resort to the classic remedies for a balance of payments deficit-deflation and depreciation. There are thus two points at which the Fund could intervene prior to the adoption of an exchange distribution system by a developing country. The first would be when reserves begin to fall, the second when consideration is given to deflation and depreciation programs. And in fact the Fund's principal activities involve interventions at both of these points. The interventions are principally in the form of provision of additional reserves. We should therefore take a brief look at the kinds of resources the Fund makes available to its members and to their utility in forestalling the adoption of an exchange distribution system in a developing country faced with a balance of payments deficit.

Upon joining the Fund, a member subscribes both gold and its own currency to the extent of its quota (Article III, 3). The proportions are 25 percent gold and 75 percent local currency. Although not wholly accurate, for present purposes we may consider the 25 percent contributed in gold as the member's "gold tranche."[1] When a member needs foreign exchange it may purchase another member's currency from the Fund in an amount equal to the purchas-

[1] According to Article XIX (j), a gold tranche purchase is one "which does not cause the Fund's holdings of the member's currency to exceed one hundred percent of its quota. . . ." For a discussion of the precise meaning of "gold tranche" see J. GOLD, THE STAND-BY ARRANGEMENTS OF THE INTERNATIONAL MONETARY FUND 13–14 (1970) (hereinafter cited as GOLD).

ing member's gold tranche. The purchase is paid for in local currency. In a sense, therefore, gold tranche purchases do not increase a member country's reserves but only allow it to recover the gold or foreign exchange equivalent of its initial deposit in the Fund. In addition to gold tranche purchases, however, members may make additional purchases up to 200 percent of their quota.[2] Purchases above the gold tranche are denominated "credit tranche" purchases. Unlike gold tranche purchases, they are not unconditional. Each credit tranche purchase must be approved by the Fund. Requests for purchases from the first credit tranche are treated "liberally." Beyond that tranche, however, purchases "require substantial justification."[3] But before going to the credit tranche a member may utilize his allotment of Special Drawing Rights (SDR's).

For reasons generally well known and discussed extensively elsewhere, the Fund's Articles of Agreement were amended in 1969 to provide for the creation of SDR's. SDR's are "unconditional reserve assets" with a value equivalent to .881671 gram of fine gold (i.e., the par value of the U.S. dollar in December 1946).[4] SDR distributions were made on January 1, 1970 (3.4 billion units), January 1, 1971, and January 1, 1972 (2.952 billion units each). SDR's are distributed to "participants" in the Special Drawing Ac-

[2] Article V,§ 3(a)(iii).

[3] Decision of the Executive Directors, No. 1477–(63/8) Feb. 27, 1963 as amended by Decision No. 2192–(66/81) Sept. 20, 1966, reprinted in GOLD 238–242, and discussed in *id.* at 16–21.

[4] See e.g., XXV INT. FIN. STAT. 7 (May 1972). In June 1974 the Executive Directors adopted a new method of valuing SDR's in terms of a "basket" of sixteen major currencies. See III IMF SURVEY 177 (1974); 251 ECONOMIST 108 (June 15, 1974).

The use of SDR's is unconditional despite the fact that the plan provides for their use for "balance of payments needs or in the light of developments in total reserves and not for the sole purpose of changing the composition of reserves." Article XXV, 2(a). For a discussion of the possible meaning of this distinction, see Note, *Legal Problems of International Monetary Reform*, 20 STANF. L. REV. 870, 933–34 (1968). For a general description of the SDR facility, see Gold, *Special Drawing Rights* (IMF Pamphlet Series No. 13, 2d ed. 1970).

count in proportion to their Fund quota. Virtually all developing countries are participants. When a developing country is in need of foreign exchange reserves it notifies the Fund that it wishes to exchange SDR's for a member's currency. The Fund then designates "the participant to receive them." The receiving participant transfers to the SDR user an amount of its currency, which must be a "currency convertible in fact," equal to the par value of the SDR's it receives.[5] The receiving state can also use SDR's for reserve acquisition, although this is unlikely since recipient states are generally those with strong balance of payments or reserve positions. SDR's may also be used in repayment for purchases from the Fund and other charges.

In a real sense the SDR system represents the creation of new reserves at the stroke of a pen. As of April 30, 1973, these reserves ("net cumulative allocations") amounted to 2,348 million units of SDR's (roughly pre-1971 dollars) for the developing country membership of the Fund. While not an amount to be casually dismissed, the figure represents less than the amount of the *trade* deficit for all developing countries in 1971. And if one excludes the oil-exporting states of the Middle East, the total SDR allocation to developing countries to the middle of 1973 represents only one third of the *trade* deficit of those countries for 1972. We are, of course, in the very early stages of the SDR system and there were good reasons for starting modestly with such a revolutionary change in the international montary system. Yet for developing countries today SDR's offer an extremely limited, though nonetheless welcome, source of assistance in times of balance of payments difficulties.[6] The limitations result from the fact that SDR allocations are tied

---

[5] Article XXV, Sec. 4.

[6] The facility is even more limited than is apparent from the figures cited since a country may only use an average of 70 percent of its SDR's over a five-year period. See Gold, *supra* note 4 at 67–70.

to country quotas. To free the SDR system from this restrictive relationship, the developing countries have sought to link the creation of SDR's to an international program of financial assistance to them.

Proposals to link reserve creation with development assistance purport to be related to the seignorage principle.[7] Seignorage is the social value gained from the use of paper as against commodity money. More simply put, seignorage is the gain from the creation of free money by the world's central banks and, in the context of our discussion, the gain that accrued from the creation of SDR's—the gain being the difference between the circulation value and the cost of creating the money. Early in the debates about international liquidity there was much discussion of how this seignorage was to be distributed. In the end the issue was resolved by prorating the SDR's in accordance with IMF quotas. The developing country champions wanted the bulk or all of the seignorage to go to developing countries. There are two major proposals for distributing the seignorage in this manner—the Stamp Plan [8] and the UNCTAD Plan.[9]

The Stamp Plan would have the IMF transfer the SDR's to the International Development Agency (IDA) instead of distributing them according to IMF quotas. The IDA would then give or lend the SDR's to the developing countries who would in turn use them to finance imports from the developed countries. The UNCTAD scheme is a slight variation. SDR's would be distributed according to IMF quota. But instead of being given "free" each member country would "buy" them in exchange for its own currency. The IMF would then pass these currencies on to the IBRD and IDA

[7] See Grubel, *The Distribution of Seignorage from International Liquidity Creation,* in R. MUNDELL AND A. SWOBODA (eds.) MONETARY PROBLEMS OF THE INTERNATIONAL ECONOMY 269 (1969).

[8] Stamp, *The Stamp Plan—1962 Version,* in J. GRUBEL (ed.) WORLD MONETARY REFORM 80 (1963).

[9] See UNCTAD, *International Monetary Issues and the Developing Countries* (1965).

and from there they would be made available to the developing countries. The UNCTAD variation is based largely on tradition. The developed countries have always acquired reserves—i.e. gold or dollars—by surrendering their currency. They would continue to do so under the UNCTAD plan. The only change would be that the beneficiaries of reserve acquisition would be the developing nations instead of the gold producers or the U.S. economy.[10]

Under both plans what is really happening is a transfer of resources to the developing countries. The advantage of these schemes is that they may facilitate such transfers by disguising them from a citizenry hostile to the prospect of more foreign aid. But they have little to do with international monetary reform—at least in the conventional sense. The possible link between aid and monetary reform was a leading issue at UNCTAD III. At the time of this writing there is no visible progress to report.[11]

Developing countries with payments deficits for whom SDR distributions fail to provide sufficient emergency reserves may resort to the credit tranches. Access has been facilitated by the creation of a new international legal form, the Stand-By Arrangement.[12] The Stand-By Arrangement has altered the procedure with regard to the credit tranches in the following way. Instead of requesting access when an emergency arises, a Stand-By user will discuss an arrangement with the Fund whereby the Fund agrees to provide a specific amount of exchange resources within a designated time period if the prospective user meets the criteria delin-

---

[10] See Machlup, *The Cloakroom Rule of International Reserves: Reserve Creation and Resources Transfer,* 79 QUART. JR. ECON. 327, 353 (1965).

[11] The question remains, however, "under study." See address by Pierre-Paul Schweitzer, Managing Director of the Fund, at the United Nations Conference on Trade and Development, Santiago, April 25, 1972, reprinted in XXIV I.F.N.S. 121, 124 (1972); ¶ 39, Outline of Reform of the IMF Committee of 20, in 3 IMF SURVEY 198 (1974). For a powerful statement of the case *pro,* see Kahn, *The International Monetary System,* 63 AMER. ECO. REV. 181 (1973).

[12] See generally GOLD.

eated in the Stand-By. In addition, Stand-By's are subject to the limits contained in the Articles of Agreement with regard to the credit tranches. These provide that within any 12-month period "ending on the date of the purchase" a member may make purchases equal to 25 percent of its quota. (Article V,3(a) (iii)). And there is a total upper limit. A member may purchase foreign exchange from the Fund to the point that "the Fund's holdings of the purchasing member's currency" do not "exceed two hundred percent of its quota." (Article V,3(a)(iii)). Within these limits members may obtain emergency reserves through the credit tranche and Stand-By mechanisms. The limitations, both monetary and qualitative, are substantial however and there are only 22 Stand-By's with a total value of 1,394 million (SDR) outstanding on April 30, 1974.[13]

The Fund provides a second source of conditional emergency reserves for developing countries through the compensatory export shortfall program. The developing countries earn their foreign exchange mainly through exports of primary products.[14] For United Nations statistical purposes they are, in fact, termed "primary producing countries." For these countries the total supply of foreign exchange available to them will be determined in large measure by the market price of their commodity exports. Except for the petroleum exporters, the prices for primary products tend to be volatile. The wholesale price per 100 pounds of Ghanaian cocoa in New York, for example, averaged $23.83 in 1964, $17.57 in 1965, $24.54 in 1966, $29.40 in 1967, $34.80 in 1968, $45.21 in 1969, $34.17 in 1970, $27.46 in the first quarter of 1971. The wholesale price per 100 pounds of Brazilian coffee in New York varied over

[13] On the limited use of the credit tranches generally, see Granade, *The Use of International Monetary Fund Facilities by Different Groups of Countries 1952–1971*, 39 So. Econ. Jr. 295 (1972).

[14] See IMF and IBRD, *The Problem of Stabilization of Prices of Primary Products* 1 (1969) (Primary products 88 percent of exports of developing countries.)

the same period from a low of $37.48 in 1968 to a high of $53.57 in 1970. The London price per 100 pounds of sisal dropped from $16.53 in 1964 to $7.01 in 1970. And the price of 100 pounds of copper in London leaped from $43.84 in 1964 to $69.22 in 1966 only to fall again to $47.98 in the first quarter of 1971. A staff study conducted jointly by the IMF and the IBRD indicates that for 38 countries studied, the average annual fluctuation in import prices was 8.8 percent in 1950–65, 6.8 percent for 1953–65 (excluding the Korean War boom). Fluctuations in export earnings were even greater, averaging 11.8 percent and 9.6 percent for the same periods.[15]

Where a Fund member encounters "payments difficulties produced by temporary export shortfalls" it may purchase foreign exchange to the extent of an additional 25 percent of its quota "where the Fund is satisfied that (a) the shortfall is of a short-term character and is largely attributable to circumstances beyond the control of the member; and, (b) the member *will cooperate* [16] with the Fund in an effort to find, where required, appropriate solutions for its balance of payments difficulties.[17]

An additional amount of exchange, to a total of 50 percent of a member's quota, may be purchased "if the Fund is satisfied that the member *has been cooperating* with the Fund in an effort to find, where required, appropriate solutions for its balance of payments difficulties." [18] At first glance it might appear that this provision gives very little to a member since, as we have seen, members always have the

---

[15] See *id.* at 40.   [16] Emphasis added.

[17] Decision No. 1477–(63/8), Feb. 27, 1963, as amended by Decision No. 2192–(66/81), Sept. 20, 1966. See note 3, *supra.* Under Decision No. 2772—(69/47) of June 25, 1969 the Fund also agreed to make resources available to members for financing buffer stocks of primary products. Purchases are limited to 50 percent of quota and an overall limitation of 75 percent is applied to purchases under this and the compensatory financing facility. As of Jan. 31, 1974 net buffer stock drawings totaled 17 million U.S. Dollars. See XXVII INT. FIN. STAT. 24 (March 1974).

[18] Decision No. 1477–(63/8), Feb. 27, 1963, as amended by Decision No. 2192–(66/81), Sept. 20, 1966.

right to purchase from the Fund, at least up to 200 percent of their quota. The important change is hidden in the obscure recesses of Article XIX(j). That Article now defines the gold tranche in such a way that purchases under the compensatory financing facility are not considered "normal" purchases. Thus a member may purchase up to 50 percent of its quota under the shortfall facility and its next purchase will be treated as if it were a gold tranche purchase. In the language of the Fund, the compensatory financing facility " 'floats' alongside the tranches." [19] The significance of this provision can be appreciated by comparing practice here with that under a normal credit tranche purchase. For purchases beyond the gold tranche purchases face criteria of increasing severity.[20] By purchasing under the shortfall scheme, a member avoids these severe criteria and is subject instead to the more flexible criteria established for the compensatory finance scheme. While the compensatory financing scheme has been of value to countries attempting to cope with an export shortfall, it has its limitations. Initially, the Fund has encountered difficulties in attempting "to ascertain currently to what extent a shortfall in export receipts is temporary." [21] The problem is that shortfall does not mean a one-year decline in export receipts, "but rather a shortfall related to the trend in export receipts over a longer period. The trend may be rising or falling, but cannot be accurately determined until several years after the event." [22] Fund officials indicated to the author that this definitional problem has now been overcome.[23] Perhaps

---

[19] GOLD 18.

[20] See Address by the Managing Director of the International Monetary Fund, Pierre-Paul Schweitzer, to the Chamber of Industry and Commerce, Stuttgart, Germany, April 28, 1971, reprinted in XXIII I.F.N.S. 129, 130 (1971).

[21] Host-Madsen, *Balance of Payments Problems of Developing Countries,* Part II, IV FIN. AND DEV. 306 (1967).

[22] *Ibid.*

[23] See International Monetary Fund, Report on Compensatory Financing 6 (1966).

more important than the definitional problem as a limitation on the use of the facility, is the fact that the balance of
payments problems of developing countries are not ordinarily the result of an export shortfall. Instead they seem
more directly related to the inflation that so often accom-
panies the development effort. It is apparently for this reason that the developing countries have made only modest
use of the facility—a total of 982.30 million (SDR) from February 1963 to April 1974.

The provision of additional reserves will not cure a balance of payments deficit resulting from inflation. It will only
postpone for some brief period the day of reckoning. The
time bought may be of considerable value in permitting the
developing countries to adjust their policies to achieve a
new equilibrium. To encourage such action the Fund, in
making available to its members resources under the credit
tranche and compensatory financing scheme, conditions
such assistance on the pursuit of policies by the bor-
rower/purchaser that will act against the inflationary cause
of the payments deficit.[24] In doing so, the Fund is carrying

[24] See Address by the Managing Director of the International Monetary Fund,
Pierre-Paul Schweitzer, to the Chamber of Industry and Commerce, Stuttgart,
Germany, April 28, 1971, reprinted in XXIII I.F.N.S. 129, 130 (1971) (". . . [I]t
came increasingly to be recognized that *internal* financial stability was a prerequisite
for the attainment of the Fund's objectives."). Katz, *Devaluation-Bias and the Bretton
Woods System,* 101 BANCA NAZIONALE DEL LAVORO QTY. 178, 183 (1972) (". . .
[T]he Fund has been able to establish effective communication with borrowing
countries concerning their current economic policies."); Fleming, The International Monetary Fund, Its Form and Functions, 6 (1964) (The Fund has found
that "if inflation is allowed to take place . . . it becomes practically impossible for
countries to fulfill their international obligations with respect to freedom of trade
and exchange stability. Therefore, the Fund in practice has directed much of its
effort to persuading countries to take steps necessary to control inflation."). But
see Fleming, *Developments in the International Payments System,* X STAFF PAPERS 461,
462 (1963) (The Bretton Woods System "imposed no specific obligation on countries to refrain from inflationary domestic policies . . ."). The Fund also makes use
of its persuasive powers with regard to developed countries. See, e.g., 239
ECONOMIST, May 15, 1971, p. xiii (". . . [I]n his budget speech of April 1969, under
some considerable pressure from Britain's anxious creditors at the International
Monetary Fund, Chancellor Roy Jenkins announced his . . . switch of emphasis

out the general admonition of the Articles of Agreement. The language of the Agreement, however, is some distance from the kinds of conditions laid down in the Stand-By's. For the Fund and for most economists these latter follow logically from the language of the Articles. Yet for a developing country the conditions may look like an interference in its affairs.

By way of illustration we may take the case of the Stand-By Arrangement between Uruguay and the Fund of February 28, 1968.[25] Uruguay was suffering from a severe inflation—137 percent domestic price increase in 1967—and equally severe balance of payments problems, which were being dealt with by a system of multiple rates and administrative controls of enormous complexity. The Fund approved a Stand-By $25 million for one year. In return, Uruguay stipulated that if during any quarterly period of the Stand-By (a) the fiscal deficit exceeded the projected limits (specified in billions of Uruguay pesos) or (b) the net foreign reserve position failed to increase by a given figure over the base period of Dec. 31, 1967, or (c) expansion of net credit generally and to the public sector did not stay within specified limits, "Uruguay would refrain from further purchases under the arrangement until new terms for further drawings were agreed to by the Fund."[26] Moreover, Uruguay was to exercise similar "restraint" if (a) new restrictions were imposed on current payments and transfers, (b) exchange transactions did not take place at one rate, (c) new trade restrictions were imposed, or (d) new bilateral payments agreements were entered into.[27] As a re-

towards monetary policy . . ."). Professor Hirschman reports that in 1949 Chile requested advice in financial management from the United Nations rather than the IMF and that the choice reflected a belief that "a United Nations mission would attach a somewhat higher priority to the need for development and the avoidance of deflation." A. HIRSCHMAN, JOURNEYS TOWARD PROGRESS 190–191 (1963).

[25] See note, *The International Monetary Fund: Its Code of Good Behavior and the Uruguayan Stabilization Program of 1968*, 10 VA. JR. INT. LAW 359 (1970).

[26] *Id.* at 389.   [27] *Id.* at 392.

sult of Uruguay's adherence to these policies, as well as a
100 percent devaluation in November 1957 and a further
25 percent devaluation in April 1968, the increase in the
consumer price index dropped to 20 percent for 1969 and
20 percent for 1970 and the exchange rate held steady
from April 1968 to December 1971 while payments enjoyed
relative freedom. The program can thus be pronounced a
success within the limits of its goals.[28] But some developing
countries believe that the goals themselves represent a dis-
torted reading of the Articles of Agreement. For the developing countries place heavy emphasis on Article I, Section
(ii) of the Articles, which provide that one of the purposes
of the Fund shall be "to contribute to the promotion and
maintenance of high levels of employment and real income
and to the development of the productive resources of all
members." [29] In their view, the Fund on occasion has
taken advantage of its role as a provider of resources to take
over the management of their economy to bring about a
deflationary situation which may help to achieve the goal of
exchange stability, but only at the expense of "high levels of
employment" and "development." [30] It is not surprising,
therefore, to find that conditional reserve assistance is the
major area of controversy between the Fund and the developing countries.

Lest the point be exaggerated, relations between the
Fund and most of its members are cordial, to say the least.
In large measure this is due to the Fund's splendid training
efforts. Many of the senior government officials in the trea-

[28] For another illustration of the workings of an IMF stabilization program, see
Bhatia, Szapary and Quinn, *Stabilization Program in Sierra Leone,* XIV STAFF PAPERS
504 (1969).

[29] See, e.g., Nair, *Exchange Control and Economic Planning in Underdeveloped Countries,* 40 IND. JR. ECON. 153, 169 (1959).

[30] See, e.g., Vernon, *A Trade Policy for the 1960's,* XXXIX FOR. AFF. 466 (1961).
(The Fund has pursued policies "too much in the tradition of the banker and too
little in the tradition of the entrepreneur. They have too easily subordinated the
objectives of growth to those of stability.").

suries and central banks with whom the Fund deals are themselves alumni of the Fund. They share a common perspective. In addition the Fund has provided technical assistance to newly independent states to enable them to establish central banks on a sound basis, and to better plan their fiscal and monetary policies. A typical attitude is reflected in the statement of the Governor of the Fund for Somalia who noted at the 1965 annual meeting that durring the past months "Somalia has maintained closer relations with the Fund. The result has been the conclusion of two Stand-By Arrangements for a total of $10.2 million; we have agreed upon a number of measures pertaining to credit, financial, and trade policies which perhaps involve sacrifices and restrictions which we have accepted in the interest of sound economic development." [31] At times, nonetheless, countries are not so willing to make the required sacrifices and the views of the Fund's officials and those of a particular country have come into sharp conflict. Colombia, for example, faced a 10 percent decline in export earnings in the winter of 1967 due to a drop in the price of coffee—Colombia's leading export. Fund officials, apparently believing that the price drop reflected a long-term trend, strongly recommended a devaluation of the peso. "On November 28 (1967), after a dramatic all-night meeting at the gloomy San Carlos Presidential Palace, [President] Lleras Restrepo expressed his disagreement with the fund's recommendations by enacting strict exchange controls that cut import authorizations from $60-million a month to $12-million in December . . . 'It is very nice for people who can afford it to be able to get dollars freely at the Central Bank, for a trip to Miami,' said Bernardo Garces, the Minister of Public Works, 'but it is not good for the country.' " [32] Colombia ap-

[31] International Monetary Fund, SUMMARY PROCEEDINGS OF THE ANNUAL MEETING, 1965, p. 120.

[32] New York Times, Feb. 5, 1967, p. 18, col. 3.

parently had unhappy experiences with the Fund before. In September 1965, Colombia implemented a plan for gradual devaluation of the peso combined with import liberalization. The latter was a basic element in Colombia's agreement with the Fund to provide support during the transition. Imports rose rapidly, mainly financed by bank credits, and by mid-1966 Colombia was again in payments trouble. The difficulties were compounded by a decline in coffee prices at the end of 1966. Exchange distribution was reintroduced in November 1966. Although atypical of the generally good relations between the Fund and its members, the Colombia case is by no means an isolated example. After President Nkrumah was overthrown in Ghana, the new government sought Fund resources for essential consumer goods and spare parts. The Fund "demanded as a condition of extending financial support that the Government begin an austerity program to cut internal spending." [33]

The Fund's willingness to extend credit to a country has been taken by many to be a certification of that government's credit worthiness. This has been a valuable benefit for most developing countries.[34] When relations with the Fund sour, however, the disputes threaten not only a country's relations with the Fund itself, but with other lenders as well. In February 1967, the press carried reports that the Government of the United Arab Republic was in arrears in

---

[33] *New York Times*, Feb. 27, 1967, p. 10 col. 3. See also A. FRUMKIN, MODERN THEORIES OF INTERNATIONAL ECONOMIC RELATIONS 332 (1969) ("It is no secret that the activities of the existing International Monetary Fund . . . imply the freest kind of intervention of these bodies in the internal affairs and in the internal and foreign policies of the borrowing countries . . .").

[34] See R. GARDNER, STERLING-DOLLAR DIPLOMACY xxvii (2d ed. 1969) (Fund's " 'Good Housekeeping's Seal of Approval' has often been decisive in persuading rich countries to come to the aid of the poor."). See also Felix, *An Alternative View of the "Monetarist"-"Structuralist" Controversy*, in HIRSCHMAN, LATIN AMERICAN ISSUES 81 n. 3 (U.S. loans "contingent on the borrower meeting IMF lending criteria.").

two payments due to the Fund. Apparently the UAR was threatened with expulsion from the Fund unless it brought its account up to date. Press reports "quoting reliable sources close to the Fund, say that the Fund has warned President Nasser that it does not think the UAR Government realises the full meaning of expulsion from the IMF, as this would virtually ban further financial aid from elsewhere in the western world." [35] This view was confirmed by press reports that the U.S. Government was holding up requests for surplus food under the Food-for-Peace program until "after discussions with the Fund are completed." [36] It is disputes such as this one that have caused one writer to say that in the postcolonial era the "International Monetary Fund fulfills the role of the colonial administration of enforcing the rules of the game." [37]

Fund officials readily concede that the policies they counsel sometimes do lead to a *temporary* setback to growth and development. If, however, those policies are followed, inflation brought to an end, and the exchange rate adjusted, the growth of output and investment is usually resumed within "a short intermission and at a higher rate than before." [38]

---

[35] IV AFR. RES. BULL. 704a (1967). A letter to the editor, 223 ECONOMIST, May 6, 1967, p. 530 took issue with the report that the Fund was objecting, *inter alia*, to " 'the wastage of resources that goes on maintaining its troops in Yemen.' " Instead the writer noted that Fund policy was that "a country unable to repay its IMF credits should not be involved in engagements abroad." The dispute between the Fund and the U.A.R. was resolved in May of 1967 with the Fund dropping its demand for devaluation and the U.A.R. pledging "economic reforms that, according to western diplomats, must have been difficult for President . . . Nasser to accept." The same sources explain the Egyptian concessions on the basis of a desperate need for foreign exchange. See Egyptians Agree to Economic Reforms, *New York Times*, May 14, 1967, p. 16, cols. 3–5.

[36] *New York Times*, Feb. 27, 1967, p. 11, col. 2.

[37] T. BALOUGH, THE ECONOMICS OF POVERTY 29 (1966). See, e.g., Bolivian Tension Tied to the Peso," *New York Times*, Nov. 26, 1972, p. 30, col. 1 (". . . International Monetary Fund . . . acts as a police force of currency.").

[38] See Fleming, *supra* note 24 at 36–37. See also Dorrance, *The Effect of Inflation on Economic Development*, X STAFF PAPERS 1, 27 (1963) ("If the analysis presented in this paper is valid, an economy experiencing inflation must be one where develop-

Moreover, it is because these sound policies are sometimes politically unpalatable that the monetary authorities of the developing countries sometimes welcome the support lent by the IMF in "strengthening their hand against political pressures."[39] And, as unpalatable as some of the Fund's recommendations may be, many seem *less* than the Agreement actually requires.[40]

This is not the occasion to attempt an evaluation of the Fund's relationships with its developing-country members. This material is relevant to our present purpose only to the extent that it indicates that the occasion when a member requests access to the conditional reserves available in the credit tranches presents an opportunity for the Fund to use

---

ment is proceeding less rapidly than it would if the economy were stable, all other conditions being similar."). But see A. HIRSCHMAN, *supra* note 24 at 222 (". . . [T]hrough the device of inflation society gains precious time for resolving social tensions that otherwise might reach the breaking point right away.").

[39] Fleming, *supra* note 24 at 35. See Sturc, *Fund Activities in Developing Countries*, 9 FIN. AND DEV. 2, 3 (June 1972) (In consultations, "members of the Fund staff . . . help officials to strengthen their determination to start on a new path."). And, e.g., "Bolivian Tension Tied to the Peso, *New York Times*, Nov. 26, 1972, p. 30, col. 1 (Long overdue devaluation "forced by the International Monetary Fund" since government was "too frightened of it."). But see A. HIRSCHMAN, *supra* note 24 at 219 (Left-wing opposition accused government of "submitting abjectly to the dictates "of the IMF in adopting conservative economic policy. This charge "unjust" since government's position was "more rigid that that of the Fund . . .").

[40] See S. DELL, A LATIN-AMERICAN COMMON MARKET? 171 (1966); R. GARDNER, *supra* note 34 at xxx. In its annual consultations with Article XIV members, the Fund is not shy about offering advice on the necessity for antiinflationary measures, including "the specific nature of the action it felt desirable." INTERNATIONAL MONETARY FUND, FOURTH ANNUAL REPORT ON EXCHANGE RESTRICTIONS 12 (1953). During 1973, 93 regular consultations were completed of which 67 were Article XIV consultations. 3 IMF SURVEY 8 (1974). "Over the years the consultation procedure has come to involve full consideration of all relevant aspects of the economic situation of the member." INTERNATIONAL MONETARY FUND, ANNUAL REPORT 1973, p. 57. And see A. HIRSCHMAN, *supra* note 24 at 223 (quoting IMF 1950 report to Chile): " 'A credit restriction to be effective . . . *must make it financially impossible for them* [businessmen] *to increase wage rates,* and it must cause a certain minimum amount of unemployment.' " Hirschman then comments that "it is [n]o wonder that many a government, faced with this kind of advice, prefers the illusion to last and the inflation to continue awhile longer." On the other hand there is occasional evidence of the IMF not "asking questions." For an anecdote involving silence with regard to a "clandestine scheme" for subsidizing exports in India, see J. BHAGWATI, TRADE, TARIFFS AND GROWTH 58 n. 26 (1969).

more than moral suasion to encourage the member to pursue "correct economic policies." If the member believes that those policies are not feasible in its present circumstances, it will be reluctant to seek the use of the Fund's resources when it finds itself in payments difficulties and will, as Colombia did, attempt to ameliorate its problems through the use of exchange distribution.

From this brief survey it appears that a developing country facing a payments deficit cannot, unless the deficit is caused by short-term phenomena, find a way out of its difficulties by reliance on the provision of additional reserves from the Fund. The amounts of Fund resources presently available unconditionally are too small and those available conditionally may be had only on terms which some countries find unacceptable. Moreover, reserves alone are not the answer. If evidence is needed to support these observations, one need only consider that of 109 developing-country members of the Fund in mid-1975, 85 were operating under the "transitional" provisions of Article XIV.

If additional reserves alone will not solve developing-country payments difficulties, attention might well be directed toward policies designed to make deflation and currency depreciation more tolerable. As for deflation not much can be said. In the debate over deflation the Fund and the developing countries have never really joined issue.

The Fund calls for discipline. The discipline may involve a threat to the very existence of the government. Certainly, the outstanding developing-country examples of growth maximization following from the imposition of domestic discipline do not manifest a high correlation with countries whose political systems could even loosely be defined as democratic.[41] Moreover, the Fund's developing-country

[41] See, e.g., Kanesa-Thasan, *Stabilizing an Economy—A Study of the Republic of Korea*, XVI STAFF PAPERS 1, 5 (1969) (". . . [W]ages of government employees were not raised despite a nearly 60 percent rise in the consumer price index.

members resent being called upon to exercise a discipline found wanting in most of the developed countries. From the vantage point of the Fund on the other hand many developing countries want to do too much, want to grow too fast. Historically the 5.2 percent growth rate achieved by most developing countries during the U.N. Development Decade (1960–70) is remarkable. Yet for the countries themselves it may appear all too low. They are in a hurry to "catch up" and are not willing to pursue policies that led to industrialization over the course of 100 to 150 years. It is difficult to see a way out of this dilemma and an attempt to soften the impact of deflationary discipline seems to offer only remote chances of success. Needless to say, the attempt should be made. And the Fund is doing useful work in assisting the developing countries in refining their systems of taxation so as to increase the policy options to a government which ought to deflate. But the going is slow as those working in the field can testify.

In the present climate of international monetary reform, a more hopeful route is to attempt to increase the palatability of exchange depreciation as an alternative to a system of exchange distribution.[42] In chapter 2 we discussed the reasons why developing countries are reluctant to devalue their currencies. These reasons were both political

---

. . ."); Frere, Per Jacobsen Lecture, Basel, Nov. 9, 1964 (". . . [M]onetary stability requires a discipline to which governments elected by universal suffrage are not always willing to submit.").

The debate between the "monetarists" (i.e., IMF) and the "structuralists" (developing countries) is fully and brilliantly explored at length in HIRSCHMAN, LATIN AMERICAN ISSUES (1961). For the classic exposition of the case of the structuralists, see Prebisch, *Economic Development or Monetary Stability: The False Dilemma,* VI ECLA BULL. 1 (1961).

[42] See Aliber, *Improving the Bretton Woods System,* in MUNDELL AND SWOBODA *supra* note 7 at 121, 129 (1969) ("The critical issue in adjustment is to devise measures that would facilitate more frequent use of the exchange rate as an instrument of adjustment. . . ."); Sohmen, *The Assignment Problem,* in *id.* at 183, 192 ("of all possible policy instruments, the exchange rate normally has the strongest 'comparative advantage' as a tool for equilibrating the balance of payments.").

and economic. From a political point of view, devaluation has come to be considered a confession of the failure of the government's economic policies and in many cases a national disgrace. In economic terms, devaluation may limit total export earnings if a substantial portion of exports are primary products for which demand is relatively inelastic. On the import side, the costs of imported foodstuffs would rise, which in some countries could generate a devastating political backlash. Although the economic points have been challenged, the case sounds persuasive. Nonetheless, having examined the various systems of exchange distribution in use in most developing countries one is forced to conclude that virtually all of them amount to de facto devaluations in economic terms. This is readily apparent with regard to the market distribution systems and multiple rate systems. It is less direct but nonetheless real with regard to administrative distribution. For in those systems the effect of the quantitative restrictions on imports is to increase the local price of goods to the point they would be at had there been a de jure devaluation. Although administrative exchange distribution does not in and of itself directly affect the export rate of exchange, all countries employing such techniques have systems for subsidizing exports of nontraditional goods. If it is thus the case that exchange distribution systems are a means of de facto devaluation, and it is difficult to escape the conclusion that they are, this means that the economic arguments against devaluation are not nearly so persuasive to decision-makers as might first appear. This is no startling conclusion as one might have guessed that since decision-makers are almost by definition politicians, it should be the political consequences of a course of action that would be their initial concern. If, then, it is the negative political consequences of devaluation that cause developing countries to utilize exchange distribution systems, a viable alternative must be one which ameliorates those political consequences.* The alternative most likely to achieve this is acceptance of a system of flexible exchange rates as the international monetary norm for developing countries.

Flexible exchange rates minimize the need for reserves. In a 1944 study undertaken for the League of Nations, Ragnar Nurkse made the point that "a poor country is less likely than a rich one to sacrifice potential imports and to tie up some of its limited wealth in an international cash reserve." [43] Experience since that time bears out the validity of this observation. It is precisely because they are unwilling to maintain "adequate reserves" that developing countries are afflicted with balance of payments crises. The level of reserves which is "adequate" is, of course, a function of the fixed exchange rate a country is attempting to maintain. Were it freed from the obligation to maintain a rate, the need for reserves would be minimal. And minimizing the level of reserves that needs to be maintained will in turn minimize the situations in which a developing country must turn to the IMF for additional reserves.

Floating exchange rates would entail a major alteration in the international monetary system established in Bretton Woods and codified in the Articles of Agreement of the International Monetary Fund.[44] The fixed par value system established in the Articles is based on the premise that the exchange rates for a currency are the basis for international concern.[45] The provisions of the Articles of Agreement concerning par values flow from this fundamental concept.

* See, e.g., Oort, Per Jacobsen Lecture, 1974, quoted in 3 IMF SURVEY 342 (1974) (Floating has the advantage of "depoliticizing and de-emphasizing decisions about exchange rate policy . . .").

[43] NURKSE, INTERNATIONAL CURRENCY EXPERIENCE 92 (LEAGUE OF NATIONS 1944).

[44] See, e.g., Southard, *Developments in the International Monetary System, Remarks Before the National Foreign Trade Convention,* New York, Nov. 15, 1971, reprinted in XXIII I.F.N.S. 385, 386 (1971) ("Operating core" of Bretton Woods system is fixed par value).

[45] See Gold, *Unauthorized Changes of Par Value and Fluctuating Exchange Rates in the Bretton Woods System,* 65 AM. JR. INT. LAW 113 (1971).

exceed 10 percent of the initial par value, the Fund shall raise no objection." [49] Larger changes give the Fund latitude to "either concur or object." [50] The Bretton Woods system therefore entails the establishment of an exchange rate for the member's currency in terms of gold or U.S. dollars (par value), a commitment to defend that par value within narrow limits, and a commitment not to change that par value unless the member is in fundamental disequilibrium, and the Fund is consulted first.

The par value system was established in part to prevent the reoccurrence of the competitive depreciations of the 1930s. As stated in Article I, among the purposes of the Fund is "to promote exchange stability, to maintain orderly exchange arrangements among members, and to avoid competitive exchange depreciation." And under the Bretton Woods system there have been no competitive depreciations of significance. Therefore it could be argued that the system has succeeded in admirable fashion.[51] To do so would, however, ignore the underlying economic situation. The competitive depreciations of the 1930s came about as reactions to a worldwide economic depression. Although the depreciations aggravated a depressed situation, they were not its primary cause. Since 1945 the world economic community has lived in an era of general prosperity and expansion with a growth rate averaging a historic high of 8 percent per annum.[52] In such a situation countries have not felt compelled to defend their interests with competitive depreciations. While the Bretton Woods system has been an additional factor to be weighed in taking a decision to depreciate, there is no way to know how the system would hold up in the face of a severe downturn in the level of world economic activity. One cannot say, therefore, that the

[49] Article IV, 5(c) (i).   [50] Article IV, 5(c) (ii) and (iii).   [51] See REPORT.
[52] See "Exchange Rates: floating, flexible, fixed," 236 ECONOMIST, Sept. 19, 70, p. 68.

When joining the Fund, the new member an
agree on the initial par value of the member's
terms of gold or "the United States dollar of the
fineness in effect on July 1, 1944." [46] Each m
agrees that "The maximum and minimum r
change transactions between the currencies of r
ing place within their territories shall not diffe
(i) in the case of spot exchange transactions, b
one percent; and (ii) in the case of other exch
tions by a margin which exceeds the margin
change transactions by more than the Fund
sonable." [47] Furthermore, "A member shall
change in the par value of its currency exce
fundamental disequilibrium" and "a change ir
of a members currency may be made . . . on
tation with the Fund." [48] If the proposed ch

[46] Articles IV, 1; XX, 4 and II, 2. This is not wholly accura
member for 13 years before agreeing on its initial par va
usual practice, however, that par values are established whe

[47] Article IV, 3. See Decision No. 3463–(71/26) of Decer
widened to 2–¼ percent temporarily).

[48] Article IV, 6(a) and (b). ". . . [I]n practice approva
without regard to the presence or absence of a 'fundament
term is not defined in the Articles of Agreement. Its meanir
through experience. . . ." OFFICER AND WILLETT (eds.)
MONETARY SYSTEM, PROBLEMS AND PROPOSALS 31 n.5 (196ς
noted that if Fund approval "were to be based upon a pro
quiry into the alleged 'fundamental disequilibrium' . . . th
wholly unworkable. The idea of a really meaningful inqui
so ridiculous as not to be capable of being taken seriou:
Forms of Exchange-Rate Flexibility, in *id.* at 202. See also F
465 ("a fuzzy and ambiguous concept."). But see Interr
The Role of Exchange Rates in the Adjustment of Internati
(hereinafter cited as REPORT) (Concept "a profound and
not necessarily require that an imbalance must have de'
payments.") And see address by Pierre-Paul Schweitzer,
Fund, to the Donaueuropaisches Institut, Vienna, Octob;
IMF SURVEY 88, 90 (1972) (". . . [T]he best definition
ance on domestic policies to correct an external imbala
quences (for example, in terms of unemployment or ir
able to the country in question. . . .' ") (quoting REPOR

par value system has prevented competitive depreciations of the kind that occurred in the 1930s. Competitive depreciations can, however, also occur in an era of general prosperity. For that prosperity is not usually shared in equal measure by all member states of the world community. It is here that the founders of the Bretton Woods system and their heirs can point with pride to the 28 years that have passed since the Conference.[53] But what has been the cost of this tranquility?

One of the costs has been that the policy of exchange rate stability has succeeded too well—to the point where countries are hesitant about depreciating their currencies when they are overvalued. Devaluation is now considered a last resort when all other policies have failed.[54] Moreover, "it is one of the many ironies and inconsistencies of modern life that, to protect fixed exchange rates—the means—we have compromised freedom of capital movements and, to some extent, of trade—the ends which the fixed rates are intended to serve." [55]

To free governments from the traumatic baggage of a devaluation, it is necessary to move in precisely the direction that practice with exchange distribution has indicated.

[53] The one sour note is "Canada's ill-starred effort to engineer a devaluation in 1961–62 . . . the first '1930s type' devaluation ["begger my neighbor"] since the Second World War. . . ." Ironically, the action was "welcomed by . . . the IMF. . . ." R. ALIBER, THE INTERNATIONAL MARKET FOR FOREIGN EXCHANGE 144 (1969). But see Johnson, *The International Monetary System and the Rule of Law,* JR. LAW AND ECON. 277, 290 (1973) ("As a broad generalization, all that they [Bretton Woods experts] succeeded in doing was to transfer fundamentally the same problems from a deflationary to an inflationary environment.").

[54] See Kahn, *supra* note 11 at 181 (1973) ("If one single reason had to be given for the deficiencies in the operations of the international monetary mechanism in the twenty years after World War II it would be the reluctance to contemplate changes in exchange rates."); REPORT at 34. See also "Exchange Rates: floating, flexible, fixed," 236 ECONOMIST, Sept. 19, 1970, p. 68 (". . . [P]ar values have tended to endow certain numbers with a holy aura. . . ."); pp. 56–57 *supra.*

[55] Joint Economic Committee, Guidelines for Improving the International Monetary System, Report, 89th Cong., First Sess., 1965, p. 18 quoted in OFFICER AND WILLETT, *supra* n. 48 at 222.

What must be done is to separate currency depreciation from devaluation. More particularly, currency depreciation must no longer be the climactic event of a balance of payments crisis awaited with anticipation by some and dreaded by others.[56] Instead depreciation (or appreciation) must be considered a normal result of the pursuit of a chosen course of economic action. To normalize currency depreciation it must be made more familiar. This requires that it occur with increased frequency. Flexible rates perform this function by allowing rates to appreciate or depreciate daily, or even with each transaction. While the changes in the rate will continue to be significant, the act of changing the rate will have its solemnity and mystery removed.

Detraumatizing alterations in the rate of exchange will not, however, make the rate of exchange an *unimportant* everyday fact of life. Quite the opposite might occur. It can become a critical fact of life. Under the present system of the adjustable peg, public discussion of government economic policy swells to a climax around the event of devaluation.[57] Intervening pessimistic reports on the movement of reserves, changes in the balance of trade, and even the cost of living receive limited circulation, deal with past events, and are not comprehensible to any but a limited elite.[58] A

[56] See, e.g., Friedman, in Contingency Planning for U.S. International Monetary Policy, Statements by Private Economists, submitted to Subcommittee on International Exchange and Payments of the Joint Economic Committee, 89th Cong., 2d Sess., p. 33 (1966) (Present system "makes a change in rates a matter of major moment and hence there is a tendency to postpone any change as long as possible."); Diaz Alejandro, Exchange Rate Devaluation in a Semi-Industrialized Country 193 (1965) (Allowing the exchange rate to "drift" would permit avoidance of "the traumatic shocks of massive devaluations.") But see Report 32 (". . . [T]rauma implicit in the act of exchange adjustment . . . [exerts] pressure for domestic corrective measures . . .").

[57] "Nobel laureate Prof. Paul Samuelson has expressed the hope that he will live to see the day when a shift in the exchange rate of a major currency does not make Page One of the New York Times." Editorial, *The Floating Pound, New York Times,* June 26, 1972, p. 30, col. 1.

[58] See Fellner, *On Limited Exchange Rate Flexibility,* in W. Fellner, Maintaining and Restoring Balance in International Payments 111 (1966) ("Exchange-rate

fluctuating exchange rate, on the other hand, is a simple concept dealing with present day events. It could become the focal point for general economic discussion in the developing countries. The functional equivalent would be the Dow Jones Average in the U.S. stock market. The Average has a significance far wider than a simple reflection of the days activity in the securities market. If the average is rising, it is widely taken as a sign that in the opinion of most "responsible" observers the government is pursuing an acceptable policy. And the Average reflects not only the government's economic policy but foreign policy as well. In short, it is a convenient focal point for discussion of the government's policies in many areas. No one indicator performs this function in the developing countries. The floating exchange rate could come quite naturally to fill this role. And if it did, it would bode well for an expansion of the number of participants in the dialogue concerning government policy—an important goal for the process of political as well as economic development.

A flexible exchange rate system would not remedy underlying payments difficulties. Rates will continually depreciate in response to continued domestic inflation. Some governments may face such a situation with equanimity, relying on the domestic effects of rate charges to deflate the economy.[59] The champions of fixed rates argue that one of the advantages of a fixed rate system is that it does not allow governments to sit back and do nothing. A fixed rate system forces them to take action to deflate in order to defend the exchange rate. But the widespread use of exchange distributions systems in developing countries is evidence of the

---

movements . . . much more readily noticeable by the public than are reserve movements.").

[59] "It will be seen that this line of reasoning once more reveals that inverted notion of the relationship between internal monetary circulation and the international payments sphere, which is characteristic of bourgeois political economy." A. FRUMKIN, *supra* note 33 at 357.

inability of these governments to exercise the requisite discipline. It has been noted that "if a country had to rely upon the discipline of the balance of payments to keep its financial house in order, then international monetary questions would be one of the lesser problems it faced." [60] This is precisely the case with developing countries. The very fact that they are developing in a political sense indicates that they do not have the capability for exercising the discipline required for deflation. Flexible rates assist them in carrying out this necessary though painful task by making deflation a consequence of market exchange rate determination. And more importantly, flexible rates restore to their economic arsenal the weapon of currency depreciation which has largely been lost because of the solemnity of the fixed rate system.[61]

To the extent that the economic arguments against depreciation carry some weight with decision-makers in developing countries, a flexible rate system facilitates exchange depreciations by assisting in dealing with those collateral problems. Recall that one of the reasons developing countries are unwilling to depreciate their currency is because of the income redistribution effect within the country. Those whose incomes are derived from exporting tend to gain at the expense of those closely allied with the import sector. Moreover, if imported goods consist in large measure of foodstuffs, the general cost of living tends to be affected in a negative way. While flexible rates do away with the shock effect of depreciation, they perform the same economic function. The only difference is in the time plane. Devaluations are abrupt changes which, though building up for some time, take place at one instant. A flexible rate would

---

[60] OFFICER AND WILLETT, *supra* note 48 at 223. But see REPORT 32.

[61] For a model in which monetary policy re rendered *more* effective under a flexible rate system, see Krueger, *The Impact of Alternative Government Policies Under Varying Exchange Systems,* 79 QRT. JR. ECON. 195 (1965).

allow the rate to drift down over time. The time advantage that flexible rates offer is not without significance. Although the income redistribution effect of a devaluation can be predicted, and offsetting tax measures introduced at the same time, predictions are not very accurate. With flexible rates the financial administrators could watch the situation develop over time and introduce offsetting measures gradually, in response to what actually takes place as opposed to what might take place. The time element is also important with regard to increases in food prices. For an abrupt increase following a devaluation can have catastrophic consequences as events in Ghana indicate.

Another economic argument for the use of flexible rates by developing countries has been developed by Professor Peter Kenen.[62] Building on prior work by Mundell,[63] Kenen seeks to answer the question of when exchange rates should be fixed and when they should fluctuate in terms of the goals of minimizing both unemployment and demand-induced wage inflation. He analyzes the question in terms of diversity of export product and the effect on the economy of exogenous disturbances, e.g., the fall in global demand for a primary product. Because developing-country exports tend to be concentrated about one critical export product, the impact of an exogenous event like the fall in the world price for that product is bound to be greater than it would be in an economy with greater export diversification. Consequently, the restoration of equilibrium will require a larger modification of the exchange rate. And this will be even more the case because developing countries have, as a rule, less well-developed fiscal and monetary policy instruments to deal with such exogenous variables than more

[62] See Kenen, *The Theory of Optimum Currency Areas: An Eclectic View*, in MUNDELL AND SWOBODA (eds.), *supra* note 7 at 41.

[63] See Mundell, *A Theory of Optimum Currency Areas*, 69 AM. ECON. REV. 657 (1961).

developed economies. Thus, Kenen concludes, the developing countries, "being less diversified and less well-equipped with policy instruments, should make more frequent changes or perhaps resort to full flexibility." [64]

The principal arguments against flexible rates are that they encourage speculation and create uncertainty. There is the danger that flexible rates "might . . . induce large speculative capital movements." [65] Note, however, that the present adjustable peg system may do more to encourage speculation than any system of flexible rates could.[66] By watching payments deficits mount up, speculators are presently in a good position to detect a situation where a currency depreciation is about to take place. For "[a]djustments [permitted under the IMF Agreement are] . . . made only *after* the disequilibrium state has become apparent to all, and . . . [this provides] a field day for speculators who could sell the weak currency short, knowing that there was no risk of its moving against them and a great chance that it would move in their favor." [67] And since changes are infrequent, when they

---

[64] Kenen, *supra* note 62 at 54.

[65] de Vries, *Twenty Years with Par Values, 1946–66*, III FIN. AND DEV. 283, 286 (1966). This was the experience in France when the franc floated from 1922–26. Capital exports "prompted by speculative anticipations of a continued fall in the exchange" resulted in rates that were "highly unstable." The fall in rates affected the trade balance so that the ratio of exports to imports fell to 93 percent for the year ending June 1926 (compared with 107 percent for the previous 12 months) and a "state of panic" developed in the French exchange market in July 1926. See R. NURKSE, *supra* note 43 at 118–120. But see Tsiang, *Fluctuating Exchange Rates in Countries with Relatively Stable Economies*, VII STAFF PAPERS 244, 271–272 (1959) ("Thus, the instability of the French franc from 1923 to 1926 was the result of an extremely elastic money supply which would have caused great instability in the economy whether the exchange rate was freely fluctuating or controlled. It therefore should not be regarded as evidence that a freely fluctuating exchange rate can, as a general rule, be expected to lead to cumulative depreciation through self-aggravating speculative capital movements . . .").

[66] See Smith, *The Present System and Its Defects*, in OFFICER AND WILLETT, *supra* note 48 at 14.

[67] P. SAMUELSON, ECONOMICS 697 n.11 (1970). See Meade, *The Future of International Trade and Payments*, THREE BANKS REVIEW, 15, 32 (June 1961) (Bretton Woods System "provides a golden opportunity for useless anti-social speculation.").

For the view that Canada's experience indicates that such speculation as ocdo come about they are usually substantial enough to encourage massive flows of capital into countries suspected of being on the verge of appreciating and out of countries at the point of depreciating. Moreover, the speculative danger of short term transfers of "hot money" generally discussed in the literature refers to transfers in and out of major currencies. Although a "run" on a freely floating developing country currency is not inconceivable, such currencies are unlikly to be attractive as even temporary havens for "hot money" given the general political instability characterizing the development process.

Even if it be conceded, however, that speculation is not a significant danger, critics of flexible rates argue that their instability adds a variable to international transactions not present under the Bretton Woods system.[68] Yet experience shows that freedom to float does not necessarily mean instability in exchange rates.[69] When the Canadian dollar floated from October 1950 through May 1961 it floated within very narrow limits. And we have other data indicating similar results. The Austro-Hungarian gulden floated against sterling from 1879–91.[70] At that time the Empire was what today might be called "semideveloped" with exports consisting mainly of agricultural products. In terms of monthly fluctuations over the entire period, the range was very much like the .87 percent experienced by Canada. On an annual basis the range never exceeded Canada's 4.17 percent. While tolerable today, the financial reporters for what

curred was stabilizing rather than destabilizing, see ALIBER, *supra* note 53 at 149. See also Fleming, *supra* note 48 at 473 (European experience in 1920's same); Hodgson, *An Analysis of Floating Exchange Rates: The Dollar-Sterling Rate, 1919–25,* 39 So. ECON. JR. 249, 254 (1972). For an elaborate model leading to the same conclusions, see Canterbery, *A Theory of Foreign Exchange Speculation Under Alternative Systems,* 79 JR. POL. ECON. 407 (1971).

[68] See Marsh, *Comment: The Currency Area Problem,* in MUNDELL AND SWOBODA, *supra* note 7 at 93 instability "the major (or only?) argument of those who oppose . . . [the floating-rate] system.").

[69] See OFFICER AND WILLETT, *supra* note 48 at 222.

[70] See Yeager, *Fluctuating Exchange Rates in the Nineteenth Century: The Experiences of Austria and Russia,* in MUNDELL AND SWOBODA, *supra* note 7 at 61.

was then Vienna's leading daily, The *Neue Freie Presse,* considered a daily fluctuation of one-half percent as a "violent convulsion." [71] Despite this experience it must be conceded that there is some likelihood that floating rates for developing countries will fluctuate within wider bands. But floating rates are a symptom not a cause of such fluctuations. The cause will be changes in the prices of primary-product exports. This was pointed out as long ago as 1938 by the Central Bank of Chile: " 'As the Latin-American countries are primarily producers of raw-materials and foodstuffs, the wide fluctuations in the prices of these products . . . may . . . make it impossible for them to maintain the principle of a rigidly stable currency." [72] The problem therefore is not that floating rates fluctuate, but that the export proceeds of developing countries fluctuate. The only advantage of a fixed-rate system in these circumstances is that it hides the symptom. It does nothing whatsoever to attack the disease.

One way in which rate fluctuations can be controlled is by government intervention in the exchange market. We have seen with regard to systems of exchange distribution that Brazilian and Indonesian monetary officials felt it necessary to intervene in systems where rates purported to be set by market demand. This is precisely the Fund's objection to floating rates. That the system would not be floating rates, but "fluctuating rates, influenced by official intervention." [73] But unlike the present system such interventions might be "arbitrary" and generate "conflicts between national policies." To bring order to this chaos, the Fund has argued,

[71] *Id.* at 73. At the time the Austro-Hungarian Government was not committed to maintaining full employment. Had it been so committed, and pursued monetary and fiscal policies to this end, the exchange rate would have been less stable. See HARROD, Discussion, in MUNDELL AND SWOBODA, *supra* note 7 at 116.

[72] Quoted in R. NURKSE, *supra* note 43 at 135.

[73] Floating with intervention is known in the trade as a "dirty float", a term attributed to the former German Finance Minister, Dr. Karl Schiller. See Officer, *International Monetary Reform,* 6 JR. ECON. ISSUES 147, 153 n.12 (1972).

would "either lead quickly back to a regime of par values, or would involve international supervision and control of national exchange rate actions." [74] This may be so in some developing countries; it may not in others. Certainly intervention is not necessarily a part of a floating-rate system. Nor do we know the degree of fluctuation that will be tolerated by the monetary authorities in developing countries. Nor do we know the degree of fluctuation that will, in fact, occur in developing-country currencies. There is certainly no substantial evidence that the possibility will become a probability. Rather, the government can intervene, as did the Bank of Canada, to "smooth" the exchange market.[75] The interventions were not at fixed points but *a posteriori* can be seen to have limited changes to ¼ of 1 percent on any given day. The aims of intervention should be "to iron out undue fluctuations in the exchanges caused by erratic movements of capital and the disturbing activities of speculators . . . [as well as] combatting seasonal exchange fluctuations." [76] So long as the goal of official stabilization activity is so limited, while permitting changes that reflect general trends, such activity would not be inconsistent with a system of floating rates.

The instability of floating rates is no more than the nor-

[74] REPORT 42. A third possibility has been suggested by Professor Meade. He proposes the creation of a Supranational Exchange Equalization authority, "which . . . would be endowed with a large fund of the various national currencies . . . [and] would be empowered on its own initiative to buy and sell these currencies in otherwise uncontrolled foreign exchange markets in order to control short-run fluctuations in exchange rates." OFFICER AND WILLETT, *supra* note 48 at 207. This proposal has been characterized as "utopian." See Fleming, *supra* note 48 at 474.

[75] See Marsh, *supra* note 68 at 94. For a description of the "smoothing" operation, see R. Aliber, *supra* note 53 at 147.

[76] R. NURKSE, *supra* note 43 at 154. On June 13, 1974 the Executive Directors of the Fund recommended that "Fund members should use their best endeavors to observe the guidelines set forth" in the "Guidelines for the Management of Floating Rates" developed by the Directors and the Deputies of the Committee of 20. See 3 IMF SURVEY 181 (1974). The interventions are to be such "as necessary to prevent or moderate sharp and disruptive fluctuations from day to day and from week to week . . ." *Id.* at 182. The guidelines are incorporated in Executive Board Decision No. 4232-(74/67).

mal result of the market system. Most prices with which we are familiar float—e.g., government bonds, stocks, automobiles, coffee—yet dealing in them is not impossible.[77]

Finally, instability of exchange rates may reflect an underlying economic instability in the country concerned. Fixed rates serve only to hide this evidence, but do nothing to cure the underlying instability.[78] Instability in the rate may also reflect changes in the political situation. In a study of the ruble, which floated against the sterling from 1879–91, Professor Leland Yeager found that the ruble fluctuated much more widely than did the *Austro-Hungarian gulden*. The extreme of a 30 percent fall in the value of the ruble occurred in 1888. This change can be correlated both with war fears and a campaign by Bismarck to ruin the credit of the Russian Government by pressuring German investors to liquidate their investments in Russia. The rate went back to normal in the summer of 1888, following the visit to St. Petersburg of the Kaiser as well as the prognosis of a bumper harvest in Russia combined with a bad harvest in the rest of the world. A system of fixed rates would have done nothing to ameliorate these underlying causes of pressure on the exchange rate.

The instability argument assumes that under the Bretton Woods system rates rarely if ever changed. Even before the rash of "floats" began in 1971 devaluations took place under that system. To cite a few examples, Sri Lanka depreciated its rupee in 1967, France its franc in 1960 and 1969, India its rupee in 1966, the U.K. the pound in 1967 and

---

[77] See Friedman, in OFFICER AND WILLETT, *supra* note 48 at 198. See also Campbell, ". . . Or a Naive Myth that Doesn't Help Canada," *New York Times*, Jan. 25, 1971, p. 48, col. 1 (". . . [w]ithout batting an eye these same corporate cats wheel and deal in raw materials and common share markets that have incredibly more price variability, and more at stake for their companies, than floating currencies probably would have.").

[78] Friedman, Statement in Contingency Planning for U.S. International Monetary Policy, Joint Economic Committee, 89th Cong., 2d Sess. (1966), in OFFICER AND WILLETT, *supra* note 48 at 198.

1972, and the United States the dollar in 1971. These are cases of formal changes in par value approved by the Fund. De facto depreciations, where par value has been "temporarily" abandoned have been more frequent. Argentina, for example, depreciated in 1962 and in the years 1964–67; Brazil in 1959–69; Chile every year from 1962–70; Korea in 1961, 1964–65, 1969, and 1970.[79] A fixed-exchange rate system allowing so many devaluations has aptly been termed a system of "hiccup rigidity." [80]

In fact, it has even been argued that the present system combines the *worst* features of both fixed and flexible rates and that it is less stable than a flexible rate system would be.[81] For one of the keystones of the fixed-rate system is the proposition that by raising interest rates, a deficit country can both deflate its economy and attract private capital so as to restore equilibrium. As to the latter, however, the system works in just the opposite direction. Fearing that the rate will depreciate to a greater extent than could be covered by the higher interest rate, capital will *flee* the deficit country. The capital outflow could then lead to a devaluation where one would not have been necessary.[82]

Given the fact that depreciations do take place under the Bretton Woods system, a businessman who ignores this fact would not long prosper. Successful participants in international trade do consider the possibility of currency depreciation and provide for it in their dealings. They buy and sell foreign exchange for future delivery at a fixed price. Foreign exchange is thus treated no differently than any other internationally traded commodity where prices change daily but business goes on becuase of a market in futures. Some have argued that such forward exchange trans-

[79] See generally de Vries, *Exchange Depreciation in Developing Countries*, XV STAFF PAPERS 560 (1968).

[80] Sohmen, *The Assignment Problem* in MUNDELL AND SWOBODA, *supra* note 7 at 194.

[81] See OFFICER AND WILLETT *supra* note 48 at 23.   [82] See *Ibid*.

actions would be costly and divert resources into the hands of those bearing the exchange risks. A response would be that dealers in foreign exchange bear little risk themselves. Their function is more the matching of supply and demand of currencies for future delivery. Since they bear little risk [83] the cost of their services is "slight." This conclusion is supported by data from the Canadian experience with flexible rates. "Empirically there exists no evidence that foreign-exchange dealers increased their share of national income when flexible rates were in effect in Canada during the period 1950–62." [84] The situation would be somewhat more difficult with regard to long-term investment in which, unlike trade transactions, the amounts and time when repatriation will be desired are presently unknown.[85] But the foreign investor bears a similar risk with the adjustable peg system. Multinational corporations have long had techniques for protecting themselves from exchange risks. In particular they "insulate themselves from currency changes by (a) asset and liability matching in host-country currencies, (b) forward hedging to cover revenue and expenditure flows between currencies, and (c) shortening the net worth of subsidiaries in forward exchange markets of suspect host country currencies." [86]

---

[83] GRUBEL, THE INTERNATIONAL MONETARY SYSTEM 112 (1969). But see Ingram, *Some Implications of the Puerto Rican Experience,* in R. COOPER (ed.), INTERNATIONAL FINANCE 87, 98 (Difficulties of French Insurance Company which purchases 30-year German bond in covering exchange risks in forward market).

[84] GRUBEL, *supra* note 83 at 112. An explanation for this phenomenon may be that there are no brokerage fees in Canada. Foreign exchange brokerage is handled by "brokers . . . on fixed salaries paid, along with rent and expenses, by the Canadian Banker's Association," R. ALIBER, *supra* note 53 at 145. It is possible that given a multitude of currencies, banks and brokers would be unwilling or unable to deal in all of them or that even if they did so the markets might be very thin so as to increase their risks and thereby their fees. See Kenen, *supra* note 62 at 45. For a suggestion that the IMF might provide forward cover in currencies not widely traded, see 241 ECONOMIST XXX (Nov. 27, 1971).

[85] Keynes believed floating rates would discourage long-term investment. See R. ALIBER, *supra* note 53 at 150.

[86] Campbell, *supra* note 77. S. ROBBINS AND R. STOBAUGH, MONEY IN THE MULTINATIONAL ENTERPRISE (1973). One of history's little ironies concerns the floating

The principal impediment to a flexible rate system for developing countries is not, as is evident, the persuasiveness of arguments about instability or speculation. It is rather the success of the status quo.[87] Central bankers who bear the day to day responsibility for monetary policy in their countries are naturally less than cavalier about jettisoning a system that seems to work tolerably well for one whose results are unknown.[88] Professor Milton Friedman, a strong advocate of floating rates, has offered another explanation of the central bankers' affection for the Bretton Woods system. He notes that "the people engaged in these activities are important people and they are all persuaded that they are engaged in important activities. It cannot be, they say to themselves, that these important activities arise simply from pegging exchange rates. They must have more basic roots. Hence, they say, it is simpleminded to believe that freeing exchange rates would eliminate the problem." [89]

---

of the rupee. Until 1873 the rupee was pegged to sterling. In that year the bimetallic standard was abandoned and the rupee was pegged to silver while sterling was pegged to gold. ". . . [A]t the time . . . it was thought that the fluctuation of the rupee was a great evil. It was thought that a floating rupee impaired trade, and more important, that it impeded British investment in the Indian infrastructure." Harrod, *Discussion,* in MUNDELL AND SWOBODA, *supra* note 7 at 115. In fact "by staying on silver after 1873, . . . India escaped the period of gold deflation which affected all gold standard countries during the last quarter of the nineteenth century." *Ibid.*

[87] "The Ministers and Governors agreed that the underlying structure of the present international monetary system—based on fixed exchange rates and the established price of gold—has proven its value as the foundation for present and future arrangements." Douglas Dillon, then U.S. Secretary of the Treasury, quoted in F. MACHLUP AND B. MALKIEL (eds.), INTERNATIONAL MONETARY ARRANGEMENTS: THE PROBLEM OF CHOICE 5 (Princeton 1964).

[88] See J. GRUBEL, *supra* note 83 at 75 ("These men carry heavy burdens of responsibility . . . reluctant to experiment with ideas for reform thought out by academicians in their ivory towers, eager to claim for themselves a place in intellectual history, but essentially unable to bear the responsibility . . . for the possibly harmful consequences of their ideas."). But see *New York Times,* Aug. 20, 1973, p. 39 (Subcommittee on International Economics of Joint Congressional Economic Committee reports "floating currency exchange rates are 'the best available alternative and are clearly superior to fixed parities.' ").

[89] Quoted in OFFICER AND WILLETT, *supra* note 48 at 226. Professor Eastman places the blame elsewhere. He notes "that politicians and bureaucrats distrust free markets." Eastman, *The Floating Dollar: A Successful Way of Life, New York Times,* Jan.

Whether one agrees with Professor Friedman's perception or not, one can question whether the central bankers
have given much attention to the idea of allowing the exchange rates of developing countries to float. For the central bankers whose attitude we account as preferring the
status quo, and for those whom Professor Friedman ridi-
cules, are generally the central bankers of Western Europe
and North America. When they think about floating rates
they think about the dollar, the pound sterling, the Deutsche
mark. It is highly unlikely that they have been troubled by
the prospect of a floating cedi or kwachwa or rupee. As one
central banker was frank to note "does it really matter what
exchange-rate system the less-developed countries adopt?
. . . Shifts in reserves to, from, or among the less-
developed countries are matters of supreme indifference to
the stability of the international monetary system." [90] Even
if central bankers did devote attention to the prospect of
these currencies floating, it is likely that they would have
analyzed the pros and cons in monetary terms. After all,
they are central bankers and monetary policy is their forte.
They would have no reason to dwell for long on the political impact of these policies, and if they did they would be
hard pressed to gather the data necessary to make even the
crudest estimate of the political impact of floating rates. Yet
if the issue were posed in the light of a choice (dilemma, if
you will) between floating rates and administrative ex-

25, 1971, p. 48, col. 1. See also 239 ECONOMIST, May 15, 1971, p. 14 ("There is a very
clear historical point of descent out of effective idealism into obstructionist nuisance
value by any bureaucracy, and it is important that this still very able commission
should realise it. The descent almost always comes when a bureaucracy (a) tries to
interfere with market forces; then (b) finds that this interference is causing so much
unnecessary trouble that dealing with this unnecessary trouble becomes its main
occupation; and then (c) decides that, as dealing with this unnecessary trouble is its
main occupation, the maintenance of the interference which causes this trouble is a
high feature of its own professional interest or even (so it kids itself) of its political
ideal.").

[90] Marsh, *supra* note 68 at 91. See also R. ALIBER, *supra* note 53 at 151.

change distribution, would there be any doubt as to where their preference would lie? [91] For most of them probably lived through the Europe of the 1930s and have first-hand knowledge of what a system of administrative exchange distribution can become. And while an economic depression is not sweeping the developing world at the present time, a process of similar impact is present. The Depression hit the world with such force that institutions of government evolved over centuries buckled and some collapsed. In the developing world there are, by and large, no such long-lived institutions. In the newly independent states the institutions are generally fragile at best. And the older developing nations are continuing a struggle to find national institutions that promise greater viability than the European transplants with which they have been wrestling for more than a century. Everywhere in the developing world the watchword is the institutionalization of change—the effort to build a governmental structure that will outlive its creator be he democratically elected President or self-appointed General. Time and again institutions are swept away, new ones reborn and swept away again. They fail for a variety of reasons. A principal reason is lack of respect for government institutions. In a sense this lack of respect can almost be equated with the absence of institutionalization. This is particularly the case if institutionalization requires legitimacy since the latter term generally means respect. Institutions that do not operate according to known rules, or that operate according to corrupt ones, are unlikely to command

[91] See GRUBEL, *supra* note 83 at 82. (Implicit in suggestions for floating rates "is the empirical judgment that greater or perfect flexibility of exchange rates would have negative welfare effects smaller than those resulting from greater exchange rate stability with all the undesirable policies necessary to maintain them."). For a rare venture into noneconomic considerations see J. BHAGWATI, *supra* note 40 at 64 ("The question of whether such programs can be implemented without causing widespread corruption and evasion . . . is a very pertinent one, and, I am afraid, one to which most experience seems to point in favor of parity changes.").

respect. In fact their presence is often counterproductive in that they generate disrespect for institutions generally. In this study we have explored typical examples of the institutional process for the distribution of foreign exchange in the developing world. In several cases we found that they fall far short of even a minimal rule of law standard and exhibit a high potential for corruption. Some suggestions have been offered which would remedy the situation. But if, as many believe, the very process of exchange distribution is antithetical to the rule of law and cannot be protected from corrupt influences, then consideration of eliminating the need for exchange distribution seems in order. It is the possibility of eliminating this potential that must be added to the balance when considering the desirability of adopting a system of flexible exchange rates in developing countries. It is not an issue that has been discussed in the voluminous literature on flexible rates. It is not a factor that can be quantified. But no decision on the question of flexible rates can reasonably be made without considering it. Note that the point made here is not that a flexible rate system should be permitted *solely* on the grounds of strengthening the rule of law and preventing corruption. Rather the suggestion is of a more modest character. It is that these considerations be *taken into account,* along with more traditional economic factors, in any consideration of international monetary reform.

If the central bankers could be persuaded that there may be some value in allowing the developing countries to pursue a system of floating rates, what changes would be needed in the Articles of Agreement? According to Fund jurisprudence, the decision to float the exchange rate is not a violation of a member's obligation not to alter its exchange rate without the concurrence of the Fund. This violation can only occur when the new par value is adopted. Until this is formally done, the Fund maintains the fiction that the old par value remains the par value. It notes, however, that "exchange transactions no longer take place at rates based on that par value." But the failure to maintain rates within the bands prescribed by Article IV, 3 is a clear violation of the Articles. As a sanction for this violation, the Fund is *authorized to declare* "the member ineligible to use the resources of the Fund" or a "member may be required to withdraw from membership in the Fund." (Article XV,2). In fact neither sanction has been invoked against a member adopting a fluctuating rate. This is in line with the Fund's general attitude of avoiding the imposition of santions: "the absence of any advantage for the international community in the severance of relations between a member and the Fund, particularly if the member was willing to remain in consultation with the Fund and showed in that way that its failure was not contumacious." [92] Herein lies the importance of the decision that a floating rate is not an unauthorized change in par value. For if it were, a member would be *automatically* "ineligible to use the resources of the Fund unless the Fund otherwise determines." (Article VI,6).

A decision not to invoke a sanction for violation of a norm, or even a consistent pattern of such decisions, may lead to the conclusion that the original norm has been modified and that a new norm has taken its place. Even if one accepts this point, the new norm with regard to floating rates can reasonably be read to indicate only that they are acceptable for short periods of time—until the currency in question finds its new level. The Fund's Executive Directors made this quite clear in their 1970 *Report on the Role of Exchange Rates,* where they noted that while the Fund had "tolerated or encouraged" fluctuating rates on occasion, "the Fund has regarded such arrangements as exceptional in character. . . ." [93] Aside from the Canadian dollar, major currencies have until recently floated for periods of a

---

[92] Gold, *supra* note 45 at 117.   [93] REPORT 28.

year or less. This is certainly not sufficient basis for one to argue that floating rates are now an equally acceptable alternative under the Articles. Or even an approved second-best system. A further consideration of developing-country economic problems indicates, however, that there is another route to the end of legitimizing floating rates under the Articles.

For even if a system of floating rates were acceptable, exchange restrictions might still be needed in developing countries. Developing countries would still have the problem of exports of local capital and flexible rates would not act as a barrier against capital flight.[94] And if capital transfers are to be controlled, scrutiny of current transactions will be necessary to ensure that they are not, in reality, disguised capital transfers. So we are right back to square one. But perhaps not if we reconsider the prohibitions on capital transfer. Despite the most comprehensive prohibitions, we know capital is being transferred out of developing countries. Although accurate figures are difficult to obtain—principally because such transfers are illegal—some indication of their volume can be gathered from the "net errors and omissions" item in the balance of payments statements. These figures are generally negative, which means that more exchange has gone out of the country than can be accounted for in the official figures for dispositions of that exchange. In 1968, the total for Chile was $88 million; Peru $88 million; India $191 million; the Philippines $103 million; and Zambia $30 million. Moreover, because these transfers are by definition illegal, they place a premium on lawless behavior and corruption. The result could be a general lack of confidence in the administration of government as a whole and the undermining of the effort to establish a rule of law. It is impossible to weigh the cost of this poten-

[94] See McKinnon, *Optimum Currency Areas*, 53 AMER. ECON. REV. 717 (1963), reprinted in R. COOPER, *supra* note 83 at 223, 231.

tially destructive effect. But it is a factor to be considered in favor of legalizing capital transfers and thereby defining away the problem. In addition one must consider the environment in which these illegal transfers take place. Because the transfers are illegal the attitude is to get one's resources out at every opportunity. If, on the other hand, capital could be freely transferred there might be more inclination to retain it at home until such time as an attractive investment opportunity presented itself, either domestic or overseas. Moreover, there is a rush to transfer funds out if one perceives an approaching devaluation which brings an instant and substantial loss. If rates floated, however, the need would be far less immediate and urgent.[95] Substantial evidence for this point is provided by the experience of Peru in 1953. At that time Peru maintained a system of dual floating rates. During 1953 "the prices of its chief exports suffered severe setbacks on the world market, while the momentum of internal inflation still continued." [96] The rate was thus under pressure on both the supply and the demand side. Yet "there was no evidence of a speculative capital flight generated by the anticipation of, or the actual continuous depreciation of, the sol during 1953." [97]

Because massive capital flight will not necessarily follow the removal of restrictions from capital transfers, because freeing capital transfers may have a safety valve effect on the rule of law, and because the restrictions of capital transfers necessitates the policing of all external payments, the removal of such retrictions ought to be seriously considered by developing countries. This is not to say, however,

[95] The Canadian experience is of some interest in this connection. Canada was "shaken by a foreign exchange crisis of extraordinary severity" in 1962 because of "public misunderstanding . . . of the transition then in process from a freely fluctuating exchange rate *to* a fixed par value." Blackwell, *Canada*, 3 FIN. AND DEV. 297, 298 (1966) (emphasis added).

[96] Tsiang, *An Experiment with a Flexible Exchange Rate System: The Case of Peru, 1950–1954*, V STAFF PAPERS 449, 465 (1957).

[97] *Id.* at 467.

that capital transfers need take place at the same rate as other overseas payments. There is a good case for commanding a premium for such transfers. The premium ought to be high enough to discourage some capital transfers.[98] Given the fact that capital transfers will now be freely permitted, a small premium may be sufficient to give capital holders pause before they do so.

If the developing countries are willing to experiment with freeing capital transfers, then the path is open for the adoption of a fluctuating rate norm under the Articles of Agreement. For although the Fund cannot approve a floating unitary rate because of the conflict with Article IV,[99] the Fund can approve a dual floating rate system as a multiple currency practice under Article VIII,3.[100] The rationale for this anomaly is none too clear. It has been suggested that the draftsmen foresaw the possible use of multiple rates in the early postwar era, and wisely decided that it should be considered a tolerable temporary aberration from the norm. A fluctuating unitary rate, on the other hand, must have been inconceivable in the sense that it was in fundamental conflict with a fixed par value system.[101] For whatever reason, the authority is clearly recognized as existing in the Fund. And "the Fund has not flinched from urging a member to allow the rate to move in accordance with market forces as the best means of achieving an ultimate stability." [102] This is evident from the exchange reforms in Latin America in the period 1954–60. Aided by technical and financial assistance from the Fund, six Latin-American countries—Chile, Bolivia, Paraguay, Peru, Argentina, and Uruguay—adopted "comprehensive stabilization pro-

---

[98] On the need for capital controls even with floating rates see McKinnon, *Optimum Currency Areas,* 53 AMER. ECON REV. 717, 722 and 723 (1963).

[99] See Gold, *The Funds Concepts of Convertibility,* 19 (IMF Pamphlet Series No. 14, 1971).

[100] *Ibid.* For a well-developed proposal along the same lines, see Fleming, *Dual Exchange Markets and Other Remedies for Disruptive Capital Flows,* 21 STAFF PAPERS 1 (1974).

[101] *Ibid.*   [102] GOLD *supra* note 45 at 128.

grams." [103] Argentina, Boliva, and Uruguay adopted single floating rates, Peru and Chile adopted dual floating rates. At the time of its reform, Paraguay adopted a single fixed rate but abandoned it a year later in favor of a floating rate. By 1960 both Peru and Chile had unified their rates and thus converted to a single-rate system. What is interesting about this history is the fact that despite its manifest lack of authority to approve a single fluctuating rate, and despite its clear authority to approve dual rates, "progress" in these countries was equated with the adoption of a *single* fluctuating rate.[104] In a sense therefore Fund policy and assistance were directed at moving countries *away* from a status in which they could legally maintain a given system under the Articles—a dual-rate system—to one in which the system was tolerated under Article XIV. The rationale for this paradox must be that the goal of Fund policy was a single fixed rate and that the Fund considered this most likely to be achieved from a status of a single floating rate as opposed to dual floating rates.

Although not clearly required by the language of Article VIII, Section 3, the Fund has interpreted its authority as limited to the granting of "temporary" approval to floating rates when they constitute a multiple currency practice.[105] This is a logical interpretation if one accepts the norm as the Article IV,3 requirement of exchanges taking place at

[103] d'A. Collings, *Recent Progress in Latin America Toward Eliminating Exchange Restrictions*, VIII STAFF PAPERS 276 (1961). See also Moore, *The Stabilization of the Bolivian Peso*, PUBLIC FINANCE 43 (1958). For the view that these "reforms" may involve nothing but a "change of names" see Konig, *Multiple Exchange Rate Policies in Latin America*, 10 JR. INTERAMER. STUD. 35, 46 (1968).

[104] Single floating rates have also been used by Afghanistan, Brazil, the Republic of China, Korea, Laos, Lebanon, the Phillipines, the Syrian Arab Republic, Thailand, and Venezuela during the last fifteen years. See Woodley, *Some Institutional Aspects of Exchange Markets in the Less-Developed Countries*, in R. ALIBER, *supra* note 53 at 177, 181.

[105] See REPORT 26. Woodley, *supra* note 104 at 182, indicates that countries that maintained relative monetary stability were those that moved from floating to fixed rates "very quickly."

par value *and* the Article VIII,2 requirement concerning the prohibition of restrictions on current payments. This is not, however, the de facto norm with regard to the developing countries. Even before the current situation, in June 1970, of the 116 Fund members, only 30 adhered to the Article IV and Article VIII norms as of April 1972. Of the remaining 86, 4 were Article VIII countries not maintaining their exchange rates with the margins required by Article IV. An additional 27 maintained their rates within the required margins but were functioning under Article XIV with regard to their current payments, 17 were Article XIV countries without a declared par value, and 38 were Article XIV countries which were not maintaining their exchange transactions within the margins required by Article IV.[106] With regard to the developing countries, therefore, the large majority do not maintain exchange rates within the bands required by Article IV, nor free current payments as provided in Article VIII. The Fund is insulated from reexamining its authority under Article VIII,3 only because most of the developing countries are operating under Article XIV. What is proposed therefore is that the Fund reconsider its Article VIII,3 authority to approve fluctuating rates as multiple currency practices with a view to eliminating the concept of "temporariness" or interpreting the word "temporary" in the same manner as the word "transitional" has been interpreted in Article XIV.[107] The Fund should then encourage developing countries to move from Article XIV status to Article VIII,3 status.

To some extent the Fund seems to do this. The Executive Directors have noted that where a government is "unable to

[106] See REPORT 26. As of April 1974 the membership had increased to 126 and the number of Article VIII countries to 41.

[107] In 1971 the Fund reaffirmed its commitment to "temporariness" indicating that it construed its authority to approve multiple currency practices to be limited to a twelve-month period. See INTERNATIONAL MONETARY FUND, TWENTIETH ANNUAL REPORT ON EXCHANGE RESTRICTIONS 1 (1971).

establish or sustain stability in its domestic finances . . . it may well be necessary to have recourse to a flexible exchange rate . . . if an open economy is to be maintained." [108] The Fund, however, considers the resort to floating rates only advisable if it will eventually lead to a fixed unitary rate.[109] The change advocated here is that the floating-rate system now be recognized as the norm for developing countries and that the temporary nature of their utilization of this system be considered coterminous with their status as developing countries.

Such a change has several attractions from an institutional point of view. First, no amendment of the Articles of Agreement is necessary. Instead a Board decision could be adopted approving in advance multiple-rate systems featuring floating rates for current and capital transactions *provided* these systems also indicate substantial compliance with Article VIII,2. The fact that this policy change does not require an amendment of the Articles should dispel one of the fears expressed by the Directors in their consideration of flexible rates.[110] Secondly, a reinterpretation of Article VIII,3 would create a category of full membership in the Fund, realistically attainable by most developing countries. The Articles, as presently interpreted, provide for only one "legitimate" membership status—Article VIII,2. The others, some 85 Fund members, dwell in various states of sin under the Agreement. This situation is undesirable for both the Fund and its developing-country members. For it puts the Fund in the position of having constantly, or at least annually, to remind developing-country members of their shortcomings in living up to the obligations under the

---

[108] REPORT 27.

[109] But see E. SOHMEN, FLEXIBLE EXCHANGE RATES 115–116 (1961) ("In recent years the administrators of the . . . Fund have tended to take the ban on fluctuating exchange rates . . . less and less seriously.").

[110] See REPORT 71.

Agreement. One would hope that this is not a task Fund officials would relish. And it naturally breeds resentment against the Fund in the developing countries. More important, perhaps, is the feeling that the Articles are yet another example of international law made by and for the developed countries that incorporate standards unlikely to be attained by most developing countries—but against which their performance is measured.[111] Finally and most importantly, a Fund move in the direction of legitimizing floating rates would encourage developing countries to move away from a system of exchange distribution with the consequent benefit of a strengthening of the rule of law in those countries. It is this gain that one finds missing in the voluminous literature on floating rates. While it is generally agreed that administrative exchange distributions are the worst of all possible systems from an economic point of view, no viable alternative is made available to the developing countries. They are confined to the nether world of Article XIV, there to experiment with different systems of exchange distribution until that "happy day" when they can become full-fledged members of the Fund. Robert Triffin warned us years ago that

Exchange freedom or stability cannot be established by mere legislation or agreements. Burying our heads in the sands of legal commitments will not protect us from the inevitable consequences

[111] See, e.g., Konig, *supra* note 103 at 51 (suggesting separate regime for developing countries to make agreement conform to "realities"). But see Address by Pierre-Paul Schweitzer, Managing Director, International Monetary Fund, at the United Nations Conference on Trade and Development Santiago, Chile, April 25, 1972, reprinted in XXIV I.F.N.S. 121, 123 (1972) ("It is sometimes argued that the rules of conduct in currency and payment relations that are suitable for developed countries are not appropriate for developing countries. I do not agree with this view. . . . Each has problems that are unique to its economic situation, but this only means that the code of conduct that should govern the system should be capable of flexible application so as to accommodate these special problems and needs.").

of international maladjustments and the balance of payments disequilibria. If we wish to restore a workable economic order we should speak a little less about enforcing stability and convertibility, and work a little more towards creating conditions under which they will become possible, and indeed attractive, to members of the Fund. . .[112]

If we continue to ignore Triffin's advice, exchange distribution in developing countries will continue to provide us with light entertainments like the proceedings before the Ollennu Commission.[113]

---

[112] Triffin, *Exchange Control and Equilibrium,* in S. HARRIS (ed.), FOREIGN ECONOMIC POLICY FOR THE UNITED STATES 413, 425 (1948).

[113] See, e.g., "Import Scandal in India Brings a Heavy Attack on Ruling Party," *New York Times,* Nov. 27, 1974, p. 10, col. 1 ("A scandal over the Government's issuing of import licenses. . . .")

Index